# CONTRABANDISTA!

# CONTRABANDISTA!

*Evert Clark
and
Nicholas Horrock*

*PRAEGER PUBLISHERS*
*New York · Washington*

BOOKS THAT MATTER

Published in the United States of America in 1973
by Praeger Publishers, Inc.
111 Fourth Avenue, New York, N.Y. 10003

© 1973 by Evert Clark and Nicholas Horrock

Library of Congress Catalog Card Number: 72-87296

Printed in the United States of America

*To our wives, who had rights of first refusal*

# Contents

The names of four people mentioned in this book have been altered to protect them. Two are agents still serving in covert assignments, and two are people who were caught up in the conspiracies but were never charged.

# CONTRABANDISTA!

# 1 The Asunción Affair

**March 25–26, 1971**

*Le Paris-Niza Motel lay a few miles* south of Asunción, dark and silent in the autumn chill. A single light beside the office door failed to pierce the deep shadows of mango trees that hid the restaurant tables casually arranged at poolside. The neat wood and stone bungalows that in sunlight flashed the clear pastel colors of a Mediterranean seaport now were only faint blurs. A gravel driveway split the high cinderblock wall to serve as the only entrance to the grounds. And arched from one part of the wall to the other, straddling the drive, was an awkward miniature Eiffel Tower. It caught just enough light to cast an eerie criss-cross of shadows along the narrow dirt road.

A hundred yards back toward the city, in shadows even deeper than Le Paris-Niza's, light frost had formed on the hood and windows of a rented American car with Paraguayan plates. The two men slumped down in the front seat seldom spoke. When they did they whispered, as if someone might hear them in this God-forsaken place.

"That goddamned tower!" Frank Mancini, the driver, said. "I've stared at it so long it looks like it belongs there. Like a plaster flamingo on a Florida lawn."

"I think you are annoyed because he doesn't come," the small, wiry Paraguayan beside him said in accented English. "I think you are bothered by the cold. I was assured he would be here tonight, and if not tonight, then tomorrow. What do you think? We pick the wrong time?"

Mancini drummed his fingers on the steering wheel, ignoring the question. The young man beside him, a Paraguayan policeman who was giving him unofficial help at great risk, knew the answer as well as Mancini did. First light was beginning to color the sky behind them, threatening to illuminate their hiding place, before Mancini spoke again.

"Damn one more wasted night!" Mancini said. "And damn you, Raúl, for being wrong again." He said it without heat. His companion knew he didn't mean it. Informants were often wrong, but sometimes they were right. When the quarry was big, you couldn't take a chance.

"And damn Auguste Joseph Ricord," Mancini said as an afterthought, "for not getting his ass back to his motel where he belongs!"

He followed this comment with a string of Italian-American expletives until the Paraguayan's eyes were wide with envy. Then, dismissing his young informant with a comradely slap on the shoulder, Mancini turned the car north and drove slowly back into the city. He would need a new approach and more help.

March in Asunción was a pleasant time in a flowered city. The Latin seasons were turned upside down, but at least in Paraguay's early autumn there was no more oppressive 100-degree heat to torment pedestrians on the wide boulevards. Cool, dry winds from the Argentine made refuge under the tiled roofs of the pink and white villas seem less urgent by day, and it was actually cool at night. Not unlike Florida at the barely perceptible change of seasons, Mancini thought. Florida. One more place he would rather be than Asunción.

Here he felt almost as useless as that unlikely tower arching over Ricord's motel driveway. A special agent of the U.S. Bureau of Narcotics and Dangerous Drugs had no powers of arrest in Asunción—not even at his own home base in Buenos Aires. He could look, listen, shiver through a useless night on a lonely road, ask questions that often produced wrong or evasive answers, pass on information that would let someone else take credit for a case. But any "bust" on foreign soil must be made by the police of the country involved—however reluctantly they might approach the task. One more year overseas, he thought, and he might go home to find most of his running mates promoted—outranking him, drawing more pay, possibly even giving him orders. For the moment, not even the prospect of collaring Ricord could alter his mood.

Mancini made the U.S. Embassy at 1776 Avenida Mariscal López in time for a quick cup of coffee. Then, taking the embassy's political officer along as diplomatic muscle, he drove the few blocks to the colonnaded Palace of Government on Calle El Paraguayo Independiente.

It was a Lilliputian palace, patterned after the Louvre but much smaller—oddly out of place in this Spanish-style city. There were other hints of France in the low-profile, landlocked capital, like the Pantheon of Heroes copied from Les Invalides in Paris. To the Frenchman Auguste Joseph Ricord, these hand-me-downs of Parisian architecture might offer a touch of home. But to Mancini they were as incongruous as his own presence here. He had heard a thousand stories of the mysterious Ricord and believed no more than a tenth of them. And he had little hope that Ricord could be pried loose from his Paraguayan protectors, even if the stories were true. Give him the chance and Mancini would take the sky-scrapered coastal cities of Rio and B.A.—or New York—over this nothing backwater of a town any time.

The agent and the embassy man walked into the dim, high-ceilinged office of Dr. Miguel Angel Bestarde, director general of the Ministry of the Interior, at precisely 8 o'clock. Early for an official call, Mancini thought, even on a matter of relative urgency. But Bestarde had said he would be ready and he was, with more coffee. Despite the embassy man's presence, Mancini decided he would make the story of M. Ricord as brief as possible. He had little patience with formalities even when his joints didn't ache for sleep.

Ten days ago, on March 15, 1971, a federal grand jury in Manhattan had returned a secret indictment against the Frenchman, charging him with conspiring to smuggle heroin into the United States. Furthermore, Mancini said, the U.S. Government had reason to believe that Auguste Ricord was the most important smuggler of narcotics on the South American continent. In addition, American officials felt that Ricord was abusing the hospitality of Paraguay to make Asunción the key transshipment point between the heroin-producing laboratories of southern France and the addict market on New York City's streets.

If Dr. Bestarde was surprised at the news or embarrassed at the implied criticism of Paraguay for harboring Ricord, he did not show it. For his part, Mancini gave no hint of his own doubts. The case that had led to Ricord's indictment was nominally a joint investigation between his own Narcotics Bureau and the Bureau of Customs—a "6J." But as far as Mancini was concerned it was primarily a Customs case, and therefore suspect. He preferred a nice, clean, simple, one-agency case—his own agency, of course—to anything those Customs kooks thought they owned.

Heroin was not a new subject to Dr. Bestarde. Several months before, these same two Americans had briefed him—first on the smuggling arrest and then on the escape from a New York jail of Enio Varela, a prominent Asunción businessman, who was suspected of having fled home to Paraguay. Now, on March 25, Varela was being linked directly to Ricord in the Americans' accusations.

Mancini's official request was relatively simple. He would like Dr. Bestarde's Policía de la Capital to monitor Ricord's movements and help identify his associates—in other words, to keep a tail on him—until copies of the indictment, a warrant for his arrest, and a formal request for his extradition could be forwarded from the United States. The agent kept his silence on what he would have preferred—an on-the-spot deportation order for Ricord, to avoid the long rigmarole of extradition proceedings.

Dr. Bestarde's reply startled the two Americans. He did not

need to point out that Paraguay's government was the oldest dictatorship on the continent. What he did say was that Paraguayan officials still held many extraordinary powers under a number of state-of-seige declarations.

"Our government," he told them matter-of-factly, "would be happy to assist by arresting Ricord for the Bureau of Narcotics and Dangerous Drugs and holding him so that he cannot escape and go into hiding."

From a government that not only sanctioned the smuggling of goods other than narcotics by *contrabandista* pilots but had actively helped to make smuggling the country's number-one industry, this came as a totally unexpected proposal. Asunción suddenly looked brighter to Frank Mancini.

Almost together, and trying hard to conceal their delight, the two Americans replied that the idea was most interesting but would have to be relayed to their superiors.

"Likewise," said Dr. Bestarde—"I, too, must consult with those above me."

It looked, despite the disclaimers, as if all three men had the same thought in mind: By keeping the affair on an informal "police-to-police" basis, the red tape that so frustrated practicing lawmen might be avoided.

They agreed that Dr. Bestarde should contact the American Embassy before 11 A.M. that day to verify his offer before taking any action.

Once back at an embassy desk, Mancini quickly telephoned the word to his regional director in Buenos Aires for relay to Washington. Then he followed up the call with Cables 495 and 497 to Buenos Aires—the first of which indiscreetly mentioned the possibility of "extrajudicial extradition proceedings."

Despite the unanimity of the morning's meeting at the Palace of Government, and despite Bestarde's promise to verify his offer before acting, the script began to fall apart long before the day was out.

A few miles outside the city a Policía de la Capital cruiser turned almost noiselessly into Le Paris-Niza's gateway. Late morning sun stole through the mango trees to dapple the chairs and tables and make bright patches across the green surface of the pool. The neat pink, yellow, and white bungalows looked innocently inviting.

Plainclothesman Salvador Victor Ibarrola, a short 280-pounder whose Gaurani Indian blood gave him a dark, powerful look, clutched a photograph in his hand and walked into the restaurant. He asked a waiter where he could find Auguste Joseph Ricord. The waiter simply pointed toward an adjoining room. There, Ibarrola met another man, who told him: "Check in the office. Someone there will read you the guest list."

In the office he showed the photograph to the pretty young French proprietress, who promptly fainted.

This was not in his instructions. Ibarrola yelled for someone to come and attend the woman and, in some embarrassment, radioed from his cruiser to his superiors to ask what to do next. "Search the facilities," an exasperated voice said.

That did no good, either. Later the plainclothesman would recall: "I went back to the lobby and suddenly I became unquiet, and I began to think maybe this man in the picture is this man I met who sent me to the office. I think he was wearing a wig or a beret then."

Feeling thwarted, upset at having made a woman faint, and not a little angry at himself, he sent the two uniformed men away. But he decided to keep a watch on the motel from the cruiser parked down the street.

At 3:30 P.M., as the shadows began to lengthen, the sound of an automobile engine suddenly split the quiet, and a red Ford Torino lurched out from under the imitation Eiffel Tower, scattering gravel as it made a skidding turn toward the south. Ahead of it lay the port city of Itá Enramada, a ferryboat ride across the Paraguay River from Argentina—a separate sovereign nation. It was almost time for the ferry to depart. For a man with reason to run, the ferry could mean freedom.

Ibarrola's cruiser made a screeching start, straining its more modest engine to catch the heavier Ford. Just short of the ferry slip itself, already past the unmanned border checkpoint that normally guarded the exit from Paraguay, the Ford skidded to a stop with the cruiser almost on top of it. Ibarrola whipped out of the police car with pistol drawn to confront—yes, he was almost sure of it, the man who had directed him to the motel office, the man in the photograph.

A small, grandfatherly sort of man in horn-rimmed glasses, brightly patterned sport shirt, and slacks. He stepped meekly from the Ford looking like a doctor out for an afternoon of golf. Auguste Joseph Ricord, this man people said was a towering giant of the illicit drug trade, who had the Ministry of the Interior and the Americans so concerned, stood less than five feet four. He was obviously in his late fifties or early sixties. Gray-white hair, what there was left of it, rimmed his ears and the back of his head and grew down his cheeks in fluffy, modish sideburns. A half-inch scar crossed his right upper lip. But a man does not have to be a criminal to acquire a scar. And he was armed only with a briefcase loaded with personal papers.

"Officer," he said quietly, "you will find that you are making a great mistake."

Within minutes Dr. Bestarde telephoned word of Ricord's apprehension to the surprised American Embassy political officer. He would explain the unannounced action, he said, if the political officer and Agent Mancini could meet with him at 5:30 P.M. He would also provide details of the arrest.

At the meeting Dr. Bestarde reported that he had consulted with the Interior Minister, who had in turn consulted with the President, General Alfredo Stroessner. It was the President himself who had ordered the arrest of Ricord, Dr. Bestarde explained.

For Mancini, the long and confusing day after a sleepless night was not over. At least there would be no more fruitless birdwatching. The bird was now in someone's hand, if not his own. But Roger C. Brewin III, the embassy's deputy chief of mission, had asked to see him. A tender toe must have been stepped on.

In circuitous but unmistakable terms, Brewin said that U.S. Ambassador J. Raymond Ylitalo was doubtful about an informal agreement to spirit Ricord away without the proper preliminaries. In the relentless war on narcotics, this kind of semi-official "snatch" had been executed before—sometimes to the anguish of diplomats who were left to pick up the pieces. Repercussions plagued harassed men who must deal with a country on a broad range of matters. The most recent episode had taken place in Panama, Brewin said, as if Mancini were not painfully aware of it. In Panama specifically, reaction against overzealous crimefighters and their short-cutting of legal procedures was endangering negotiations over American control of the Panama Canal.

Ambassador Ylitalo, Brewin said, was particularly concerned over Mancini's Cable 495 and its reference to "extrajudicial extradition proceedings." Henceforth, Mancini was to submit all outgoing messages to Brewin for clearance. And he was not to route the word of Ricord's arrest through State Department channels in Washington "because of possible embarrassment."

Christ! Mancini thought. Any way you read it, *that's* a chewing out. But he left it unsaid. And he kept his mouth shut about the irony of the Paraguayan Government's overcooperating while his own embassy turned Nervous Nellie. He walked out into the darkened street, brooding. Tomorrow—if I can sleep tonight—will be just another screwed-up day in the life of your friendly narc. To think I could have been a sky marshal. . . . With his luck, he reflected, he would have been hijacked to Asunción.

The outer walls of Tacumbu Penitentiary had crumbled in spots, giving them the same shabby look as too many other official buildings in Asunción. But inside, in a wing conveniently away from other prisoners, M. Ricord's cell was surprisingly comfortable. The room itself measured at least nine by twelve feet, and a telephone and private bathroom gave his accommodations something of the hominess of a bungalow at Le Paris-Niza.

The diminutive Frenchman straddled the seat of a straight chair, turned so that its back faced his Paraguayan captors. He folded his arms across the top of the chair back and rested his chin on his arms. He was by turns polite and indignant, putting his glasses on, removing them, waving them to emphasize a point.

He had never set foot in the United States, he said, and for anyone to accuse him of conspiring to smuggle narcotics into New York City was preposterous.

"That is a lie made up by the Americans," he said calmly. "Their government is rotten from top to bottom and they have chosen me to make me the victim of an absurd plot involving drugs. If they want to stop the drug business, let them put their own officials in jail."

The polite, almost casual interrogation was interrupted by the arrival of Ricord's dinner. It was not prison fare but an example of Le Paris-Niza's modest French cuisine, brought to him by Maria Ana Elena Bonsignour, usually called Ana Elena or Hélène, a slender, dark-blonde woman of thirty-three who Ricord said was his niece. With her was a beautiful girl of fifteen, Josefina Brigita, or Josephine Brigitte, Ricord—Auguste Joseph's daughter.

The questioning would resume in the morning.

Special Agent Frank Mancini got an early start, but Friday, March 26, quickly began to look like the flip side of the day before. He was still shaving when a Bureau of Narcotics official in Washington informed him by phone that formal extradition—rather than a swift deportation—should be sought for his potential prisoner.

By the time he had worried a tough steak and eggs into an unpalatable mess on his plate and settled for toast and coffee, he decided the hell with it. If that was what they wanted, that was what they'd get. Visions of a weekend back in Buenos Aires, with no official duties except to write a report of his trip and make out his expense account, gradually lifted his gloom. With Ricord safely in a cell, he wouldn't be needed here.

But at the embassy another call was waiting. It had now been decided, the same official said over another lousy connection from Washington, that an "informal police-to-police transfer" seemed more desirable. Obviously, the State Department and the narcs were at war again. Round One to the diplomats: Do it the formal way. Round Two to the narcs: Do it quick. A quick transfer would mean flying to the States immediately with his prisoner and his last clean shirt. He would lose the weekend at home. Still, he might trade it for a letter of commendation that could mean a promotion despite his field assignment. Hurray for the narcs.

Leaving the intergovernmental arrangements to the embassy's political officer, Mancini set about trying to arrange the "informal transfer." He conferred with the U.S. military group commander. If the Air Force cargo jet now unloading military supplies for the Paraguayans at the airport outside of town could delay its departure, Mancini might have a top-priority passenger for them.

"I'll do all I can," the commander said, "—but it will have to be cleared by higher authority."

Great, Mancini muttered under his breath, turning away. Now let the Pentagon add to the confusion. Did these bastards want Ricord or not? It had taken the Justice Department's Bureau of Narcotics and the Treasury Department's Customs Agency Service years to crack the mystery of Ricord's identity and finally "make" him in a case. President Nixon had called the heroin plague the nation's number one domestic problem. The bureau's strategic intelligence office in Washington believed that Ricord was the top operator in the newly developed "Latin connection" linking Marseilles and Manhattan. The Paraguayans had even defied all predictions by cooperating with U.S. officials. And now the big thinkers up the line couldn't decide what to do next. I should have been a building guard, Mancini thought. Nobody hijacks buildings.

Auguste Ricord sat on the side of his bed. This time the colonel of police had the straight-backed chair. Perhaps unconsciously, he sat straddling its seat, arms resting on the chair back as Ricord had the evening before. Ricord still protested his innocence in various tones and various ways. But he seemed almost undisturbed by the gentle questioning, his eyes twinkling with something like amusement.

The colonel was fascinated. The mantle of heroin kingpin did not seem to fit this little Frenchman. No fool, the colonel had done his homework. Or so he thought. Ricord lived in a one-story house on Alberdi Street, in a quiet, middle-class residential neighborhood, with Ana Elena and Brigitte. They appeared to lead the most normal of lives. Neighbors had assured the colonel personally that there were no late night revelries, no clandestine visits from sinister-looking men.

And Le Paris-Niza with its ludicrous little Eiffel Tower was, after all, a respectable place. He knew it himself. Tourist maps of

Asunción, tailored largely for North American visitors, did not list its restaurant among the top half-dozen, but prominent Paraguayans knew that it served some of the best food in the capital. And weren't those imperious fellows from the American Embassy sometimes seen there? Hardly the place to be a pivot in the global heroin trade.

". . . the Americans say I have $15 million, when my whole fortune consists of $20,000 which I have in a Swiss bank and which is the result of the sale of property. . . " his prisoner was saying.

Like many of Ricord's protestations, the statement had the appearance of truth. Charmed by his well-mannered prisoner, the colonel thought again of Alberdi Street and found himself quite ready to believe that the Americans had accused the wrong man.

*Excerpt from a report on the items found in the attaché case of Auguste Joseph Ricord upon his capture, 3/25/71:*

A review of the suspect's personal papers indicates two accounts in his name at the Union Des Banques Suisses, 1 Place Street, François, Lausanne, Switzerland. Account no.———* and deposit account no.———. Also indicated, present or former account in the names of Auguste José [sic] Ricord and Ana Elena Bonsignour with the Bank of Boston International, 2 Wall Street, New York, 10005. Account no.———. Also, account in Ricord's name in First National City at New York City, Account no.———.

*Excerpt from a report prepared some months later by a special agent in New York City and forwarded to the chief of enforcement, Customs Bureau, in Washington:*

Ricord has three U.S. and two Swiss bank accounts. Jeopardy assessments against the three domestic accounts will yield $75,000.

The sweltering, grassy prairie stretching north and west from Asunción, called El Chaco Boreal, may once have been an inland sea. Now it has few natural resources and fewer inhabitants. Some roads and many sluggish rivers criss-cross it, but for all

---

* The numbers have been deleted because of ongoing federal investigations.

practical purposes it is a primitive, hostile land best navigated by airplane. The Chaco is chiefly renowned for a hardwood tree that yields almost indestructible railroad ties and—like the chestnut trees of Corsica—a tanning extract necessary for turning cattle hides into leather.

Had Auguste Joseph Ricord been born a Paraguayan he might have been called after that tree—"quebracho" or "ax-breaker." If the pattern of international police records, put together often with hindsight and at the loss of a few lives, was any guide, he was nothing like a doctor out for a golfing afternoon. Nor was he merely the grandfatherly-looking owner of a pleasant motel thousands of miles from his native land.

Ricord had come to Asunción several years before, a man on the run. He had been on the run much of his life. But the records showed that he was a man of cunning, not fear. Even when others forced the timing, each move had been well executed, each flight calculated to ensure continued freedom.

Though police dossiers listed many crimes in many cities, what they really said was that M. Ricord always got away. On several continents, in the underworlds of a half-dozen national capitals, he was known as a criminal tough enough to break the ax of any lawman who tried to cut him down.

The hardening of Auguste Joseph Ricord began early and in the most likely of places. He was French Corsican, born to Pierre and Josephine Ricord in the storied port of Marseilles on April 26, 1911. Until the Germans destroyed much of it in World War II, Marseilles was a city of dark and light, sun-splashed but sinister, its intricate network of steep and narrow streets roamed by seafaring men of many nations and few scruples. The milieu undoubtedly had its effect on young Auguste Ricord, most law-enforcement men believe.

A French narcotics agent who has tracked Ricord across three continents contests this judgment. He argues that Marseilles is a maligned city: "If there are 100 narcotics traffickers in Marseilles, there are 120 in Le Havre, 150 in Bordeaux, and 75 in Barcelona." "A Frenchman will tell you," this official says, " 'Marseilles did not give the reputation to Marseilles. New York did not give the reputation to New York.' "

But the same agent will not argue about Ricord's reputation.

That, he agrees, has been earned. Two weeks before his sixteenth birthday, in 1927, young Ricord was convicted of theft and extortion. The details of the affair are lost in the less than fastidious files of the Marseilles police. But by November his "rap sheet" had already collected its second entry, "Violence, unauthorized possession of firearm," and Ricord left Marseilles for a city where a young man inclined toward trouble would be less noticeable. Not yet seventeen, on the run for the first time, he quickly added a third type of crime to his growing record: "11/15/27. Paris, France. Possession and sale of stolen property."

Someone scanning the French Sûreté's dossier on Auguste Ricord might momentarily conclude that a burst of adolescent passions lay behind his early troubles. For almost a decade after the Paris incident, no new offenses appeared after the name. When finally a new violation did appear on the books it was a relatively minor one: "Hunting infraction." A year later, however, on January 3, 1939, serious crime again became a part of the Ricord pattern. Police in Paris arrested him for unauthorized possession of a side arm.

An arrest report dated 3/27/71 from the Paris police to an American narcotics enforcement agency states: "From this time on he lived from proceeds earned from prostitution but was never arrested for it." France was at war with Germany. Crimes of low priority like prostitution and men of little consequence like Ricord were forgotten. World statesmen and diplomats and French generals had no interest, the police little more. Yet men with the talent to direct prostitution rings and the cleverness not to be caught can be of great interest to a conquering army. When the Nazis marched into Paris in June of 1940 they quickly sealed unwritten alliances with certain figures of the capital's criminal world. One of them was Auguste Joseph Ricord.

An American agency's one-page summary of Auguste Joseph Ricord's criminal biography describes him as a "member of the Gestapo in Occupied France." Another agency's files indicate that Ricord worked not directly for the Gestapo but as a chauffeur for the Parti Populaire Français, a fascistic, violently anti-Communist group that demanded the alliance of France with Germany and Italy. A narcotics enforcement official in Washington, in an interview after Ricord's 1971 arrest in Paraguay, said: "If he wasn't working for the Gestapo, he was posing as one of them—shaking people down." An intelligence official of the same agency said: "I'm afraid no one did a field investigation on Ricord and the Germans while it was still timely."

In the immediate postwar years, however, the French Government had no doubts about Ricord's wartime alliances. One excerpt from a French intelligence report, which demonstrates Ricord's skill at slipping out of trouble as easily as he slipped in, states: "On 9/9/42 he was charged with violence and sentenced, but was released by order of the German occupation forces. Just before the Liberation he went to Italy for refuge."

To the French, the diminutive Corsican was no longer the petty hoodlum, challenged by authority for violence, thievery, and the use of women and firearms. He had become a hated collaborator of the Third Reich—and an international fugitive.

In July, 1950, when Ricord was thirty-nine, the Permanent Military Court of Paris sentenced him to death *in absentia* for his Nazi associations. A year later the civilian court of Eure-et-Loir converted this harsh military judgment to the relatively benign sentence of twenty years' hard labor and 10 years' banishment from his homeland for an aggravated theft some years before. With an irony that must have amused Ricord, the statute of limitations would have caused this sentence to hang over his head until October, 1971—eight months after his arrest on the dusty road to Itá Enramada—except that both the military and the civilian crimes were later proscribed by a general amnesty.

It was a long trail from the labyrinthine streets of his Marseilles boyhood to a collaborator's sentence of death. But Ricord had not followed the path of crime without learning. The key words in his sentence of death were *"in absentia."*

From wartime Paris, Ricord apparently made his way to Milan. Like so much of his furtive life, not even that is certain. He passed through Germany and Austria on the way, then left Milan for Buenos Aires just before Christmas in 1948. But there also are indications that he sought asylum in Spain as early as 1944, left there for Rio de Janeiro in 1946 or 1947, and made his way from Rio to Buenos Aires.

In any case, long before the military court ordered his death,

Auguste Joseph Ricord was safely in the Argentine capital, lured by a cosmopolitan city that is the European immigrant's beacon on the South American continent.

Ricord did not find the New World hostile to a man of his political sympathies, as postwar Europe had become. A few years before, a group of Argentine Army officers who modeled themselves after Germany's National Socialists had seized control of the government. Buenos Aires, the City of Fair Winds, had become not only a postwar refuge for escaped Nazis but—of greater interest to Ricord—a collecting place for their former French collaborators as well. Ricord became an Argentine citizen.

Somewhere along the way he had left behind a wife, probably in Paris. In Buenos Aires he eventually acquired another wife, a buxom young German-born nightclub stripper named Ingebord Cabski—though intelligence officials insist that no record of a formal marriage can be found. Ingebord bore him Josephine Brigitte (or Josefina Brigita in Spanish) before they separated in 1960.

"When Ricord arrived in Argentina he covered himself so well he just disappeared," a Bureau of Narcotics official said. "It's surprising how little is in the files." Careful reconstruction, however, has shown that something drew Ricord almost immediately to Buenos Aires's rugged dockside area. It may have been nostalgia for Marseilles—or a simple desire to be near routes of escape. ("Look at Le Paris-Niza many years later," a State Department official said. "It, too, was suspiciously near a border.")

Whatever Ricord had done for the Nazis, he later boasted from his Tacumbu cell that he left France for Italy and South America "with more than $100,000 in my pockets." Narcotics officials have been told that he and his half-sister, Maria Traversa Bonsignour, sold a restaurant called the Navarin for $40,000 before they fled from Paris.

In the New World, with Maria's help, Ricord quickly became a multiple restaurateur. But he began by buying a nightclub, Le Fetiche, and then another, the Lido. At one time or another he owned and operated restaurants called El Nido, Chez Danielle, L'Etoile, the Bar el Sol (later renamed L'Auberge Provençale), the M. André, and the Pompidor.

The Bar el Sol on Marconi Street, in the close-in dockside

suburb of Olivos, would become a familiar name to narcotics intelligence agents on three continents. But in the 1950s it was unknown to them. Had they been aware earlier of its existence and
the activities of its patrons they might have saved thousands of
man-hours and millions of dollars.

Close associations, particularly among men who consider themselves comrades-in-arms, do not die easily. From the back streets
of Paris and the police mugbooks of Marseilles, familiar faces
converged on the Bar el Sol in the decade after the war. In the
words of a seasoned French narcotics agent, Auguste Ricord became "the switchplate" for a constant flow of traffic. Like the
switching mechanism at the junction of many pairs of railroad
tracks, he received a steady procession of European fugitives and
skillfully dispatched each one to his next destination.

If a man needed a new identity, "M. André" could provide
identity cards. If the fugitive was, for the moment, a man without
a country, "Cori" could produce a "funny passport." If the passport—real or faked or stolen—was already in the fugitive's possession, it was nothing for "Dédé" (a diminutive of André) to
acquire a "funny visa" to accompany it. A man with papers but
needing cash might be told where to acquire it—using his own
illicit skills, of course.

M. André, Cori, and Dédé all were Auguste Joseph Ricord, using the convenience of the alias and the code name—tricks he had
learned as a young man in Paris.

In an underworld, as in an upperworld of bankers or presidents,
fraternity or union brothers, there are bonds based on common
backgrounds, common nationalities, common interests—at the
very least, earned trust. Many trusted men—but only these—were
sent from Marseilles and Algiers, Milan and Casablanca, Rome
and Barcelona to the bar at 380 Marconi Street in the postwar
years with simple instructions: "See M. André." If the proprietor was not around, bartender Joe Bouillon (once married
to singer Josephine Baker) was there as a steersman in the night,
always able to find the navigator's star and point the wandering
new arrival onto a safe course.

An excerpt from a French police report describing Ricord's
activities in those years states: "He used to frequent the Maison

des Anciens Combattants Français, which then became a veritable haven for international gangsters. . . . One of his principal associates is Christian David, the murderer of the Paris Police Commissaire Gallibert." For a man who kept such company, Ricord stayed remarkably free of trouble. Just as he had kept his name off French police blotters for a decade before World War II, he now avoided making a postwar record in South America. But from an ocean away, the ever watchful French police observed that he had lost none of his talent for whoremongering. One intelligence report noted: "His major source of revenue [in Buenos Aires] came from his interest in prostitution." This revenue, by some estimates, ran as high as $3 million a year. Ricord's business, anchored in Buenos Aires but spreading into neighboring Brazil and Uruguay and as far north as Caracas, Venezuela, provided his many old and new acquaintances with income and employment—not to mention women, many of them impressive young beauties imported from France. As the French Sûreté put it, Ricord become an expert at "harboring international criminals who were channeled into his prostitution syndicate."

Finally, in 1957, trouble appeared to have found him in his Argentine refuge. It seemed that even his collaborator's past might be catching up with him. Two close associates sought by Paris police for a triple murder at the Hotel Pigalle in Paris—François Lucien Capezza and Jean Lunardi—were traced to Buenos Aires through Interpol, the international police information-swapping organization. Under questioning, they "flipped" on Ricord, telling officials how and where his prostitution network was operated. Whoring was prohibited within the Buenos Aires city limits, but Ricord had taken advantage of legal technicalities to ring the city with suburban establishments. The Argentine police arrested Ricord for corruption and criminal association. But his wartime history intervened. The French, claiming a prior and much more important interest, asked that M. Ricord be handed over to them.

The kind of Interpol lookout notice that trapped Capezza and Lunardi is color-coded, according to the severity of the crime for which a man is wanted. The red box in the upper right-hand corner of Auguste Ricord's flyer made it tantamount to an arrest warrant in whatever country he might be found. But an Interpol notice does not list political crimes such as collaboration with an occupying German army—the charge for which France really wanted Ricord.

The French request for extradition fell on hostile ears. Argentina is, with Uruguay, the most Europeanized of the Latin countries. By no means all of its immigrants were lured by the promise of riches; many left their homelands to escape from political oppression—or prosecution for political crimes. The Argentine Government was not quick to extradite a man to the Old World, even if the crime for which he was sought seemed nonpolitical. Sympathy lay with the immigrants. Furthermore, M. Ricord was now a citizen. Argentina turned the French down, and Ricord was released. He promptly left for Montevideo, Uruguay.

In Montevideo, Auguste Ricord became Lucien Darguelles— but again the relentless French police authorities sought his extradition. Again, however, Ricord seems to have had more influence than his would-be captors. Uruguay, like Argentina, refused the extradition demand.

Late in 1958, still haunted by France's long-distance pursuit and still traveling, Ricord surfaced in swinging Caracas as the owner of a nightclub called Le Domino. Caracas was thousands of miles north of the risky Buenos Aires–Montevideo circuit and half a lifetime from Marseilles. It was a city with plenty of action, where protection came high even to the experienced buyer. But not too high for Ricord. According to a French dossier compiled in 1971, "Le Domino was very active in prostitution."

Again, an entry marked by brevity, as if an artist could catch only an occasional glimpse of a man he wished to sketch in great detail. By now the Ricord rap sheet carried almost as many aliases as it did crimes. Some were variations on his real name, such as August José Gallese (his parents' name). Others were variations on the "Lucien Darguelles" he had used in Uruguay—Lucien Dorguelle, Lucio Maria Darguelles, or Lucien Gegelles. And to M. André and Cori and Dédé had been added terms of honor that comrades give a man who has led them in war or survived decades of battling with the police—"El Commandante" (The Chief) and "L'Ancêtre" (The Old One).

American intelligence files are as unsuccessful at capturing the full face and profile of Auguste Ricord in the Caracas years as are the French dossiers. Generalizations abound in lieu of specific dates, activities, and places. It is known that a decade after his flight to Caracas Ricord boldly returned to Argentina (some intelligence analysts believe he moved in and out all the time) and walked right back into trouble. Again two old acquaintances almost led to his downfall. Lucien Sarti, wanted for the murder of a Belgian policeman, and Francisco Chiappe, under sentence of death for another murder, had fled Europe and found their way to the South American "switchplate" who might offer them shelter, connections, and perhaps permanent employment. In 1968 Sarti and Chiappe held up a money exchange. Argentine police arrested them and Ricord. Though none of them went to jail for that crime, a search of their restaurant near the Rio de la Plata Football Stadium in Buenos Aires turned up a cache of arms, including machine guns. Ricord was declared *persona non grata* and kicked out of Argentina.

Throughout the years from his first arrest in 1927, at the age of sixteen, until the late 1960s there had been no hint of involvement in narcotics, despite Ricord's origins in Marseilles and his abundantly obvious ties with Corsican underworld figures.

*Excerpt from a French intelligence report made available to Customs agents in New York City early in 1971:*

Subsequently [to his sojourn at Le Domino in Caracas], Ricord set up a large organization trafficking in narcotics to the United States. His protégés acted as carriers. Regardless of the numerous arrests [of carriers], his business is excellent and he has established himself as the owner of the Paris-Nice Restaurant located in the outskirts of Asunción, Paraguay . . ."

The Aeropuerto Internacional Presidente General Stroessner outside of Asunción is small by New York or London standards but it deserves the term international. Built largely with U.S. aid, it is served by a trim four-lane highway that U.S. money also helped to buy. A 9,000-foot runway easily accommodates the sleek Boeing 707s and the lesser planes of half a dozen airlines, among them Braniff and Aerolineas Argentinas. Although the Paraguayan capital lies almost 1,000 miles from the sea by riverboat—the most common form of travel—modern aviation has modified its isolation.

Across the field from the glaring white concrete-and-steel terminal building on the day after Ricord's arrest, a U.S. Air Force C-141 jet transport unloaded cargo. It was there on a routine assignment, but if it had not been, another military jet probably would have been available. At a certain working level, agents of the Bureau of Narcotics and the Customs Agency Service were quite capable of contingency planning with their military counterparts, even if their superiors did not always let them execute the plans.

The C-141's commander had already been notified by the embassy that by nightfall he might have a high-priority civilian passenger—a Frenchman. He had dragged out the unloading as much as possible to allow more time, as requested. If the passenger showed, the commander understood, the plane was to make a nonstop flight direct to Homestead Air Force Base near Miami, avoiding the legal complications that might arise if it set down on the soil of another country.

Standing in the shadow of the giant wing, out of the bright glare reflecting from the plane's smooth aluminum skin, Mancini now explained that there might be some snags.

"The Frenchman is wanted in the States for smuggling, but he's never been there. The Paraguayans find that strange. They don't have a conspiracy law. They have no narcotics laws at all, and as you know, ordinary smuggling is their stock-in-trade, so they see nothing wrong with it. The embassy is into this thing but it's waffling—Ricord hasn't been convicted of anything here *or* back home yet. We have an extradition treaty with Paraguay, but unfortunately it doesn't say anything about narcotics.

"And while your beautiful daylight fades, Treasury, Justice, State, and the Defense Department are busy countermanding my orders faster than I get new ones. We want this little Frog—but we're having trouble with our protocols. Anyway, we appreciate all you're doing and can do."

The night of March 26, 1971, came, but the civilian passenger did not appear and the C-141 departed.

# 2  An Abundance of
#### Oscilloscopes

## 1966–67

       *The visit from Paul Chastagnier fell*
across Gregor Sobol's tranquil life like the deep, cold shadow of a
New York skyscraper on a November afternoon. It brought with
it disquieting memories of a less certain, less comfortable time.

Sobol was not a rich man, nor had he been unusually lucky.
Yet he had few complaints. Even the prospect of being almost
forty did not bother him as he had thought it would. No pot belly
marred his tall, trim figure. The same women who noticed his
youthful build and commented on his dark eyes were kind enough
to overlook the thinning of his dark hair.

Gregor Sobol had been a boy of twelve when war convulsed
Europe in 1939—young enough to escape military service throughout the years of fighting. When the Soviet Union turned Hungary
into a Communist satellite after the war, fate had already intervened in Sobol's behalf again. He was safely in Ecuador.

Now he had become a New Yorker, one of a multitude of immigrants who find in lower Manhattan a place of livelihood, a

23

home, and the sense of peace that comes to a man who has stopped traveling. He had a small apartment on West Twenty-seventh Street and, as the export sales manager of a million-dollar-a-year business, an acceptable amount of responsibility and a good income.

Sobol had met Paul Chastagnier in Ecuador. They had, in fact, been business partners for a time, operating a French restaurant there. But that had been fourteen years ago, a time and place that seemed almost as remote to Gregor Sobol now as the Budapest of his childhood memories. Now, Chastagnier was saying, he had returned to his native France and he, too, was in the export business. He proposed that he ship French-manufactured electro-cardiograph machines to Sobol for sale in America. Sobol declined, pointing out that he was in management now, not sales, and that his company was interested in exporting, not importing. Chastagnier seemed to accept this explanation and again departed from Sobol's life. That was in the late autumn of 1965.

The letter from Chastagnier a year later was harder to brush away than the personal visit had been. It said that Chastagnier was consigning to Sobol's company two shipments of oscillo-scopes, electronic instruments the size of a desk-top television set, used to monitor variations in electrical current. The letter added that the Frenchman would arrive in New York soon to pick up the merchandise himself.

This time there was no proposal that Sobol become directly involved by attempting to sell the instruments. It appeared to be a straightforward commercial shipping arrangement, leaving Sobol no alternative but to face once more the man who was an unwelcome reminder of harder, less pleasant years.

About the time of Chastagnier's first visit to Gregor Sobol in Manhattan, Parisians were engrossed by a sensational kidnapping that was to remain a *cause célèbre* for more than two years.

The victim was Mehdi Ben Barka, fiery leader of a dissident political party in Morocco, who had been living in exile in the French capital. The abduction was laid to two members of the Paris narcotics squad. They protested that they had acted at the request of an Orly Airport official who was also a French counterespionage agent. He in turn protested that he had simply been trying to do the Moroccan secret police a favor.

Ben Barka was traced to the home of a French gangster, but there the trail ended. Ben Barka was never seen again; the gangster and several of his associates caught a plane to Morocco.

When the French police finally took what critics said was a belated interest in the whole affair, they happened across a friend of the missing gangster living in a Montparnasse hotel owned by the gangster's wife. For more than a year they kept a diligent watch on the friend, hoping he would lead them to the gangster—and perhaps to an explanation of Ben Barka's kidnapping and possible murder. Instead, their months of unrewarding surveillance told them only that the friend bought oscilloscopes in what seemed to be extraordinary numbers—and that his name was Paul Chastagnier.

Air France Flight 055, a Boeing 707 direct from Paris, made a less than perfect landing on a windswept runway at John F. Kennedy International Airport in New York and taxied past soot-blackened mounds of snow to the warmth of the International Arrivals Building. Time: 1:26 p.m., December 22, 1966, a Thursday. In three days it would be Christmas, or Noël, depending on a passenger's point of origin.

A neatly dressed Frenchman of about fifty was just closing the last of his expensive suitcases when something about him caused the Customs inspector to ask him to step aside. Seven months earlier, a Bureau of Narcotics liaison man, who admitted that the reliability of his informant was unknown, had asked Customs to alert inspectors to watch for three Frenchmen. They were suspected of having smuggled heroin into the city by commercial jetliner. Until now, the alert had produced nothing.

Mistakenly, the inspector thought the dapper Frenchman standing before him was a particular suspect mentioned in the months-old notice. In fact, the man was Paul Chastagnier—who also, as it happened, was named in the alert.

A polite search of Chastagnier and his luggage in a detention room off the vast, open Customs inspection area had almost ended when Bureau of Narcotics agent Albert Garofalo, alerted by Customs, walked into the room. Chastagnier looked slightly startled. Then he regained his composure and smiled as if he had been dealt four aces.

"I recognize you," he said to Garofalo. "You frequented the Station Bar and the Olympic Bar in Marseilles." There was a note of triumph and superiority in his voice, as if he had caught Garofalo cracking a safe. Obviously, he knew Garofalo was a narc.

To Garofalo, Chastagnier looked much like a dozen other Frenchmen he might have seen in Marseilles or Paris, or right in this same building for that matter. The face meant nothing special. But the agent knew the Station Bar and the Olympic Bar well enough—his investigation of heroin laboratories in the Marseilles area had taken him to both more than once. The Frenchman could easily have noticed him there. Which meant that other patrons must also have seen through his cover, Garofalo thought.

The search ended. Both the man and his luggage were clean. There was nothing to do but release him, with apologies, and watch to see what happened next.

Chastagnier gathered up his bags, stopped to make a brief phone call from a pay booth, and then walked quickly to the street. As he hailed a cab, Garofalo and another agent raced for the car they had left almost a block away. But the incredibly tangled traffic around the JFK parking area was no place for fast wheel-work. Their man disappeared into a sea of automobiles.

Back to Square One: What else had the Customs inspector learned before Garofalo got there? The agents were told that among Chastagnier's effects was a small slip of paper bearing a penciled message. It had not seemed important, but if he recalled correctly the message had said:

"Meeting—Café des Sports, 51st St. & 7th Ave."

"Thanks for the memory," Garofalo said, heading again for the street. The inspector shrugged and went back to his post.

The agents had lost their man once, but they might pick him up at his meeting. Again, however, the odds seemed to be with Chastagnier. Garofalo and his companion fought their way up the Van Wyck, across the Long Island Expressway and through the Queens Midtown Tunnel, turned north and took Forty-ninth Street across town toward Seventh. But they cruised the area around Fifty-first and Seventh for ten minutes without seeing a Café des Sports. They were about to stop and consult that most reliable of sources, a phone book, when Garofalo noticed the Hotel Taft and decided on a hunch to check it out. He had tried better bets and lost, but he had tried longer shots and won. This time he came up winners.

Paul Chastagnier had filled out the usual I-94 Immigration and Naturalization Service form on the plane, noting that he would be staying with a friend in Ridgefield, Connecticut. But the desk clerk said that a Paul Chastagnier had checked into the Taft only half an hour before. He had gone out almost immediately, however, and the switchboard operator said she did not think he had made or received any telephone calls.

With only that to go on, the two weary agents watched the Taft until three o'clock on Friday morning. If Chastagnier returned, he did it without their seeing him. Maybe he was in Ridgefield after all. He had come into New York clean, there were no charges outstanding, and the agents decided to chuck it without calling for replacements. Only two more shopping days until Christmas, and manpower wasn't that cheap.


Gregor Sobol's office in the grimy building at 90 West Street, almost at the southern tip of Manhattan Island, overlooked the gray Hudson River and the depressingly dirty Central Railroad of New Jersey passenger station on the river's opposite shore. Heavy traffic from the Brooklyn-Battery Tunnel and the West Side Highway kept the windows at a steady rattle that Sobol had long since ceased to hear. But the ringing of his phone on the afternoon of December 22 startled him. He winced, as he had done every time it rang for the past several days—knowing the call was overdue, knowing it would inevitably come, wishing the Frenchman would have the grace not to spoil the holidays.

It was Chastagnier. In his pleasant, fluid accent, he was asking

Sobol to meet him in the Hotel Taft lobby at 6 P.M. Chastagnier was more than an old acquaintance and former partner now. He was a customer, and Sobol agreed.

Chastagnier wore a dark blue overcoat, dark gray hat, and soft leather gloves. Obviously, he didn't mean to stay indoors. Politely, he ushered Sobol out of the hotel, and they began to walk, aimlessly as far as Sobol could see. But Chastagnier was deliberately using the privacy that a sidewalk crowd provides: An enemy might follow them but would not hear their words. The Frenchman explained that four oscilloscopes had arrived at JFK as air freight two days earlier, on Air France Flight 077. His own flight that day had brought in a shipment of six more. Addressee for both sets of instruments: Gregor Sobol, 90 West Street, N.Y.C.

"Then it's as good as done," Sobol thought.

But Chastagnier was worried about clearing the shipments through Customs—he hoped there would be no undue delays. Sobol, the experienced export man, explained that the heavier load at Christmastime and the holiday atmosphere that depleted the working ranks would undoubtedly mean a longer clearance time than usual. "Yes," Chastagnier said. He still seemed unusually fretful.

They had drifted north and east as they walked, but Sobol had been unaware that his companion had a destination in mind. When they reached an apartment building at 135 East Fifty-seventh Street, however, Chastagnier paused, took Sobol's arm, and said, "There is someone you must meet." Sobol was glad to leave the December chill for any reason. The Frenchman must have ice in his veins.

In apartment 8B, Chastagnier introduced Sobol to Albert Larrain, a saturnine man who spoke English with a Spanish accent. Senor Larrain, said Chastagnier, owned an interest in a horse-racing stable in South America. The two abruptly began discussing the oscilloscopes, ignoring Sobol as if he were a piece of the furniture. He was getting that feeling again that he always got around Paul Chastagnier, a feeling that he was being used. Only once, perhaps sensing his mood, did the host even acknowledge

Sobol's presence. Midway through the conversation, Larrain turned to him and said, "You will be rewarded for your help." Sobol grunted a reply, thinking Larrain would say more, but the remark went unexplained.

*Excerpt from a memorandum dated 12/27/66 from an American narcotics agent in Paris to his home office in New York:*

The French Sûreté officers mentioned South America as a possible source of the merchandise, although they are not convinced that narcotics are involved.

They further stated that apparently something occurred which delayed the delivery of whatever merchandise it may be, because according to [an] informant, they were afraid something was wrong and even thought the American Bureau of Narcotics was on to them.

The Sûreté informant was wrong. Customs had let Chastagnier pass through, Bureau of Narcotics Agent Garofalo had long since lost his trail, and the only thing holding up his shipments was the Christmas holiday.

That same afternoon, two days after Christmas, two large cartons containing ten oscilloscopes were delivered to Gregor Sobol's office. Chastagnier, still fretful over the delay, telephoned shortly afterward—as he had on the 23d and the 24th and the 26th.

"They're here," Sobol said.

But Chastagnier did not come for the packages. Instead, the phone rang again an hour later, and this time it was Albert Larrain's voice. He said Chastagnier had asked him to make the pickup. He was in the neighborhood and wondered if he could come up now. For some reason that eluded him, Sobol asked Larrain to wait until after 5 o'clock, when all the employees would be gone.

At 5:10 P.M. Larrain walked in, accompanied by a tall, thin young man with very blond hair and a large scar on the left side of his face. Larrain did not bother to introduce the young man, who Sobol was to learn later was an Argentine living in New York. The name didn't matter. Sobol would always think of him as the Scarred Man.

With no formalities, Larrain and the Scarred Man took the large cartons one at a time down to a waiting taxicab, leaving the second time without a thanks or good-by.

On Wednesday the 28th, Chastagnier took Sobol to Larrain's Fifty-seventh Street apartment again. This time Sobol was introduced to another Latin American, identified only as "Luis the Argentine." Luis was as different from the Scarred Man as anyone could be. He was impeccably dressed in a hand-tailored beige suit that had a look of the subtropics about it. He appeared to be in his fifties and was as short and chunky as the Scarred Man was tall and thin. From the conversation, Sobol gathered that Luis, too, had racing-stable interests. And something in what the other men said—Sobol was again left out of the conversation—led him to believe that whatever the game was here, Luis was the boss for Latin America.

Larrain opened a large satchel and, without explanation, handed $2,000 to a surprised Gregor Sobol. He assumed this must be the reward mentioned a few days earlier. But all he could think of to say was, "It's not safe to have so much money around the house."

Larrain laughed. "If you think that is a lot of money," he said, "look over here." He crossed the room and opened a large dresser drawer. It was completely filled with U.S. currency. (The Scarred Man told Sobol later that he had come to Larrain's apartment on the day after Christmas to find the entire living-room floor covered with stacks of bills. On another occasion, Larrain had two paper shopping bags filled with money.)

Gregor Sobol, Hungarian refugee, once-satisfied export sales manager, now faced what he had tried to force from his mind since Paul Chastagnier's first visit in the autumn of the year before—Chastagnier was trouble, expensive trouble. Not even oscilloscopes of solid gold could command this kind of money. Sobol's confusion and dismay showed clearly in his soulful brown eyes.

Chastagnier laughed gently. Taking a certain delight in toying with his pigeon, he at last began to explain to Sobol. He said that Larrain and the Scarred Man had taken the oscilloscopes to the Scarred Man's apartment the day before "to unload them."

The load, Chastagnier said, was ten kilograms (twenty-two pounds) of heroin of a great purity, prepared in one of Marseilles's finest laboratories. Each oscilloscope had concealed a kilogram. Diluted, or "whacked," by as much as 16-to-1 with anything from Epsom salts to milk sugar or talcum powder, the heroin would be packaged in individual doses and sold on Manhattan's streets for more than $2 million. Despite his shock, Sobol found himself calculating rapidly that his $2,000 was only a tenth of 1 per cent of $2 million.

But Chastagnier was still talking. Pure heroin delivered by a smuggler to a New York receiver was selling for a mere $11,000 or $12,000 per kilo, he said. The white powder would pass down through many hands toward the retail market, multiplying its value at each step as the risk of being busted for "pushing" it to addicts grew closer. Thus the transportation organization that Chastagnier represented would receive only about $120,000 for the risks its members had taken.

Again Sobol's mind was calculating automatically despite himself. His $2,000 now looked closer to 2 per cent. But that was no consolation. Without leaving the spot where he stood, Gregor Sobol suddenly felt like a man on the run. He knew that never again would he feel the sense of safety, the tranquillity of having finally put down roots.

In microseconds, the incriminating events and bits of evidence flashed through his mind. He was now as much a part of the trouble as Chastagnier. There was the letter from the Frenchman consigning the oscilloscopes to his company—undoubtedly Chastagnier would have kept a carbon copy. There were the Customs records, the air cargo waybills bearing his signature of receipt, the cartons stenciled "Attn. G. Sobol." The links to Chastagnier going back fifteen years in Ecuador. His own failure to press Chastagnier on why he had picked Sobol's company, why the Frenchman had been so anxious about the Customs clearance, why ordinary oscilloscopes seemed so dear.

Most frightening, Sobol realized, was that he must have preferred all along not to ask Chastagnier the hard questions. By his inaction, he had helped make himself a pigeon, and an accomplice.

On the same day that Sobol's life began to splinter in the living room on East Fifty-seventh Street, narcotics officials in New York received another in the fusillade of cablegrams from their American counterparts in Paris. For some days the traffic had been heavy, and Chastagnier's name had been prominent in almost every message.

The cable that day contained yet another reference to the Frenchman. The information was on the mark this time, but six days too late:

"CHASTAGNIER BELIEVED TO HAVE LEFT PARIS VIA AIR FRANCE DEC. 22, 1966, AT 10 A.M. PARIS TIME NOT CARRYING MERCHANDISE. INQUIRIES CONTINUE AT PARIS."

Adding to the confusion was another cryptic reference to a continent that had never before seemed important in the heroin smuggling trade:

"ORIGIN OF MERCHANDISE BELIEVED TO BE SOUTH AMERICA."

There was no elaboration.

Almost unnoticed, overshadowed by the mention of Chastagnier—who at least was known to have reached New York—was a second name that would soon assume great significance:

"OTHER SUSPECT STILL AT PARIS, FELIPE SPADARO, AKA [also known as] JOJO, 45, SPEAKS ENGLISH WITH ACCENT. ENGAGED TO 'MRS. FELIPE' IN NEW YORK. USES POST OFFICE FOR MAIL. SOME DELAY RECEIVING DELIVERY."


At a meeting in Larrain's apartment on December 29, plans for taking the money for the heroin back to France were discussed, argued about, rediscussed. It was finally decided that the cash, a little more than $100,000, should be divided between two couriers. Chastagnier thought that he should be one of them and the Scarred Man the other. The Scarred Man would carry the larger amount. If he were caught, the organization would lose a lot of money. But he was less important to the organization than Chastagnier, and it was the rule that the less important the man, the more risk he must be prepared to take.

They also discussed the wisdom of taking the same plane. Although Chastagnier did not say so, he preferred to keep an eye on the Scarred Man, who was younger, inexperienced as a money courier, and inclined to be impetuous. To cover up his motive, he

said that the Scarred Man should take his pretty young wife with
him to help avoid suspicion. They would travel as a couple; Chastagnier would travel on the same plane but pretend not to know
them. No one was likely to connect a French citizen and an Argentine couple.

Early in January, Luis the Argentine handed the Scarred Man
$76,000 and a generous wad of expense money and told him to
take the heroin proceeds to a certain hotel in Paris. There, Luis
said, the $76,000 should be turned over to "Pepe"—who would
actually be Paul Chastagnier—and a man named Felipe Spadaro,
the same man the cable of December 28 had identified as "other
suspect still at Paris."

Luis also had a word of caution for his young friend. The
Scarred Man was to resist any urging by Chastagnier or Felipe
that he bring back a load of heroin on his return trip. Customs
agents had busted too many heroin couriers lately, and this was
not a good time to take extra chances.

The Scarred Man and his wife boarded the Air France flight on
January 4 and saw Chastagnier already seated near the rear of the
tourist cabin. They carefully avoided any sign of recognition. As
the flight neared Paris, however, they were surprised to have
Chastagnier suddenly standing in the aisle beside their seats, lean-
ing close to the Scarred Man. He whispered that they should take
a taxi to the hotel Luis had mentioned and wait for him to call.
The young Argentine was again impressed at the way the organization worked. He would not see Chastagnier and Felipe Spadaro at
the hotel after all—it probably had never really been planned
that he would. And he had not been notified of the actual plan
until the last moment. If the thought of skipping with the
$76,000 had crossed his mind—and it had—he now forgot it. He
would not try to defy the efficiency of this machine—at least not
yet.

At Chastagnier's home, the Scarred Man and his wife were
introduced to Felipe Spadaro and a man called Etienne. The
three older men almost smothered the Scarred Man with praise
for his successful delivery of the $76,000. He knew what they
meant without their saying it specifically. His height, his near-
white blond hair, and the scarred face meant that he was noticed

almost everywhere he went. To keep his cool and arouse no suspicion when he knew that the eye of every Customs and Immigration man he passed must be on him was the sign of a very promising neophyte. Perhaps his size and his marred good looks worked for him rather than against him, distracting the official mind from any thought that he might be a smuggler.

True to Luis the Argentine's prediction, the others tried to persuade him to take a quantity of heroin back to New York, concealed in small packages taped to his shins. He told them of Luis's warning and flatly refused. Now he was not so sure about the group's efficiency—it seemed to him unwise to even think of carrying contraband cash in one direction and heroin in the other within a very few days.

The older men were put out at his refusal. But in his brashness he pointed out that Luis was in New York, not they, and they must trust the man on the scene. Chastagnier, Spadaro, and Etienne grudgingly agreed. For now, oscilloscopes were safer. Without even scolding him for his impertinence, Chastagnier suggested that the Scarred Man and his wife take the remainder of the expense money and spend a few weeks on the Continent. It might be prudent, in view of what Luis had said.

Narcotics enforcement officers, like the smugglers they pursue, tend to be creatures of habit. If the professional criminal has an MO (*modus operandi*), or standard way of operating, so does his counterpart on the other side of the law.

For hundreds of years, the smuggler of any item of high value —money, watches, diamonds, or gold—had commonly carried his goods with him, unwilling to trust it out of his sight. More recently, this had been even more true of heroin. Its extremely high value for its bulk and weight made concealment unusually profitable and relatively easy. Merchant seamen reached the docks of New York and Baltimore and Philadelphia in great numbers. A heroin courier among them could be confident that overworked Customs inspectors and understaffed narcotics squads might easily miss him.

Often a courier had small packets of "the white stuff" or "the shit," as it was called, taped to his body under his clothing. Until the mid-1960s the U.S. market was relatively small; large amounts of capital were not needed to operate a ring, and heroin in adequate amounts could be supplied simply by increasing the number of individual couriers. Customs agents were less well trained and less alert to heroin because mass addiction was not then a widespread, critical problem.

The "body carry"—known to narcotics enforcers as "bellying it in"—was a favorite. It put only the low-paid courier at risk. He did not need a group of confederates, just the man who handed him the packet in Marseilles or Bordeaux and the man who paid him for it at the other end of the voyage. A second favored way to slip contraband in was among a courier's personal effects—in a raincoat pocket, a toilet kit, or a suitcase, sometimes with a false bottom or false sides.

The reason for preferring these methods was simple—the heroin was always "chaperoned," accompanied by a personal guard as if it were a shipment of fine diamonds or small gold coins. And with his pay waiting for him in the port of destination, a courier would guard his "load" with great attention.

The use of commercial cargo—transported out of the smuggler's sight and out of his control, passing through many pairs of hands —had not become a common method of moving heroin even as late in the modern American heroin epidemic as December of 1966.

"I can only think of two or three loads that came in with any imagination before that time," an experienced Customs agent in New York recalled. "In 1965 or 1966 there was the Nebbia case— ninety-five kilos or pounds, I forget which, came in from Europe packed in the walls of a home freezer, shipped by a warrant officer who was being transferred back to the States. That and one other—the 'French Connection' car.

"In 1966 there was another nice load also hidden in a car on a ship, but that was then bellied off in small amounts."

It was natural in the days of Gregor Sobol and Paul Chastagnier for Customs inspectors and agents of the Bureau of Narcotics, which still concentrated on busting street pushers and users, to focus on people rather than on inanimate objects such as oscilloscopes.

Even so, it has always been axiomatic among Customs men that the smuggler will think of something first. He will never abandon a centuries-old route or technique, but he will always be looking for new ones. Often he uses the new for months or years before discovery finally tells the Customs inspector what he has been failing to watch for.

The advent of the Boeing 707 and Douglas DC-8 long-range jets late in the 1950s was, in a way, American ingenuity's gift to the smuggler. The jets dramatically shortened delivery times across the Atlantic, proving stout competition to the slower voyage by sea. Airline stewardesses and even pilots would occasionally agree to a "one-timer," hauling a single load of contraband and quitting with their winnings. More often, the specially recruited courier, fitted out with air fare, expense money, false documents, and a special heroin "girdle," replaced the lowly seaman as the primary carrier. It was all quite easy. The explosive growth of air travel brought about by the jets and by the increase in tourism among affluent Americans and West Europeans of necessity made Customs procedures more cursory than ever before.

Swifter delivery meant that a greater volume of goods could be brought to market. So the purveyors of heroin now also made certain that the demand was stimulated. "It only took one to hook one," as they said. Addiction began to double and triple each year, especially in the main market place of New York.

Only the speed of transport and the volume of smuggling increased at first, however. The classical carrying patterns remained —for a time—much the same.

Just as they were slow to spot the use of commercial cargo for drug smuggling when men like Paul Chastagnier began to pioneer it, so were narcotics agents disinclined to believe that such a valuable commodity as heroin would be diverted from the standard routes. For decades, Turkish opium had moved either as raw opium or its illicit by-product, morphine base, to Marseilles. From the heroin laboratories—little larger than a mountain whisky still—of Marseilles, the white gold-dust then came directly to New York or another Eastern port, or very occasionally through Montreal or Toronto to the United States.

A detour of thousands of miles to South America made no

sense. It was so alien to logic—and to ingrained habits of thought —that agents tended to ignore occasional vague references to a Latin connection. Auguste Ricord could build his cartel virtually free of suspicion.

"As far back as '64, '65, there were rumors that South America was involved. But nobody knew anything then, so the easiest thing to do was laugh it off," a Customs agent too young to have made that mistake said.

Thus a memorandum from an agent in Paris, dated January 12, 1967 ("Spadaro reportedly left France, probably for South America") and a cable of March 6 ("STRONGLY BELIEVE SPADARO LEFT FRANCE FOR SOUTH AMERICA") made no particular impression in New York.

It probably meant only that a much-mentioned suspect had gone into hiding to cool off for a while.

Latin America's importance was still unrecognized. But certain Narcotics Bureau and Customs agents in New York were about to be hit right between the eyes with the potential of using cargo to conceal bulk shipments of heroin.

The March 6 cable had been one of an unprecedented flow that had continued since shortly before the Christmas holidays. One message, at the end of February, had shown a remarkable if not totally accurate understanding of Paul Chastagnier's new game:

"CHASTAGNIER SHIPMENT POSSIBLY 10 ITEMS ELECTRONIC EQUIP- MENT, EACH SEPARATELY BOXED, EXPECTED FOR MARCH 10, 11, OR 12 WITH PART OF ABOVE OR SECOND SHIPMENT TO FOLLOW ABOUT ONE WEEK LATER.

"DUMMY COMPANY RESPONSIBLE FOR SHIPMENTS," this cable read, "BELIEVED TO BE SOCIETE FRANCAIS APPLICATION ELECTRONIC AT 3 RUE DE L'ETAPE AT CHENNEVIERES, FRANCE 9. BOXES OF ELECTRONIC EQUIPMENT MAY BE CARRIED BY COURIER AND DECLARED AT CUS- TOMS."

The cable also showed the accuracy of hindsight:

"CHECK INCOMING PARIS FLIGHTS TO NEW YORK BETWEEN 12/22 AND 12/26/66 FOR REPRESENTATIVE OF YOUNG ELECTRONICS OR S.F.A.E. DECLARING BOXES AND PAYING DUTY ON SAME."

The ten oscilloscopes that had arrived by Air France and passed through Gregor Sobol's hands might have gone undetected at the time, but somebody had been on to them.

Finally, the cable contained an alert:

"CHASTAGNIER MAY DEPART FOR NEW YORK ON MARCH 2. REQUEST SURVEILLANCE ONLY."

No Chastagnier was among the passengers of incoming Paris flights on the second of March. Six days later, however, as agents continued to monitor the flow of traffic from France, a short chunky man with brown hair and blue eyes landed at JFK aboard Air France Flight 017. He fitted the description of "Etienne," a 46-year-old native of Bordeaux who had been mentioned in a late-December cable along with Chastagnier and Spadaro.

This man the agents knew much about, if only from the cable traffic. Under another name, he had stayed with his mistress at the Hotel Claridge in Paris in mid-December and had met there with Paul Chastagnier. Etienne, who spoke Spanish as well as French, had lived in Bordeaux until 1947. Then he had gone to Caracas, Venezuela, to work as a cook. He had become a partner in the ownership of a bar in Caracas and of a restaurant in Ciudad Bolívar. Some time later he had come to the United States, returned to Caracas in 1961 to liquidate his business, and moved back to the United States in 1963. The next year, New York police had charged him with stealing $3,000 from a prostitute. But Etienne had made restitution and the charges had been dropped.

The agents also knew that Etienne had been in New York again as recently as mid-January—and that he had been back in Paris late in February at the same address as Felipe Spadaro.

As Etienne passed through Customs inspection with no trouble, he was met by a tall, slender redhead whose hair was styled in an extreme upsweep. She was twenty-five or thirty—a bit too old to be the mistress who had been seen with Etienne in Paris. The woman wore heavily smoked sunglasses and a dark green coat with a fur collar—a lovely target for surveillance, almost impossible to lose.

But agents who tailed the couple to 425 East Sixty-third Street and watched them for several days finally had to conclude that they were scoring zero in a serious narcotics investigation.

"Surveillance indicates they spend most of the time inside the apartment," one agent's report noted. "Take occasional walks. Frequent French restaurant in area."

"These offenses," a senior narcotics official said sarcastically, "are not indictable. Cool this surveillance."

On the same day that Etienne arrived, March 8, yet another cable from Paris indicated that someone in France was rapidly acquiring a thorough knowledge of the Chastagnier operation. The message also reflected a degree of Franco-American cooperation that had not always been there in narcotics cases:

"CHASTAGNIER CONTACTED THE 'CENTRADE CO.' AT ANNECY, FRANCE, TO ASK ABOUT HIS ORDER OF OSCILLOSCOPES FOR THE U.S. ASKED TO BE NOTIFIED SOON AS INTERMEDIARY RECEIVED THEM. IT IS LEARNED THAT CHASTAGNIER HAS PLACED THREE ORDERS FOR OSCILLOSCOPES FROM CENTRADE, TWO THIS MONTH (ONE FOR 12 OSCILLOSCOPES, ONE FOR 10 OSCILLOSCOPES) AND ORDER NEXT MONTH FOR 25. SEEMS THIS DELIVERY WILL BE MADE MARCH 13.

"FRENCH POLICE AND CUSTOMS READY TO SEIZE ALL FRENCH [suspects] AND LET PART OF SHIPMENT THROUGH."

Even if the instruments were later thrown away, forty-seven more oscilloscopes, each carrying a single kilogram of heroin, would be worth $600,000 more to the smugglers. On the street, the greatly diluted heroin would be worth more than $10 million. To earn their share, Chastagnier and his cohorts had only to see the shipment in New York and safely in the hands of receivers.

Two days later the agents in Paris again demonstrated that their sources were well informed—if a little tardy in reporting. This time they cabled that they had learned that Gregor Sobol's firm was the addressee for four oscilloscopes shipped December 20 and December 22 by air freight.

The message conveyed the strong belief that the transformers in the oscilloscopes were removed and replaced by one kilo of heroin, the weight of the transformers. Actually, as the New York agents would soon learn, the technique was to remove steel parts, replace them with much lighter aluminum parts, and add two half-kilo bags of heroin per oscilloscope to balance out the weight.

*Excerpt from a cable from Paris to New York dated 2/14/67:*

FELIPE SPADARO BELIEVED AT NEW YORK WILL BE A KEY FIGURE IN
THIS CASE ALONG WITH GREGOR SOBOL. INDICATIONS THAT DELIVERY
WILL BE MADE TO N.Y. ON OR ABOUT MARCH 20.

On the morning of March 20 at Orly Airfield in Paris two large
boxes were delivered to the air freight office. French customs officials and narcotics agents, in the presence of American narcotics
men, seized one box and opened it. Inside were six oscilloscopes.
Inside the oscilloscopes were six kilograms of high-quality heroin.
Heroin and oscilloscopes were officially confiscated.

Arrangements were then made to put the second box aboard
Air France Flight 015, due to depart from Orly early the next day
and to arrive at New York about noon on the same date. The
case, after months of waiting and false starts, seemed in the drug-
fighters' jargon "about to go down."

*Excerpt from a cable dated 3/21/67, Paris to New York:*

FRENCH OFFICER EMILE ANGLES ABOARD FLIGHT 015. REQUEST
GAROFALO MEET HIM. ARRESTS ARE NOW UNDER WAY AT FRANCE
BUT NO INFORMATION WILL BE RELEASED FOR AT LEAST 24 HOURS.
ATTEMPT WILL BE MADE TO DELAY RELEASE INFORMATION OF THESE
ARRESTS UNTIL NOTIFIED OF SEIZURE AT DISTRICT 2 [New York].
CHASTAGNIER HAS BEEN ARRESTED AT HIS HOME IN PARIS.

At 1:05 P.M. on March 21 a package containing six oscilloscopes
arrived at John F. Kennedy International Airport aboard Air
France Flight 015, as scheduled.

It was taken immediately to a private Customs office in the International Arrivals Building. Customs and Bureau of Narcotics
agents did the honors. They carefully opened the carton in a manner that would allow it to be expertly resealed. Part of the heroin
was replaced, but some of it had to remain under continuous surveillance if a sound case was to be made against those who received it. The rest was destined for a safe in Customs Agency
Service intelligence headquarters at 201 Varick Street in lower
Manhattan, not thirty blocks from Gregor Sobol's office.

The oscilloscopes were then moved back to Air France's cargo terminal. Under ordinary procedure, the instruments would make their way to the addressee, probably on the next day.

Suddenly, on the morning of March 22, a Wednesday, the case threatened to explode right in the faces of the long-suffering agents. Paris, where the clock was almost half a day ahead of New York's, fired off a bad-news cable:

"INFORMATION REACHED FRENCH PRESS A.M. . . . BY A SMALL NEWSPAPER. . . . ALL MIXED BUT CLEARLY MENTIONS OSCILLO-SCOPES. . . . DUE TO ABOVE OUR COLLEAGUES MUST NOW GIVE FULL INFORMATION TO THE PRESS."

The cable named six men who had already been arrested in France, including Chastagnier. It also said "our colleagues" (French police) reported that all suspects were cooperating fully, and added that further arrests were anticipated.

Fine for that end—but it meant that the entire New York case was endangered by the premature leak of the French arrests.

The scene at JFK became one of ordered frenzy. On the chance that a member of the smuggling ring had inside contacts, the package of oscilloscopes would have to be put through all the proper formalities. The "official" Customs examination and the release of the shipment were "completed expeditiously," as a later report understated it.

At 1:30 P.M. on the 22d, the telephone on Gregor Sobol's desk rang once, twice, three times. By now he was resigned to his role as an underpaid stooge for his one-time friend Chastagnier, but he could not shake his sense of dread. This call, he assumed, would tell him that two packages of oscilloscopes had arrived, consigned to his company.

"Hello, Sobol here."

"Monsieur Sobol," a woman's voice said. "I am calling for Agence France Presse, the New York office. What comment have you on your arrest and those of Paul Chastagnier and the others for violation of narcotics smuggling laws—"

The swift teletype communications of the French news agency had already brought the word from Paris to New York City and directly into Gregor Sobol's right ear.

Stunned beyond belief, Sobol said nothing. He held the

phone out before him, staring at it as if it had done him gross physical harm. Frantically he searched his mind for some explanation of this incredibly bad bit of information. Why was Chastagnier not here to tell him what to do?

Finally he replaced the phone gently in its cradle, shutting off the woman's insistent "Monsieur Sobol? Monsieur Sobol—"

He stood for a moment, sat down, stood again, a man in shock.

At 1:32 P.M. a genuine delivery man and a narcotics agent dressed to look like one walked into Gregor Sobol's office carrying a package of six oscilloscopes.

Sobol would not have believed a moment before that anything could shake him more than the woman's phone call had. Now the presence of the two men and the appearance of the incriminating package reduced him almost to incoherence. Only one box—the woman's information must have been right. The other box must have been seized or there would have been no arrests for her to question him about.

Reflexes acted for him as he scribbled a quick "Recd. 3/22/67 G. Sobol" on the yellow waybill and pushed it back across the desk toward the genuine delivery man.

The sense of relief that flooded over him as the two men turned and walked out of his office was only momentary. He sat for a long time, staring at the badly painted landscape on the wall calendar opposite him without seeing it. His only thought was that he could not think, only sit as if his body were made of lead.

At last, at 3:15 P.M., Gregor Sobol pulled on his overcoat, took his hat and walked to the elevator, oblivious of the man who stepped into the elevator and rode down the eleven floors with him. He was totally unaware that the man was Leonard S. Schrier, special agent, Bureau of Narcotics.

Not until Sobol reached the door to the street did he show signs of caution. Looking nervously up and down West Street, he stepped out and began walking east across Rector Street, past the Trinity Church, toward Lower Broadway. He turned into an office building at Broadway and Wall Street and walked directly to a waiting elevator. Agent Schrier, a dozen paces behind him, decided not to risk a second elevator ride with his quarry in so short a time.

A few minutes later Sobol stepped out of another elevator, left the building and began walking north on Broadway. It was impossible to guess why he had gone into the building. He had not been inside long enough to conduct much business, unless it was perhaps to pass a warning. But Schrier was sure that Sobol still had not made him as a tail.

At 120 Broadway, Sobol cast a quick awkward glance over his shoulder and ducked into the doorway. Just as he was about to enter the elevator, Schrier decided this game must stop before the hunted spotted the hunter. He stepped quickly over to Sobol and placed him under arrest. Sobol was amazed at his sense of relief. It seemed even greater than the feeling he had had when the two delivery men had left his office without arresting him.

Schrier and another agent took Sobol to the Bureau of Narcotics' New York headquarters at 90 Church Street for questioning. To move things along, they told him all about Chastagnier's arrest in France. Ordinarily, Sobol might have chosen not to believe them. But the phone call, immediately followed by the delivery of the oscilloscopes, had shaken him badly. He began to spill out all he knew—or so it seemed at the time.

He had been on his way to his safe-deposit box to get his passport, he said, when he felt Schrier's hand on his shoulder.

"Look," Sobol said to the agents. "I'm a businessman. If I were to cooperate with the government and tell you what you want to know, what would you do for me?"

A question Schrier and his partner had heard so often that the answer was automatic: "We can promise you nothing. However, it could not help but weigh in your favor."

Sobol "communicated," as narcotics officers say. But he tried as hard as his muddled mind would let him not to tell them anything important that they might not have guessed already. And some of what he said didn't seem to track with what the agents already knew.

In the scenario that Sobol now laid out, it was Felipe Spadaro —not Albert Larrain and the Scarred Man—who came to his office to claim the first oscilloscope packages in late December. He obligingly identified Felipe—correctly—from photographs that the agents showed him. And he insisted that the December deliveries were the first oscilloscopes he had dealt with. (Later,

Sobol was to contradict a part of this story by telling other agents that he did not meet Felipe until early March, when Albert Larrain introduced him by phone. In this version, the three of them then went to dinner at La Grenouille, where "the restaurant staff often bowed to Spadaro and addressed him as 'Mr. DuPont,' an alias given to wealthy people." As was often the case, his interrogators were never certain that they had ascertained the truth of many less important points in either version of his story.)

For now, however, Sobol declined to give Schrier and his buddy any inkling of where they might find Felipe. Further muddying the story, he told them that Albert Larrain had come with Felipe to collect the oscilloscopes in December. He indicated that Larrain probably was the "customer." And he made no mention of the Scarred Man or Luis the Argentine.

That night, as the agents searched Sobol's office with Sobol there, the dreaded telephone on the desk began to ring again. Sobol looked at it as a trapped animal looks at a hunter. Only at the agents' insistence did he answer it. It was Felipe. He had indeed come to New York again, just as the March 14 cable from Paris had predicted.

Coached by the whispering agents, a trembling Sobol tried to coax Felipe into coming to West Street at 8 o'clock the next morning to pick up the oscilloscopes.

To the surprise of all three men, Felipe agreed, then hung up. But the agents who waited for him all through the morning of Saturday the 23d waited in vain. It had been a worthwhile try, but something in Sobol's voice the night before must have served as a warning.

The Scarred Man had never enjoyed Europe so much. He was very much in love with his pretty wife, for now at least, and he was still basking in the praise that Chastagnier, Spadaro, and Etienne had heaped on him for his cool first run at being a money courier.

Then the letter from Luis arrived. It warned him that the New York Police Department was looking for him but did not say why. It urged him to go to Buenos Aires for an indefinite stay, until he got further word. But the young Argentine refused to believe the truth of the letter. He sent his wife to Buenos Aires, but he caught the next plane for New York, determined to find out what was up. Luis would not have written him without some reason.

In New York, he began a lonely wait. He had goofed. Repeatedly he had been told never to initiate a contact with Luis, and he sat in his hotel room for almost a day before he realized that Luis would have no way of knowing he was back. On the second day he resorted to a gamble. He would drop into a couple of places where both he and Luis were known, be seen, and hope that the word would filter back to Luis. He would drop around again a few days later to see if Luis had left a message. After all, he thought grimly, who can miss this face? He would just have to chance that the cops didn't know his haunts.

It worked, and late in March a bartender told him to meet Luis at the Argentine Cafe at 1626 Broadway. The Scarred Man knew he was in for a certain amount of hell but he had underestimated Luis's wrath. First came the reprimand for defying his elder's advice and returning to New York. Second came a royal chewing out for visiting bars where both men were known—it was the kind of risk that pros did not take, Luis said. The Scarred Man had thought it was a clever, if dangerous, way out of his dilemma but he said nothing.

To hammer home the lesson, Luis now gave him the shocker: He told him of the arrest of Sobol and the seizure of the heroin; of the six arrests in France that had included Paul Chastagnier's. Furthermore, Luis said angrily, the Scarred Man had been replaced in the organization until he could earn back his job.

The lecture was working too well. The younger man's contrition and disappointment were so obvious that Luis decided to reverse his field and teach this young jerk still another lesson: Never concede defeat. After all, Luis pointed out, the two of them were still free, and Albert Larrain and Felipe Spadaro had also escaped. In case Sobol talked, they must all exercise extreme caution. But at least they were free for now.

He did not know about Spadaro, but he knew why the agents who went to East Fifty-seventh Street for Larrain had found only an empty apartment—no suspect, no heroin, no shopping bags or dresser drawers crammed with currency. Although the premature leak of news from Paris had not come in time to save Gregor Sobol, Larrain's mother had heard about the French arrests on television. She had immediately called her son and pleaded with him to flee to Europe or, better still, to Buenos Aires.

"For once," Luis said, smiling for the first time, "Albert took his old mother's advice."

The New York agents had been denied anything like the *grande coup* that the French had pulled off in Paris. The news leak had badly damaged the American effort. But something about the case, something vaguely apparent but not quite there, like a name on the tip of the tongue, nagged at the Customs men who sifted through the growing pile of documents. These papers, the bureaucratic manifestation of the Oscilloscope Case, would have to be reviewed and reviewed, almost like shuffling a deck of cards until the right one came up, until the answer was there.

Late in March, as a senior agent leafed through the stack of cable traffic from Paris for what seemed like the hundredth time, it came to him: They had been focusing much too hard on New York and Paris. Grabbing a lined yellow pad, he began to make a rough listing of unusual things that the case had revealed:

"References to Spadaro going to South America."

"References to South America as possible source of merchandise."

"Etienne in Paris kept in phone contact with man in Hamburg who arrived from Argentina 1/3/67."

"Chastagnier address book: 'Ph. Spadaro, Monasterio 1054 Vincente Lopez, Buenos Aires.'"

He turned to a younger man at the next desk and said, "We've got to know a lot more about South America. Particularly B.A. I want Sobol interrogated until we get some answers. Get Narcotics into this, too—they've got men overseas and we haven't. Check Interpol, anything you can think of. Make it top priority and don't come back until you've got something."

Early in April, the senior agent was able to make important additions to his list:

"Sobol first met Chastagnier in Ecuador."

"Two suspects previously unknown to us, 'The Scarred Man' and 'Luis the Argentine,' both Argentinians."

"Albert Larrain and Luis the Argentine may have race stables in Latin America. Larrain may be Latin, not French."

Within the month, Felipe Spadaro, who had been unwilling to risk any border crossings for the moment, was found holed up in a midtown Manhattan hotel and arrested. On May 4 a federal grand jury indicted him for conspiring to smuggle heroin into the United States. Four months later, when his bail was reduced from $50,000 to $20,000, friends posted it and Spadaro promptly fled the country.

Albert Larrain was arrested some time later in Spain. When Spanish narcotics agents interrogated him on December 3, 1967, he told them a wild tale of a Buenos Aires–based drug smuggling ring run by French Corsicans and Latins. His account was sketchy and even the names were not complete—"Domingo," "Michel," "Raymundo," "Marcelo," "Beto."

Larrain also mentioned a "Monsieur André," who he said ran the operation. The names meant nothing to the Spanish and they forwarded them to the United States, where Larrain was wanted

There was nothing for the Customs agents to do but add the nicknames to their somewhat crude nickname file, kept on three-by-five index cards, and hope to piece the information together later with other bits and pieces.

But the Oscilloscope Case had alerted them, swinging their gaze from the traditional Turkey-Marseilles-New York pattern to a new compass heading, almost due south toward Latin America and specifically Buenos Aires, the City of Fair Winds.

No one in the Spadaro Chastagnier organization ever knew just how much Gregor Sobol might have talked. But the group's monitors in New York passed along the word that Sobol was never tried for narcotics smuggling. The only charge he finally answered to was an income-tax count, and he served no time in prison—a privilege rarely accorded to anyone but a cooperative witness.

# 3    *The Latin Transfer*

*1968*

*The westbound 707 jet droned* through the September night high above Indiana. Richard M. Nixon, his nomination as Republican Presidential candidate only four weeks behind him, was headed for his home territory of California and some tough campaigning.

Candidate Nixon's crisply efficient organization was well aware of a growing public concern about drug abuse—and a public belief that addicts committed many of the street crimes that in the summer of 1968 had exploded into a major political issue. The campaign aides knew, too, of California's particular sensitivity about drugs because of its common border with Mexico.

Teletype from RN INDIANAPOLIS (the candidate's plane) to RN NY (the candidate's campaign headquarters in New York City) late on the night of September 12, 1968: "WE HAVE MESSAGE FROM BUCHANAN FOR MARTIN POLLNER.

"VITAL THAT WE GET SOME BACKGROUND ON THE NARCOTICS PROBLEM IN THIS COUNTRY AS WELL AS INFORMATION REQUESTED ON THE TIJUANA BORDER PROBLEM. END."

"Buchanan" was Pat Buchanan, a young speechwriter later to

serve with Nixon in the White House. Martin Pollner was a tough young ex-federal prosecutor in New York who was executive director of Nixon's Advisory Committee on Crime and Law Enforcement and a member of the Nixon law firm, later to join the Nixon Administration to direct law enforcement in the Treasury Department.

The Buchanan message was received by a secretary in New York and telephoned to Pollner's Westchester County home at 3 A.M. on Friday the 13th. Despite the hour, Pollner immediately called John W. Dean III in Washington for assistance. Dean, a Nixon supporter, was counsel for the National Commission on Reform of Federal Criminal Laws, later to become President Nixon's counsel in the White House.

Pollner then dressed, drove to the Nixon campaign office in Manhattan, and began working on a four-page memorandum to Buchanan headed "Potential Materials and Recommendations for RN's Position on Narcotics and Drug Abuse." With the help of Pete Velde, a young lawyer who was also to be brought into the Administration after Nixon's election, Pollner managed to send off the memo the same day and to follow it with another headed: "Narcotics Problem in Southern California."

The position papers recommended that Nixon advocate a balanced program of research, law enforcement, rehabilitation, and education. They included specific proposals.

On Monday the 16th, Buchanan in California sent Pollner in New York a teletype message headed, "RUSH RUSH". It began:

"FOLLOWING DRAFT NEEDS CLEARANCE FROM YOU—AS SOON AS POSSIBLE."

The draft of a proposed Nixon speech opened with the candidate's thoughts about a letter he had recently received from a 19-year-old girl drug addict. It went on to discuss the general problem ("narcotics are the modern curse of American youth . . .") and to propose certain changes.

"I recommend that we triple the number of Customs Agents in this country from 331 to 1,000," the draft said. "This is not any irresponsible recommendation. It was urged upon this country by the President's [Johnson's] own Crime Commission, and as President of the United States in January of 1969 I will follow through with that recommendation—and I will take the executive steps necessary to make our borders more secure against the pestilence of narcotics."

Richard Nixon delivered the speech, only slightly altered from the draft, that same day at Anaheim, California. Almost a year later, in July, 1969, White House aide Arthur Burns read through all the Nixon campaign speeches and pledges involving Treasury Department matters and put them into an "action program," which the new President submitted to Congress shortly afterward.

Late in December, 1969, the Congress approved an appropriation of $8.75 million for 915 more Treasury men and equipment. It was a significant step, designed to help bring the Customs lawmen into a somewhat better balance against the smugglers and peddlers.

But it came very late.

In the spring of 1967, when Gregor Sobol and Felipe Spadaro were arrested in the Oscilloscope Case, the Customs Agency Service had only four agents specializing in narcotics enforcement in New York City. On any given day, a smuggling ring far less powerful than Auguste Ricord's could "shotgun" half a dozen heroin couriers into the city by plane and outnumber the narcotics investigators man for man.

The Oscilloscope Case and then the arrest of Ange Luccarotti on May 6, 1967, two days after Spadaro's indictment, marked the beginning of change. It was not dramatic change. The Oscilloscope Case "started opening up this whole South American thing," as one agent put it. The Ange Lucarrotti case slowly began to shift Customs heroin enforcement in New York from the more ordinary police procedures into something resembling a smoothly functioning intelligence operation. It also helped make Albert W. Seeley a legend among the younger agents who would come along when the much-delayed buildup of Customs forces began after the Nixon election.

Seeley, a serious, almost doleful man, hard-talking and 100 per cent a cop, as a detective had for a number of years with the New York Police Department specialized in fighting organized crime. When he became a Customs special agent in 1962, the amount of heroin being smuggled into the United States was what he would call "no big deal." But he pursued each narcotics suspect as if the man were the head of a worldwide Mafia.

"I get very enthusiastic when I get into enforcement in junk," Seeley says. "We got three tools. We catch 'em with the junk, we catch 'em with the money after the sale, or we catch 'em with false documents, like a phony passport. One false document and he can get five years. Two counts and it doubles. He talks about the junk or gets five to ten years for the phony papers. It works like a charm."

But Ange Luccarotti never talked. He flew into New York City from Rome aboard a Greek airliner with a false Belgian passport and with three kilograms of heroin taped to his body, intended for a Cuban receiver. Luccarotti was obviously something of an internationalist even among drug smugglers.

For his crimes and his silence he got ten years in Leavenworth. And Seeley got an idea. The agents were being run to death by the constantly rising numbers of individual heroin cases—but it seemed highly unlikely that the cases were as unrelated as they appeared. Behind the scattered, single operations there must be system, organization, superior planning, and financing. It was time to fight that kind of fire with better planning, organizing, and sleuthing on the legal side of this battle.

Seeley, a cop in the oldest and truest sense of the word, doing what his training and upbringing in the world's hardest city and his private view of morality call for him to do, is as tough a man as Auguste Ricord, playing for the opposite side. A real ax-breaker. Some of his young subordinates would pronounce it "ass-breaker," but they would also do almost anything Seeley ordered. At the time of Spadaro and Luccarotti, however, there were no young subordinates—only special agent Al Seeley and three other men.

To Seeley, the way a smuggler worked was the key to the man's downfall. Seeley was a student of patterns. Luccarotti wouldn't help him, so he helped himself. He began pulling flight manifests, not only for Ange Luccarotti's plane but for those of every suspect in any recent case who had used the airlines as a means of travel. He checked back through the Immigration and

Naturalization Service's I-94 forms, filled out by incoming aliens, to see how often the suspects had entered the United States, where they had stayed, for how long. He scoured through hotel records to see if X and Y, who might not seem to be related in crime, had used the same hotel, entered the country at the same time, left on the same plane.

He was looking for the designs of crime the hard way—"strictly a non-television-show type of investigation," another agent said, "without computers, without a bloody thing."

The patterns were there to be found. A suspect named Joannas "Wigsy" Muñoz, the investigation revealed, packed and boarded the same plane with Luccarotti but got off ahead of him—probably "riding shotgun" on Luccarotti to warn the organization if Luccarotti got busted at Customs. Joe Bouillon, who was busted in Boston five months later as he tried to "belly in" three kilos of heroin, also was caught as a consequence of Seeley's paper work. So was René Santamaria, arrested a year later in New York.

As single couriers, these were not important men. But years of similar painstaking piecing together would lead to many more arrests—and prove that "Wigsy" Muñoz and René Santamaria were lieutenants of a French Corsican named Auguste Joseph Ricord, a name Seeley had never heard when he began the Luccarotti investigation.

For a case that produced only one immediate defendant, the Luccarotti arrest had become a gold mine. Chemical analysis even disclosed that Luccarotti's heroin came from the same French "laboratory" as the heroin in the Oscilloscope Case. Pieces were beginning to fall together.

"The Luccarotti case was Day One of the formation of the nucleus that became this narcotics intelligent unit," a younger agent said five years later. "Seeley started the whole thing of travel patterns, hotel patterns—it was the mother case. One guy we caught because of it even had a map and the address of an apartment used in the Oscilloscope Case. Everything comes out of this. The case has never really stopped—and the guy never cooperated! That's what makes it brilliant!"

Within months, Seeley's group could not keep pace with the rapidly expanding workload of cross-checking, counter-referencing, and arrests stemming from the unrelenting growth in new cases.

"They asked for and got the assistance of four drones," the younger agent said. "That's when us CPOs got in." A CPO is a Customs patrol officer. He is a law-enforcement man, and he carries a gun. But until a few years ago he was no match for an international narcotics syndicate.

"To be a good Customs patrol officer," one of them who became a narcotics agent said, "you had to know all about values of goods, excess property, country of origin, prohibitions against agricultural imports, products that were decreed to be on the Food and Drug Administration blacklist—on and on and on, even to the regulations against ships pumping their bilges in the harbor. It had little to do with heroin.

"The beauty of the whole thing is that when they organized this thing, they fell on Albert. He has a fantastic organization in his brains. You ask him a question and he sputters on for ten minutes. But then the answer will come out, the whole goddamn thing is coming forth in its proper framework and perspective."

To put Auguste Ricord in his proper framework and perspective, however, was to take even a man like Seeley a very long time.

In April, 1967, a pretty young woman named Susan came to the door of Jack Grosby's apartment at 44 West Seventy-second Street and said she had an urgent message from Felipe.

Grosby took her coat, offered her a drink, and eased his 6-foot 3-inch frame into an armchair to listen. He had known Felipe Spadaro for several years. He even knew that Felipe's business was narcotics. The two of them had gone to the Cassius Clay-Zora Folley fight at Madison Square Garden, accompanied by Luis the Argentine and a Frenchman about Grosby's own age named Pierre "Bibi" Ricord. Grosby and Felipe and Luis had had dinner with Albert Larrain at the Argentine Restaurant on Broadway only two months before Felipe's arrest and Larrain's flight from the country. They had talked about importing and breeding race horses, a project in which all of them but Felipe were intensely interested.

Although Grosby was a born gambler, he had steered clear of

drugs. Horses were his passion, anywhere in the world that they ran. But he would not let Felipe down just because this business of narcotics had gotten his friend into some trouble. He had already provided Felipe with a lawyer and he had even served as a translator in the intricate legal matters growing out of Felipe's arrest.

Trying to keep his mind off the girl's full, clearly etched breasts and concentrate on what she was saying, Grosby asked what the message was.

Another favor. The judge had set Felipe's bail at $75,000, reduced it later to $50,000, but demanded that it be posted in cash —rather than accept the usual 10 per cent down and the word of a bondsman—because of the serious nature of the crime. But all Felipe's money was elsewhere. Felipe wanted Grosby to fly to Buenos Aires and raise the money among Felipe's "family" there.

"It's done," Grosby said, getting to his feet. "I'll call you when I get back. Leave me your phone number and tell Felipe not to worry." Too bad she's Felipe's woman, he thought. If Felipe were to be put away for awhile . . . But if he knew Felipe, the little Frenchman would leave that bail money as a present for Uncle Sam and disappear as fast as a dime bag of heroin flushed down a tenement toilet.

Jacob Grodnitzky, alias Jack Grosby, had been born in Argentina forty-one years before. His square-shouldered frame carried his 220 pounds well, and the brown eyes and dirty blond hair gave him a look typical of many Argentinians—taller, stronger, and often fairer than their European ancestors. He thought he knew Buenos Aires as he knew his racing charts, but the Bar el Sol at 380 Marconi Street in the suburb of Olivos was new to him —as was most of what he learned there.

His first surprise was that the man he knew as Felipe Spadaro was not Felipe Spadaro but Louis Bonsignour. Louis's mother, Maria Traversa Bonsignour, ran the bar and its French restaurant for her half-brother—a man named Auguste Joseph Ricord.

Then who, Grosby asked, was the Pierre "Bibi" Ricord whom he had met at the Clay-Folley fight in New York? Maria only smiled and said, "another of Auguste's many nephews." Grosby could not interpret the smile, so he let it pass. Patience would bring him answers that too many questions might not.

He had already learned without asking that Louis had once been married to a woman named Isabel Spadaro and had fashioned his alias from that. Despite the scores of men he had known who had used names other than their own, Grosby could not break the habit. He kept thinking of Louis Bonsignour as Felipe Spadaro and referring to him that way, though the family repeatedly corrected him.

Grosby's second surprise came when the family would not believe his story. He had flown four thousand miles to help Felipe beat a narcotics smuggling rap and Felipe's—or Louis's—own relatives would not believe that a judge might release Louis, even temporarily.

Obviously, Maria said, overestimating what narcotics agents knew of her son at that time, Louis was too important for the United States to let him go free for $50,000. Also, Grosby had not yet earned their trust—they said it to him bluntly, in so many words. No, they would not give this tall, smooth stranger even half of $50,000. His story was too preposterous.

Jack Grosby, gambler, flew back to New York empty-handed.

Before August, Felipe/Louis's lawyer had succeeded in getting another judge to lower the bail to $20,000. Susan soon showed up again at Jack Grosby's apartment, and he found himself wishing she would talk about anything but Felipe. She is not beautiful, he thought, but if I can walk away from a woman because she is only very pretty, I'm crazier than I think.

Susan's request was the same as before—Felipe was losing a great deal more than time sitting in jail, he was losing money— but this time, Susan said, she was prepared to arm Grosby with information that would convince the family he was Felipe's trusted friend and convince them as well that Felipe could and must be freed. Furthermore, she said, Felipe had told her to tell Grosby he would be rewarded. Felipe had emphasized that, she said, and she knew that he meant it.

Grosby did not doubt her. And he already had learned a thing or two. If you kept still, bail could be reduced, even in narcotics cases. He had made some contacts in Buenos Aires that he knew might be useful someday, even though Felipe's family had turned him away the first time. And the gambler in him was intrigued by Felipe's promise of a reward. He would go.

This time the "family" he met went beyond Louis Bonsignour's cautious blood relatives. In a lawyer's office at 1800 Calle La Valle, he sat down with Auguste Ricord, Luis the Argentine, whom he already knew, and five men introduced only as François, Domingo, Jean-Pierre, Marcelo, and Michel.

Like Ricord, four of the men who used only one name each were French Corsicans. Grosby was not so sure about Michel, a man of medium build whose dark, straight hair was covered by a toupée that looked unnaturally black over his unhealthy gray complexion.

Grosby felt like an intruder at a meeting of a board of directors. But he left Buenos Aires with the $20,000 and a strong impression that he had met some very important, if almost nameless, men.

When Felipe Spadaro/Louis Bonsignour's bail was posted he proved out Grosby's hunch—he fled the country, leaving the U.S. Treasury richer by $20,000 and the narcotics agents poorer by one defendant.

Grosby was not worried. He had his reward to look forward to. And his gambler's instincts told him that Susan probably was still in New York.

It was in December, 1967, not long after Spadaro/Bonsignour's disappearance, that Albert Larrain told the Spanish narcotics agents who arrested him in Madrid the strange, sketchy story of a Buenos Aires based heroin smuggling ring. If the Customs agents to whom the story was passed had been inclined to disbelieve it, the Montreal–New York "shotgunning" in that same month would certainly have changed their minds.

It began when a French Corsican using a false passport was arrested by Customs officers at Rouse's Point on the New York border as he rode a train from Montreal toward New York City. Six kilograms of heroin were found in the false bottom of his suitcase. He had reached Montreal from France three days before. The Corsican said he was to meet a man at Grand Central Station in New York and give him the heroin. They were to identify each other by presenting matching halves of a 10-franc note.

The arrest on the train led the agents to a second courier, already in New York; then to four more arrivals from Montreal—whose false-bottomed suitcases yielded twenty more kilograms of heroin. Before it was over, twenty arrests had been made in Montreal and New York, fifteen couriers were in custody, and some sixty-eight kilograms of heroin had been confiscated, all in a thirty-six-hour period.

It was a fantastically bold and extensive use of the single-courier method of delivery, firing them in like shotgun pellets, and a very big haul of heroin for those days. But what intrigued the Customs agents most was that one man—who was photographed in Grand Central but warned by a colleague in time to get away—turned out to be Lucien Sarti. Interpol records had him down as the killer of a Belgian policeman who had fled Europe and was believed to be living in South America.

The photograph was "the first indication Sarti's in junk," an agent later recalled. "He's controlling fifteen or twenty couriers and all that heroin, a staggering amount for that time, and we don't even know he's in junk!"

Almost as interesting was the discovery that most of the couriers carried U.S. visas in their passports—all issued in Buenos Aires. The scattered Latin threads, first picked up in the Oscilloscope and Luccarotti cases, were rapidly beginning to knit themselves into a rough fabric.

One year after the arrests of Gregor Sobol and Felipe Spadaro, in March, 1968, Jack Grosby received a letter from his old friend Felipe. It asked him to meet Felipe in Madrid. Obviously, the time had come to discuss reward, and Grosby flew to Spain.

There were several days of conferences among Grosby and Spadaro, two Frenchmen, both about sixty years old, and two nameless Italian-Americans. The aim of the talks was to persuade Grosby that he should buy a boat capable of crossing the Atlantic and use it to take back 200 kilograms of heroin—almost $2.5 million worth to the smugglers and a staggering $44 million worth at street prices. Grosby found it hard to believe that even a heroin epidemic could eat up such quantities. But it was the risk that made him refuse, not once but repeatedly.

At last the five men saw that they could not wear him down. He was told that other ways would be found to make him useful. He was to return to New York and wait for "Billy" to contact him.

In the same month, Billy appeared in Manhattan, handing Grosby a Swiss postcard to identify himself, just as Felipe and the strange quartet in Madrid had said he would. He soon began delivering 6-kilogram loads of heroin to Grosby, and to a friend of Grosby's named Daniel Mitnik, at frequent intervals.

Grosby the gambler was now in junk. He would turn his shipments over to a man with a Spanish name for $11,000 per kilo. The Spaniard in turn delivered them to "Jimmy," a New Yorker suspected of being a Mafioso—but that part was no concern of Grosby's. Each 6-kilo load brought Grosby $66,000. He took out his "expenses" and returned $54,600 to his old friend, Felipe. It was simple, and more certain than the horses.

One day in May, when the operation was still less than two months old, Billy was stopped and searched by police. Billy was clean, but he didn't come around any more. Instead, the next delivery was made by a short, hazel-eyed Belgian who called himself "Victor."

Victor, a man in his mid fifties, had been recruited in Europe by a man he knew only as "Robert," a Swiss who told him to go to New York, live in certain hotels for short periods of time and await telephone calls from Robert from Geneva, telling him where and how to pick up the heroin. Victor was also initiated into the high finance of the heroin world—Robert instructed him on how to dispose of the $450,000 he would collect for the 6- and 12-kilogram loads each month.

The switch in delivery boys made no difference to Grosby, whose income was growing so fast he found it necessary to fly to Switzerland twice to bank a total of $120,000. (The sum did not include the $68,000 in cash in his safe-deposit box at the First National City Bank at Seventy-second and Broadway.)

Things were going exceedingly well for Gentleman Jack Grosby, a long-time horse fancier, who had found a new and infinitely more profitable kind of horse to back.

Trans World Airlines Flight 709 from London seemed to float across the shimmering heat waves rising from the green Virginia countryside as it made a straight-in approach to Dulles International Airport outside Washington, D.C. The sleek aluminum tube taxied to a halt and disgorged its passengers directly into an air-conditioned mobile lounge for a cocooned ride to the futuristic terminal building. There, still more mechanically cooled and dried air would help them fight off the syrupy humidity of a Southern July.

A TWA servicing crew climbed aboard the 707 to clean out the seat-back pouches, the ashtrays, and the lavatories before the flight continued on to Saint Louis, Denver, and San Francisco. Refueling began, and a truck pulled up beneath the galley door with metal chests filled with trays of food.

At the rear of the passenger cabin, the worker assigned to clean a lavatory saw a string across the top of the towel-disposal bin and did the natural thing. He pulled it. Up came a man's black nylon sock stuffed with plastic bags filled with a white powder. What the hell is this? he thought. It must weigh a pound if it weighs an ounce. He called his coworkers to come and share his find.

The Customs port investigator found the sock even more interesting. He knew that Dulles was not a favorite gateway for European heroin. But what other kind of white powder, unless it was cocaine, would anyone hide in a sock, hung on a string in the dirty towel bin of an airplane washroom? He field-tested a sample with a portable narcotics detection kit and was not surprised to get what agents called "positive results." It was heroin.

The investigator dumped the rest of the powder, replaced it with Epsom salts, and called in Customs Agent George Festa. Both men knew that this much heroin never simply got lost and seldom traveled alone. The only conclusion was that the person for whom it was intended had not yet claimed his prize. The only thing to do was to hang it back in the towel bin and see who came to take the bait.

When Flight 709 climbed out of Dulles and banked gently toward the west, the sock was back in its place and George Festa had a seat conveniently near the lavatory where he could see who entered and left. If that sock isn't claimed before Frisco, he thought, I may be in for a long day.

The minute the seat belt sign went off, Festa decided he would lead the inevitable parade of passengers to the john. Out of curiosity, he reached into the dirty towel bin to check his bait— and came up with the first string of narcotic sausages he had ever seen. Seven more socks—each stuffed almost to the splitting point with heroin, strung together by their ends like so many cylinders of pork. In their excitement over the single sock, the agents had almost missed the mother lode. My God! There's a small fortune here! Festa said to himself.

Sausage like this would surely draw flies—but only flies who knew where to look. Festa hastily replaced the treasure, completed the mission that had really brought him to the washroom, and returned to his seat.

Each time another passenger finished using the lavatory, Festa had to simulate another call of nature and go in to check that the heroin was still there. In the games that lawmen sometimes had to play he had felt foolish many times before, but nothing like this. The stewardess, warned of his mission when he came aboard, knew what his problem was. But he feared that some passenger was bound to notice his frequent visits and begin to wonder about his physical—or mental—condition.

Festa kept up his in-again, out-again routine all the way to Saint Louis, certain that by now he must have aroused the smuggler's suspicion. Fortunately, he was wrong.

Forty minutes after they left Saint Louis on the leg to Denver, a short hazel-eyed man in his fifties went into the lavatory carrying a suitcase. Jack Grosby would have recognized the man as Victor. But George Festa could only reflect that very few passengers took their suitcases with them into a jetliner's compact washroom.

As soon as the man slid back the bolt that changed the door

sign from "Occupied" to "Vacant" and walked back to his seat,
Festa was up and into the lavatory again. No mistake about it—
this fly had taken the sausage.

Patience cannot be trained into an agent. It has to be learned.
As the Rocky Mountains finally came into view. beneath the left
wing, George Festa wondered if his patience could carry him
across the Rockies and all the way to San Francisco. He never had
to find out.

At Denver, Victor got off the plane, walked into the terminal
and headed directly for a bank of public lockers. He placed the
suitcase in Locker 517, pocketed the key and walked away—unaware that Festa, another Customs agent, an agent of the Bureau
of Narcotics, and two Denver detectives were now watching him.

As the others carefully followed Victor around the terminal,
Festa stayed behind to "sit on the load." If the sausage—presum-
ing it was in Victor's suitcase, and it had damned well better be—
went unsurveilled for even a moment, the agent could not legally
catch his fly.

When the public address system announced the imminent departure of United Airlines Flight 178 for New York, the agents
saw Victor walk quickly back to the locker, remove the suitcase,
and head for the United boarding gate. Festa, the other Customs
man, and the narcotics agent followed him aboard, trying not to
look like a parade of narcs.

Festa had now traveled two-thirds of the way across the continent only to be heading back east. Flight 178 was due at John F.
Kennedy International Airport at 6:10 the next morning, Saturday, July 27, 1968. There goes another weekend, Festa thought.
He wondered if he would qualify for United's 100,000-Mile Club
before this case went down. He suspected not—an embarrassingly
large percentage of the world's heroin shipments stopped right
where this plane was headed—in little old New York.

Shortly after the plane left Denver, the agents who had stayed
behind notified their counterparts in Manhattan. A little after
5 A.M. on Saturday, as the early sun began to heat the long runways and asphalt taxi strips that would later give off the smell of
kerosene and oil and rubber, three men from Customs and a
Bureau of Narcotics agent drove up to United's terminal at JFK.

As Victor walked into the terminal building, one of the Customs men who had arrived with him walked right behind. He gave the waiting agents a barely perceptible nod in Victor's direction to identify the quarry. Victor went directly out of the building, turned suddenly as if he had forgotten something, walked back into the terminal and pretended to make a phone call.

Clearly, the fly with the sausage was taking unusual precautions. He seemed to sense that he was being followed—not too surprising, since seven pairs of eyes now watched his every move. It's amazing, Festa thought, how much we're all trying to look like ordinary passengers. Like most policemen, he prided himself in thinking he could always spot another policeman. He wondered, as he had so often before during a surveillance, whether smugglers always thought they could spot cops, too.

Victor hung up the phone, walked quickly out of the terminal, and hopped into a taxi. It was time to move, before he was lost from sight. Two Customs agents stepped up to the cab and placed the hazel-eyed Belgian under arrest.

The fly and his sausage were taken to the Customs office in the International Arrivals Building, the white powder was proved to be heroin, and Victor was advised that he could remain silent, that anything he did say could be used against him, that he could call an attorney if he wished. But Victor said he would like to cooperate. He said he was staying in Room 1240 at the Belmont Plaza at Forty-ninth Street and Lexington Avenue in Manhattan, and he suggested that the agents take him there.

Festa and two other agents drove him in a Customs car to a corner a few blocks away from the Belmont Plaza. Then, in case someone was waiting for him at the hotel, they handed him his suitcase, stuffed him into a taxi, and discreetly followed him to Forty-ninth and Lexington.

Inside the Belmont they followed him to Room 1240, while three other Customs men and two Bureau of Narcotics agents signed into Rooms 1237 and 1239, across the hall. They had no idea how long the vigil might last.

A search of other luggage in Victor's room turned up fourteen thousand-dollar bills and a sealed package, wrapped in brown paper and marked "30." Victor said the package should contain

$30,000 more. Two Customs agents and a narcotics agent who was called into the room witnessed the counting and initialed the package. If Victor were convicted on a narcotics count, the crime-related money would become the property of the U.S. Treasury.

Victor now disclosed that his real name was Willie Wouters, that he had been born in Belgium, that he had just passed his fifty-fourth birthday eleven days before. He told how "Robert" had sent him to New York a month before, on June 25. And then he startled the agents by describing to them in considerable detail just what they had been missing.

Two, three, or four times a week since his arrival, he said, he had removed heroin from TWA Flights 709 or 711 each time they arrived from Europe. He said that he worked with Jean Marc Montoya, a thirty-one-year-old Frenchman, who also pulled heroin sausages off TWA planes several times a week. Montoya's heroin went either to Victor or to Montoya's own customer.

In fact, Victor said, Montoya had been aboard Flight 709 with him all the way from Dulles to Denver on the day before. He had stayed aboard the plane all the way to San Francisco to lift another six kilograms of heroin from the very same plane, and he was due back in New York with it at any time.

It was an ingenious scheme. Overseas flights would reach international gateways such as New York and Washington with heroin—but no heroin couriers—aboard. That way, no courier and no cargo needed to pass through a Customs inspection, risking possible search. Who would think to search the airplane itself?

A pick-up man would then board the plane as a domestic passenger, flying on from the gateway to an inland city. Or he might get on at some intermediate stop, such as Saint Louis. Either way, his flight was not an international one, and there was no question of having to pass through Customs or Immigration procedures. The pick-up man could then make his way back to New York— still an unsuspected and uninspected domestic traveler.

Victor was now chirping like a bird and the agents liked his song. He told how, when he had a load to deliver to his receiver, he telephoned a man named Jack. Jack or his man, Daniel Mitnik, usually paid for the load the day after receiving it, Victor said.

It was not yet noon and the agents already knew more about

this specific case and the general smuggling technique than they sometimes learned in months of surveillance and office brain work.

At 11:30 A.M. Victor's phone rang. It was Montoya, back from San Francisco with $66,000 worth of heroin. Victor told the Frenchman to call him back at 8 o'clock that night because he would not accept the heroin in the daylight hours.

That afternoon the agents took Victor before a U.S. Commissioner for arraignment. They explained his cooperative attitude, and the Commissioner released Victor on his own recognizance. It seemed safe enough with the squad of protectors he had. The agents promised to return him by the following Tuesday.

At 8:10 P.M. the telephone in Room 1240 rang again. Montoya agreed to meet Victor in the hotel's drugstore ten minutes later. With five agents trying to look like disinterested drugstore customers, Victor sat at the food counter until the young Frenchman arrived, carrying a black handbag.

Montoya joined Victor at the counter, setting the handbag down at their feet, between the two stools. After fifteen minutes of conversation that the anxious agents could not hear, Victor stood up, picked up the handbag, walked out of the drugstore, and went to his room.

If he had tried to warn Montoya in any way, he was playing a very cool game. The agents thought he had not. Maybe misery loved company and Victor didn't mind seeing someone else collared. Maybe he was simply afraid to do anything but cooperate.

He said that Montoya had moved from the Roger Smith Hotel, two blocks south of the Belmont at Lexington and Forty-seventh, to the sedate Barclay Hotel at Lexington and Forty-eighth.

Victor also told a bizarre-sounding tale of traveling heroin. TWA aircraft No. 765, he said, had arrived in Saint Louis on July 20 carrying twelve kilos of heroin in two lavatories. But he and Montoya had been delayed in New York by bad weather and had never been able to board that plane and pick off their sausages.

In the interim, the plane had made several crossings of the North Atlantic, both ways, with the small fortune in smack still aboard. Victor said he had told Montoya as they sat in the drugstore a few moments before to go out to JFK International and try to locate the plane, which was believed to be back there now.

Saturday night was winding down fast and the agents did not know how much to believe Victor. But the last thirty hours had proved once again that almost anything was possible in the smuggling of narcotics, so they knew they must continue to check him out.

In the meantime, they went about the job of repacking Victor's suitcase. They put half a kilo of the heroin Victor had retrieved on the way to Denver and half a kilo of Montoya's San Francisco heroin into the bag. It would be delivered to Victor's receiver, and at least a portion of the heroin—the critical evidence—must travel the route intended for it as far as possible. They would substitute white flour for the rest of the heroin—that way, if something went wrong, most of the load would still be in their hands. But some of the junk must go the whole route—after all, there was no federal law against carrying white flour around in a suitcase.

While the repacking was going on, Agent Al Seeley went through the kind of time-consuming but vital street-pounding that had been a part of his whole life as a cop. To be certain that Victor was not crossing them, and that Montoya did not get away, he had to know whether Montoya had shifted hotels, as Victor had said.

At least the area was small, easy on the feet. With his usual thoroughness, Seeley checked not only the Roger Smith and the Barclay but the nearby Hotel Lexington, which Victor had not mentioned. As usual, Seeley came up not only with a smuggler's pattern—pick a hotel, stay a few days, move on—but with something extra as well. The picture was this:

On July 11, a man registered at the Lexington as Marc Montoya of 19 rue de la Jacquière, Paris 17e, France. He was assigned to Room 914. On July 23 he checked out. At 10:43 A.M. on the same day—thirteen minutes after the Marc Montoya checked out of the Lexington—a man using that name checked into Room 408 at the Roger Smith. Three days later—on the day that a TWA employee found the sock of heroin at Dulles—Montoya checked out of the Roger Smith. But on Saturday, back from San Francisco, he returned to the Roger Smith, picked up his luggage, and departed. A few minutes later he had checked into the Barclay —making Victor a reliable informant up to now, and not a liar.

Sunday morning catches midtown Manhattan at its very best, empty and quiet by comparison with the shoving crowds and raucous traffic that make midweek a hassle. It is a time to buy a Sunday paper, take a stroll, sit in a park and feel as if the city belongs only to you. For Victor, alias Willie Wouters, and his bleary-eyed baby-sitters, such an opportunity was wasted. At 8:10 A.M. the phone in Room 1240 of the Belmont rang again, reminding them all that any day might be a working day in the business of smuggling narcotics or the business of trying to stop it.

It was the man known as Robert, calling from Geneva. He told Victor not to give the $44,000 he had to anyone until he received further orders. Victor was also told to go to Saint Louis on Monday and again on Wednesday to pick up single loads of six kilograms from the washrooms of TWA Flight 709 on each of those days. And he was told that on Friday, the London–Washington–Saint Louis–Denver–San Francisco flight would carry a double load.

Again, the simplicity and the enormity of what they had stumbled into left the agents annoyed but grudgingly admiring of the way this crew operated. The same controlled curiosity that makes a man complete a difficult acrostic or stay with a game of chess to the checkmate drove them forward, toward the mind behind this scheme.

Between 3 and 5:15 that afternoon the only things to break the boredom in Room 1240 were three phone calls from Marc Montoya. On the third call he told Victor he had located TWA aircraft No. 765 but that he did not intend to travel aboard it because it was about to leave for Rome, Italy. Unless he could get at it before the plane left, the unclaimed heroin would have to make still another trans-Atlantic crossing.

The agents in the room notified their superiors. At Kennedy Airport, two Customs agents found aircraft 765, arranged to board it, and searched the lavatories. In two of them, the agents found more narcotic sausages—but left the socks in their places.

At 5:25 P.M., Jean Marc Montoya walked up to a ticket agent near TWA gate Number One carrying a TWA handbag. He talked for a moment to the agent and then the two of them walked to the plane and boarded it by a door usually used only by employees. Within a few minutes they stepped down from the plane, walked together into the terminal, and separated.

Montoya made a phone call, stopped to have a cup of coffee, and then boarded a bus about to leave for downtown New York. The agents climbed aboard the bus, arrested him, advised him of his rights, and took him to the Customs office in the International Arrivals Building where Victor had been only the day before. The TWA handbag yielded three packages of heroin.

Told about Victor's arrest and cooperation, Montoya too decided to sing. He took the agents back aboard aircraft 765 and showed them how he had taken the three packages from the lavatory designated "C" in the coach section. A search of Lavatory C produced more socks, stuffed with nine more packages of heroin. And Lavatory D, across the aisle, had yet another sausage of socks with twelve more packages of heroin inside them! The plane had been a flying storehouse of heroin. The agents found themselves wondering how TWA passengers found room enough for their dirty towels.

Twenty-four half-kilo packages in all, or twelve full kilograms of heroin—worth $132,000 to their New York receiver or more than $5 million when "the shit" hit the streets (and by the time it had been adulterated with the kinds of crud that some middlemen would whack it with, that's just what it would be). To think that these guys were pulling socks out of towel bins three and four times a week! Earlier, the agents had been impressed. Now they were beginning to be numbed by the measures of weight and dollars.

The Belmont Plaza end of the case was hardly stagnating. Victor went downstairs to the hotel drugstore at 7:30 P.M. and, following the agents' instructions, placed his call to the man named Jack—just as he had done in the past when he was ready to make a turnover.

Jack said he would send his man, Mitnik. Victor was to be outside the hotel in approximately twenty minutes.

Eight o'clock. A blue 1968 Ford, New York license 726442, pulled up in front of the hotel. Victor hefted the suitcase containing twenty-two packages of flour and two packages of heroin into the car and climbed in behind it. The agents moved in.

Daniel Mitnik was startled, but he had his story ready. He was not about to join Victor and Montoya in song. He said he had never seen Victor in his life until two days before, when they happened to meet in the Belmont Plaza bar. They had talked for about twenty minutes. Before they parted, Victor had asked him if he would meet him at the hotel at 8 P.M. on Sunday and "drive him some place."

No, he didn't know where. No, it did not seem odd to him. "I like people," he explained. No, he did not have any heroin in his apartment. "If you don't believe me," he protested, "you can come and search it." The agents thought that was a splendid idea. It was something they would have done without the invitation.

By 8:45 P.M., as the last light of the long Sunday evening was dying, Mitnik and three Customs agents pulled up in front of Mitnik's apartment house at 8215 Brittain Avenue in the Elmhurst section of Queens.

Mitnik was right; there was no heroin. The $410 in a desk drawer in the bedroom was not necessarily suspicious. But the $13,000 in the white cloth bag, hidden beneath dirty clothes in a cardboard box in the closet, definitely was. Like another smuggler or a glassine packet of heroin, the money was taken into custody.

Fifteen minutes before Mitnik and his keepers arrived at his Queens apartment, there was action in midtown Manhattan. Two Customs agents and a narcotics bureau man walked into apartment 2H at 44 West Seventy-second Street and bagged Jacob Grodnitzky, alias Jack Crosby, fancier of fast horses and fine women—or was it the other way around? They had followed the simple expedient of tracing the man whom Victor knew only as "Jack" by checking out the phone number Victor had called from the Belmont Plaza drugstore.

Grosby and the other defendants now got "the Varick Street treatment."

The massive gray sandstone building at 201 Varick Street on the southern edge of Greenwich Village, like a woman of the streets, finds it difficult to conceal the past. It is an old Customs warehouse, long ago converted into an office building to save the taxpayers money. Unlike the brilliant white Casa del Custom that dominates the riverboat passenger's first view of Asunción, it sits blocks away from the giant cranes of any dockside.

"Varick Street," as the agents know it with dread and some affection, still has its concrete loading platforms along the King Street side. But the grimy cargo bays that once housed steamer trunks and bales of cargo held for inspection are now used to park the agents' cars. The block-long monument to the days of ocean liners is down at heel, slow of elevator, depressing to the soul. Flaking, lime-green paint, obviously government-issue, does nothing to make the walls more hospitable. It hides dirt well but ages gracelessly. The walls, in fact, seem to be closing in on rows of cluttered desks that might have been scavenged at an eviction sale. Wood and glass partitions break up the open floor areas without beginning to hide the huge concrete pillars that make the building's past unforgettable. Only the men themselves bring life to this institutional cavern in lower Manhattan.

The Narcotics Intelligence Unit is in Room 352, which is not much of a room but another area, bounded by wood and glass partitions. Past the "Restricted Area" signs and beyond the maze of corridors, Room 352 has the unmistakable air of a roomful of cops. It is habitable but not uplifting, with a rundown but grimly professional atmosphere.

Here, Jack Grosby, Willie Wouters, Jean Marc Montoya, and Daniel Mitnik were photographed, fingerprinted, and questioned. Then they were scattered out to detention homes for what law-enforcement men call "safekeeping."

From a Friday afternoon in the Virginia countryside to a Sunday night in Manhattan, one of the most important heroin cases in recent years had gone down. Most of the agents would never forget it, for it was soon to open even wider windows.

Jack Grosby had now come full circle. His two flying trips to Argentina to raise Felipe Spadaro's bail had put him into junk, and junk had put him into jail. Now he needed $100,000 in cash to get out—the bail that the courts had set on each defendant in "the TWA Case."

But in the meantime his captors were getting to know him. And their admiration of his skills continued to increase. For it was Grosby who had developed the ingenious use of the TWA washrooms for smuggling heroin.

"Grosby also devised 'the pregnant woman carry,'" a young agent said enthusiastically. "A woman courier would strap a big load around her abdomen in a special girdle, like she was pregnant, board a European plane to an East Coast port but continue on into the interior, where there was no Customs. It was so simple it was insulting!"

Smuggling is more of an art and a game of wits than a science. But the modern smuggler has moved his trade a long way toward the scientific: He studies the system, determines its flaws, uses them to his advantage as Grosby had done with the TWA flights. Methods, far more than the contraband itself, are the smuggler's stock in trade. Security men at the British Overseas Airways Corporation once looked the other way as their own plane crewmen flew out of Hong Kong for Tokyo with a watch—or sometimes several—on each wrist. The duty on watches wasn't that much, and it seemed like a confiscatory tax, anyway. Then, in 1950, both the security officers and the flight crews learned with mutual shock that the sellers of the watches had been removing the works and filling the cases with heroin. The crewmen, with only a little larceny in their hearts, had become unwitting narcotics couriers and the airline's own policemen, by ignoring the seemingly harmless watch-peddling, had become their accomplices. The practice was stopped, but the heroin smugglers simply moved on to other methods.

New techniques are so highly valued that some organized smuggling rings hire "idea men" who specialize in inventing new ways to conceal and transport. When an idea succeeds, it may work for years before a customs inspector or a border guard tumbles to it. It was once a common saying among U.S. Customs officers that most contraband was discovered only "by look and luck." But when heroin flared into the public consciousness the way it did in the late 1960s, look and luck would no longer do. "Listen" helped, when smugglers were apprehended and talked. But the real improvement was in intelligence as the narcs, especially Al Seeley, began to play the game as thoroughly and systematically as the smugglers were doing, despite the lawmen's disadvantage in terms of manpower and money.

In a neat but crowded office of the Bureau of Customs headquarters, 2100 K Street, N.W., in Washington, Special Agent Bill Knierem uses the hindsight of the 1970s to explain the transition from "look and luck" to "intelligence, informants, and investigation."

A small, intense, dedicated man, he is the supreme briefer, firing it out staccato, ammunition belts of information running through his machine-gun mind almost too fast for the listener to handle.

"From '62 to '67 it was all bodies and suitcases," he says, moving around the charts on the easel as if the smugglers are about to get ahead of him. "They get it in France, they go to the U.S., Canada, Mexico. We are getting beat. They also begin to ship it from Europe in freezers, in oscilloscopes. Automobiles get knocked off. They are full of it. The French must have been saying, 'You Customs guys got no imagination at all.'

" '60 to '68 was still a good period for federal law enforcement. Then the red lines (he points to the smuggling routes marked in red on his flip chart) begin to fan out. Fort Lauderdale, Boston, Washington, et cetera. It's no longer just New York and Montreal—they're coming in everywhere."

The lines on the map leading up from Buenos Aires and Asunción and Caracas through Panama and into the United States are still an embarrassment, even though they have now been discovered.

"We were looking at Marseilles and Barcelona and New York and Montreal," Bill Knierem says, "and they were hitting us underneath, from Latin America. We ought to be ashamed there. We were looking the wrong way. It was basically a failure in law enforcement."

In the heroin business, there are no complainants. The supplier, the smuggler, the receiver, the pusher, and the addict are allied in one thing—silence. Or at least they once were.

"The Corsicans used to send over hardened criminals," Knierem explains. "We called 'em mules. They didn't know who the real supplier was or who the receiver was to be and they didn't give a damn if they got busted. They could always beat us with body carriers and suitcases as long as the quantities were small and the couriers were plenty.

"But then we started to notice some changes. All the mules were of European parentage, but many were being recruited from the underworld in South America, issued visas in Buenos Aires, taken to France, loaded up and sent on in. Pimps, pickpockets—you name it."

Intelligence work like Al Seeley's developed patterns, the investigators' favorite word. Many of the mules carried false passports and visas.

"They might beat a junk rap and we'd get 'em on false documents. As we knocked more of them off, the Corsicans started putting a little higher class of guy in as mules, higher education and living standards," Knierem explains.

"When *they* get arrested they get *afraid*. Some are a lot smarter than the people we were arresting fifteen years ago. There are larger loads now and they are putting into it people who are not so happy to sit in a jail. They say, 'If I lose the money and I lose the load, I don't need fifteen years . . .'

"They are talking to us a little more now and that helps."

Jack Grosby was a deviser of patterns and Al Seeley was an observer of them. But a Grosby had to devise a new technique before a Seeley could study it. As usual, the smuggler stayed one jump ahead.

One shortcut, therefore, was to study the smuggler himself—learn what he was like, what drew him into the business, how he thought, where he traveled, what his associates might be like.

Frank DeSantis, a young assistant of Seeley's with admiration for his boss's skills, got to know Grosby well. DeSantis was a Customs agent of the early heroin-boom days, as young and as mod as some of the millionaire-smugglers he pursued.

None of Seeley's white shirts and narrow black ties for him. The sideburns were there and the purple striped shirt with the wide purple tie that made the .357 magnum in his belt look glaringly out of place. With his lean frame and chiseled features and quick, graceful movements, he looked more like the pro basketballer than the heroin hunter. If he lacked Seeley's passionate disgust with the narcotics smuggler, he still had a sense of great adventure—and an impatience for the score that matched Seeley's deeper feelings about making a case.

As he admired Seeley, he also admired the high-rolling smugglers who more and more often were straying into the Customs web.

"Jack Grosby's been at every race track in the world," Frankie said, "including Russia, Czechoslovakia, Poland—all over—South America, Hong Kong." He said it with a kind of awe. "He had two personal interests—horses and money, and he was successful and ingenious at both.

"He judged a country by the people he met at its race tracks. But Jack's *big* thing in life was money. He didn't have to bet, like some guys do, but when he bet he won.

"He's a very intelligent man—not a muscle man. It's more finesse."

As the agents got to know Grosby, they concluded that "he really didn't like to handle junk," Frankie said. "That's why he hired guys to take it off the planes—so he didn't have to touch it."

In the long interrogations and plain old bull sessions with Grosby, the agents learned a lot. Grosby knew about bail from his experience with Felipe Spadaro—he simply cooled it until his lawyer could get his bail cut in half, to $50,000. The man who posted the $50,000 for him was a suspect in the Oscilloscope Case of the year before and in other narcotics cases. But more interesting to the narcs, intensive investigation revealed that $10,000 of the bail money was originally in the form of a check signed "Leon Baptistin Bonsignour"—or Felipe Spadaro/Louis Bonsignour, nephew and employee of Auguste Joseph Ricord.

The summer of '68 was long, hot, and productive, despite some setbacks. While Presidential candidates campaigned and cops and hippies rioted in Chicago, agents of the Customs Bureau and the

Bureau of Narcotics questioned and requestioned new suspects and old.

A Customs man will say: "We often supply the intelligence and then Narcotics gets the credit by making the bust." And a Bureau of Narcotics man will say with equal conviction: "Sure, Customs makes a lot of big cases, but they're usually acting on intelligence passed on by us."

Both are right. And in the summer of '68, both were very active. They even cooperated a little more than usual.

A few months earlier, the Scarred Man—sought for a year in the Oscilloscope Case—had finally been arrested. He was now reinterrogated. Jack Grosby was "talked to" at great length, then watched carefully after he made bail. In August, two prisoners in the Federal Penitentiary at Atlanta, Georgia, both narcotics violators, were reinterviewed by Bureau of Narcotics Agent Anthony Pohl, a man whose skills were recognized by intelligence officers and smugglers alike.

From it all, a slightly clearer picture of the Latin scene was slowly taking shape.

*Item:* Etienne of the Oscilloscope Case once told the Scarred Man that he and four other French people had banded together with a group of Latins to smuggle heroin to the United States. The other French were Felipe Spadaro; his mother, Maria Traversa Bonsignour; Paul Chastagnier; and a man called André Ricord. The operation had been initiated by Luis the Argentine, who had introduced the French (some of whom lived in France, some in Argentina) to the right people in Latin America.

*Item:* Louis, an Atlanta prisoner, said that Auguste Ricord controlled South American narcotics traffic, buying heroin in France from his old friend Joe Orsini through Ricord's nephew, Felipe Spadaro (or Louis Bonsignour). By the prisoner's account, Ricord also sent Chilean and Bolivian cocaine to Orsini's "labs" in France to be purified. It was then returned to South America and Ricord's men smuggled it to the United States.

*Excerpt from an agent's report, based on an interrogation in the summer of 1968:*

The smuggling methods [Ricord] utilizes and the instructions given to the couriers remind one of the operations of the French underground during the German occupation. As a member of the French Gestapo, Ricord must have appreciated the efficiency of these methods . . . and he now utilizes to his advantage the methods he at one time was fighting.

On September 6, 1968, Jack Grosby jumped bail. He went directly to Buenos Aires, where his old friend Felipe and Felipe's companions welcomed him as a hero. He had earned his stripes by jumping a high federal bail on a narcotics charge and becoming a fugitive from the United States—a mark of *machismo* and distinction, not unlike a Mafioso's "making his bones" by killing a man.

With Felipe, his uncle Auguste Ricord, and two Ricord lieutenants called Jean-Pierre and François, Grosby celebrated his new status in, naturally enough, a French restaurant in Buenos Aires.

Jean-Pierre was the stocky Corsican gunman also known as Christian David, wanted in Paris for the murder of Police Commissaire Gallibert—who, when he was shot, was investigating the kidnapping and murder of the Moroccan political exile, Mehdi Ben Barka. David was now Auguste Ricord's bodyguard.

François was Francisco Chiappe, a bulky, 6-foot Corsican also under sentence of death for murder in Europe. It was the investigation of the robbery of an Argentine money exchange by Chiappe and Lucien Sarti—killer of a Belgian policeman and smuggler of heroin into Grand Central Station—that had uncovered a cache of arms in a Buenos Aires restaurant and led to Ricord's second ouster from Argentina in the turbulent year 1968.

On November 17, 1968, in Le Berthus—a small town on the border between France and Spain—Felipe Spadaro, wanted in the Oscilloscope Case, was arrested by French police and, like Louis Bonsignour, sentenced to several years in prison for violating a French law.

On April 29, 1969, in Madrid, Albert Larrain, wanted in the Oscilloscope Case, was interrogated by an agent of the U.S. Bureau of Narcotics. Larrain credited Spadaro/Bonsignour with organizing and controlling all narcotics traffic between France and Spain on one end, South America in the middle, and the United States on the receiving end. He also said that "the power man" of the organization was Auguste Ricord, "who recently re-settled in Asunción."

On December 6, 1969, in the McAlpin Hotel in Manhattan, detectives of the New York Police Department Narcotics Bureau's Special Investigating Unit were arresting two Chileans and an Argentine in a heroin case when in walked another Chilean, fresh off a Lan Chile Airlines flight from Santiago. The two 5-quart wine jugs he was carrying proved to have about a glass of wine each in the part of the bottle above their woven reed jackets. Beneath glass partitions, each jug also had five kilograms of cocaine. One cop couldn't resist saying, "Yeez! They're putting snow [cocaine] in their wine now! That ought to get ya higher than the Andes!"

Special agents of the Customs Agency Service narcotics unit, which by late 1969 numbered sixteen men, were called in. Believing "the wine-bottle MO" too good to be used only once, they alerted all Customs inspectors.

Two days later another Chilean stepped off Argentine Airlines Flight 300 from Buenos Aires at JFK Airport carrying two jugs of wine. This time the bottom half of each jug contained three kilograms of heroin.

Fully awake by now to the dimensions of the Latin Connection, agents working under Al Seeley instituted a relentless check of I-94 immigration forms and airline passenger manifests on planes arriving from South America ("we pulled all the decks from all of those flights"). And new patterns began to take shape.

*Excerpt from a report by Customs Special Agent Al Seeley:*

This investigation formed the basis on which South American traffickers who had merged with French-Corsican elements in South America were identified.

In January of 1970, at 201 Varick Street, a large piece of white cardboard was stapled to the top frame of a blackboard in the

Narcotics Intelligence Unit, Room 352. As time passed, case names and defendants' names were penciled onto the cardboard, one or a few at a time, and dotted lines drawn to connect cases with common defendants or common techniques. Nobody remembers who first started calling it "the Condor Chart." But much of what is known about Latin American drug-smuggling came from its dotted lines.

# 4   *Contrabandista!*

*1950–70*

The night club in Asunción's modernistic Hotel Guarani was cool and quiet, not yet alive with the warmth of liquor-filled bodies and the excited chatter of late evening guests. The American spoke to the Paraguayan in low, intense tones.

"The bananas will come by mixer," the American said. "They will include bread, big bread, butter, and eggs. From Sylvia they can go by grinder or mixer to Caroline, Claudia, and Patricia. Mary is fishing, but Claudia's umpire may make trouble. Now, this is important you must ask Eleanor for sixty yards of red. The remainder will be in black. Joseph and Elias have guaranteed that the vegetables will include celery. Hughes is ready and the teams are ready.—"

The two men were pilots, and the American was speaking in code—the code of the *contrabandistas,* the men who fly any kind of contraband goods into Latin America. It was safe and convenient. He could speak it on a street corner or into a telephone or use it in a cablegram without fear that a hostile government or a rival group would fathom its meaning. But just in case, the code was often changed.

Translated, what the American had said was this:

"The cigarettes will come [to Asunción] by plane. They will include Kents, Kent 100s, True 100s, and Newports. From Asunción they can go by boat or plane to Argentina, Brazil, and Uruguay. Paraguay has agreed but Brazil's government may make trouble. And you must ask officials in Montevideo for sixty days' credit. The remainder will be in cash. . . ."

And so on.

In the code, "vegetables" were the documents that would accompany the planeload of cigarettes. Joseph and Elias—code names for two prominent Asunción businessmen—had guaranteed that the documents would include "celery"—bribe money, or *mordida*, to be used on reluctant border guards or customs officials if necessary.

"Hughes is ready and the teams are ready" simply meant that shippers in Miami (Hughes) and the major American cigarette companies (teams), from which the cigarettes would be bought wholesale, were set for that particular shipment to fly south.

Literally every day, *contrabandista* planes leave Southern Florida's many airfields for Latin America. They are oil-streaked Lockheed Constellations, the light planes of Cessna and Beech and Piper, converted World War II B-25 and B-26 bombers, creaking Douglas DC-3's built in the 'thirties and replaced part by part—almost anything that will still fly. Most of the pilots are very good, usually superior to their machines.

The cargo is often tobacco. In 1969, Paraguay was the world's leading importer of American-made cigarettes—even though it grows and exports some tobacco of its own. But the load could also be whisky. In 1971, Paraguay imported more Scotch whisky than any other country in the world. Yet the tiny, land-locked nation is no larger than the State of Montana and has only 2.5 million people.

*Contrabandista* cargos are not limited, however, to smokes and booze. A load might just as well consist of transistor radios, Levis, television sets, wigs, stereos, or—a favorite in Peru—women's

Bikini panties. In short, any commodity manufactured in the industrial north and desired by consumers in the agricultural south.

It is a simple question of supply and demand, with the airplane serving as the mode of transportation. Profit is the natural motive. A pair of Levi jeans bought for $4 in the United States will bring $12 on the Latin market. Tobacco mark-ups are even higher. "When a pack of cigarettes bought in the U.S. for 18 cents wholesale can be sold under the counter in Latin America for 75 cents, a load of 100,000 cases of cigarettes is better than gold" an American official observed.

A narcotics intelligence officer who has made a thorough study of contraband flying said: "The *contrabandista* system in Latin America is well established, with many pilots involved. It is a highly profitable way to move contraband. They make one-way trips, primarily—cargo only goes south. They occasionally fly to the U.S. with a load of jewelry or antiques or emeralds, but ordinarily planes are empty going north. It is a semilegitimate undertaking for pilots. It is not against U.S. law; it is winked at and certainly even condoned in Latin America."

That is the irony of the term *"contrabandista."* Most of the merchandise is not contraband as it leaves the United States. It is legitimate cargo, legally purchased and legally shipped—at least as the plane clears the end of a Florida runway.

At Panama, things change. Panama has a duty-free zone where goods may be bought tax free. Most of what passes through in transient aircraft, however, should be subject to an import tax. But Panama also has several hundred small, unpoliced airports— as well as many officials who have learned how to turn their backs and hold out upturned palms at the same time.

*Contrabandista* pilots bend the law a bit further as they short-hop down the western coast of South America, through Ecuador, Peru, and Chile, paralleling the spine of the Andes Mountains. "Unofficial" landing fields and friendly customs collectors mean that a properly planned and executed flight can make it all the way south to Antofagasta, Chile, just below the Tropic of Capricorn with only the cost of gas, food, lodging, and a little *mordida* here and there.

The ancient Connies and even the tiny Cessnas and Beeches

then turn eastward to follow the railroad through mountain passes 12,000 feet high, avoiding the 22,000-foot Andean peaks. After a stop at Salta, Argentina, on the eastern slopes of the forbidding Andes, the home base of Asunción is almost due east across the flat, sparsely inhabited Argentine chaco.

Until the mid-1960s, contraband flying was wide open to anyone and done strictly for private profit. Then a rocky economy and a restless military made it seem wise for the government to institutionalize what was already going on. President Alfredo Stroessner's dominant Colorado Party had no trouble pushing through a law that levied a small tax on *contrabandista* goods intended for consumption in Paraguay. A tax would raise revenue to keep the army in uniforms and equipment and keep the generals' mind off thoughts of a coup. That was the theory. But when a plane landed at the Presidente Stroessner Airport outside Asunción and duly declared its load, the merchandise always seemed to be labeled "in transit"—and therefore not subject to tax. Besides, to land at Asunción was to take much of the fun out of *contrabandista* flying, as well as some of the profit. No more night landings with only the headlights of two automobiles as beacons; no more bullets from the *policia* to pray about on the way down in the darkness.

Most of the pilots preferred to fan out across the rolling hills to the south and east, find the broad valleys, and land on the uncharted grass and clay strips of the great *estancias. Mordida* paid to an estate owner was cheaper than the tax, and it also avoided the hocus-pocus of labeling everything "in transit."

The new approach could be said to have worked, in part. Despite many evasions of the law, the Paraguayan Government raises perhaps a third of its revenue from money paid over the counter or under the table by *contrabandista* groups. The generals have larger budgets to allocate, more genuine work to occupy their time. Perhaps more to the point, most of the better landing strips are located on the *estancias* of Paraguay's leading businessmen and political figures—who, in many cases, are also the generals. It is a set of arrangements that seems to please almost everyone. A shaky economy is bolstered, many leading citizens grow wealthy, top military figures make so much money to retire on that the *contrabandista* system is considered a kind of informal, paid-in-advance retirement plan.

Pilots sometimes become rich, though they and their planes are basically considered a cost of doing business—and some of the men and machines exist in near-servitude to the financiers of the system.

Consumers throughout the southern half of Latin America are pleased, even if they do not know of the *contrabandistas* as such. The goods they can buy are not always cheap, but at least they are available.

American cigarette companies make millions. In Paraguay it is widely believed that these companies created the *contrabandista* system—and it is universally accepted that if they didn't, they should have.

Legality and morality are seldom mentioned in a discussion of *contrabandistas.* Paraguay considers itself a kind of bonded warehouse, a customs-free stopover point for goods destined primarily for Brazil and Argentina and to a lesser extent for Uruguay. The merchandise is not contraband as it leaves the United States; for all practical purposes it still is not while it sits "in transit" in Paraguay, except that some of it has escaped the local tax.

Only when the loads, divided up into single- and twin-engined Cessnas and Beeches and museum-piece Lockheed Lodestars, are hedge-hopped illegally across the borders to isolated landing fields in the final markets does the cargo again become contraband, since no import duty is being paid in the receiving countries. The governments of the "victim" countries lose out but seem to care little. Their officials too can collect *mordida.* A man smart and tough enough can even carve out a permanent piece of the action—offering the smugglers a protected landing strip or guaranteeing safe transit from the clandestine field to the city markets.

It is a fact of life and a way of life. From the time that these lands were Spanish and Portuguese colonies, smuggling of one kind or another has been an adjunct to legitimate commerce.

Even if the neighboring countries raised violent objections, Paraguay probably would stand its ground. Asunción was founded in 1537, seven decades before the first permanent English colony was established at Jamestown, Virginia. In more than four centuries, fierce pride and independence have seen the Paraguayans through many adversities. The tiny nation threw off the Spanish yoke in 1811, before most of the other Latin countries. In the devastating War of the Triple Alliance in the 1860s, Paraguay lost half its population but staved off the combined armies of Argentina, Brazil, and Uruguay. And in the mid-1930s, it wrested a vast chunk of the disputed Chaco Boreal, which forms the western two-thirds of the country, from neighboring Bolivia. The bloody Chaco War exhausted Paraguay but left it independent—and produced some of the military heroes who help run the country today.

The waterways that converge to form the mighty Rio de la Plata at Buenos Aires and Montevideo link Asunción to the sea, but it is a tedious river journey of more than 1,000 miles. Paraguay's long years of isolation produced a strong and stubborn people, and a country with, by Latin standards, a certain stability. President Stroessner's conservative, authoritarian rule has lasted for the past eighteen years, longer than that of any other South American government, and it is the not-always-secret envy of other Latin leaders. If Stroessner maintains power partly by defying his giant neighbors on such matters as *contrabandistas* and by keeping his generals in the proper balance of power, that is simply the way it is. He has even been able to relax things a bit since the early 1960s and allow political parties other than his own Colorado Party to take part in elections.

Hernandarias, 300 kilometers almost due east of Asunción, is a clandestine airstrip, isolated and difficult to reach except by air. Its convenience to borders, however, could not be greater. It lies only a few kilometers from the beautiful Iguacu Falls, where Argentina, Brazil, and Paraguay come together.

Dozens of aircraft land there each week—most of them *avionetas*, or small planes. But the hard clay landing strip, more than 3,000 feet long, easily accommodates the four-engine Lockheed Constellations and Douglas DC-6s that arrive several times a week with the big loads.

"One pilot," said a Customs agent in New York, "has described Hernandarias as a sort of fly-in, fly-out, cash-and-carry supermarket."

Though Hernandarias does not appear on many maps, its fame is widespread in southern Latin America. Even details of its ownership, management, and day-to-day operations sometimes appear in print, complete down to details of the way the *avionetas* land with their identification numbers covered over by pieces of cloth and tape.

The airstrip is said to be owned by General Andres Rodriguez, commandant of the Paraguayan cavalry—one of two generals who for many years wielded most of the power in Paraguay not concentrated directly in the hands of President Stroessner.

The operation of Hernandarias is said to be managed by an official of Alto Parana, the province within which it lies. He is said to be an associate of a well-known Asunción cigarette dealer, Miguel Angel Napout. The owner of an Asunción-based air taxi service is said to "front" for the whole operation. The essential political protector for Napout and his organization, according to this version, is the director general of civil aeronautics for Paraguay.

Whoever controls Hernandarias, the pilots who fly there, drones of the *contrabandista* hives, often find their aircraft seized for ransom if they fail to keep up their landing fees and other financial commitments.

Much closer to Asunción, there is another airstrip near the town of Santa Elena, on the *estancia* of the late General Patricio Col man, a wounded hero of the Chaco War who until his death in mid-1972 balanced on President Stroessner's seesaw of power with General Rodriguez.

A Customs agent whose study of Latin American smuggling has twice taken him to Asunción explained the Paraguayan power balance this way:

"Stroessner, I understand, is a very honest man. Underneath him he had two strong, conflicting generals who didn't trust each other—Rodriguez and General Patricio Colman. They were both staunch anti-Commies and you will notice Paraguay has had no problem with insurgency and terror groups like some other Latin countries. So these two guys were underneath and Stroessner's sitting shakily up there . . ."

General Colman was the protector and *padrinazgo*, or god-father, of a young Asunción businessman named Enio Anibal

Varela-Segovia. The two most important ties in the Latin American culture are blood kinship and the godfather, or *compadre* (literally "co-father"), relationship. A godfather has extensive obligations, and the bond and duties of the relationship are reciprocal for a lifetime. Varela would have owed General Colman as much as General Colman would have owed Varela.

In a country as small as Paraguay, with its highly concentrated wealth and power, strong ties of birth, business, or *padrinazgo* were more than enough for a young man to get ahead. Enio Varela apparently also took some shortcuts.

Varela was born in San José, a village 100 miles east of Asunción, in June, 1936. By the time the *contrabandista* system became institutionalized he was a businessman in his middle thirties with a wife and three daughters and all the right connections in the capital. Once a clerk to a big cigarette importer, he had had one kind of tie or another to Miguel Angel Napout and almost every other name that was big in the Paraguayan tobacco trade. He had also developed a reputation for being somewhere else when financial discrepancies or the hijacking of contraband loads was discovered.

"I figure he screwed people for $2 million," a Customs agent said. "He started his career as a clerk-accountant for Hymie Gerlich, alias Chaim Erlich, who is documented in Interpol files. Varela screwed him for $600,000 in cash. There was a parting of the ways . . . "

The Paraguayan Government, or key figures within it, often provided phony paperwork to cover shipments of whisky and cigarettes that—because of some slip-up or other—got confiscated.

"Varela was involved in this smuggling," the Customs agent said. "He worked out of Asunción and Hernandarias near the Argentine border. He was the biggest in the business. But he screwed Philip Morris, Liggett and Myers, American Tobacco, Brown and Williamson for $10,000, $25,000, $50,000 and so on. He ended up on the blacklist of some. It was a very risky business, but very profitable."

Enio Varela did not limit his talents to other shippers and the cigarette companies. Because of Paraguay's questionable financial stability, the American companies often did business with money exchanges in New York, Asunción, Buenos Aires, and Montevideo instead of banks. The exchange houses extracted higher interest rates and service charges than banks, but asked fewer questions. They seemed to come out on the long end of many deals.

*Contrabandista* pilots were often exceptionally skilled in the air and addicted to their trade, but real innocents at business dealings. They were sometimes surprised to find their only means of livelihood—their planes—taken over by exchange houses for non-payment of small debts they didn't know they owed. But Varela, according to Customs intelligence officers, was one *contrabandista* operator who turned the tables: He took one money exchange house for a quarter of a million dollars.

Those in law enforcement who study smuggling have been surprised to find that modern organizations employ not only idea men but "bribers"—men who do nothing but seek out and subvert the key officials at the proper levels of government.

This, too, Varela understood. One of his friends, protectors, and financiers was a slender, distinguished Frenchman of sixty-five named Pierre Joseph Travers. In November, 1967, Travers had appeared in Asunción, a step ahead of the French police. His Interpol lookout said that he had "fiddled the accounts and embezzled the funds" of DeLitra and Company in Paris, traders in gold and precious metals. Travers had been DeLitra's managing director. Now, he was in South America, and 100 million francs were missing from DeLitra. It was said to have been the biggest embezzlement in the history of France.

But Travers knew of Paraguay's attitude toward the so-called right of refuge. Along with the *contrabandista* system, it was considered one of the country's two main resources.

Nazis who fled Argentina after the fall of dictator Juan Perón in 1955 had made excellent use of Paraguay's right of refuge. A "petit Nazi" who had need of forgetfulness and nothing else might come to live in Asunción for a payment of $20,000 to $30,000. If he also needed a small measure of protection from anyone who might seek him out, the price could be $50,000 to $60,000. If he needed complete anonymity, protection, and physical security—as did a chief medical officer from the Auschwitz concentration camp—the price was $100,000; for such a fee a man could live out his days on certain of the great *estancias*, which the journal *Paris Match* once called "true little autonomous republics where no one can enter without a password."

Pierre Travers did not need such thorough security. The rumors that he paid certain Paraguayan officials $5 million for the privilege of making Paraguay his new home have never been proved. In fact, just after his arrival he spent a short time in the very same jail cell that was later to be occupied by Auguste Joseph Ricord. In that short period, fear that Paraguay might waive the right of refuge and allow his deportation or extradition paralyzed many an old Nazi and many others who had capitalized on Paraguay's generosity. But Travers was soon free, and he is still there.

Even without the example of his friend Travers, Enio Varela fully understood the moral climate of his country. He would have agreed with a narcotics intelligence official's assessment of what conditions must exist in a country for it to become a haven for smugglers and other violators of the law—"a lax or corrupt government, protection by powerful individuals—in some other instances, a lack of sophistication, lack of resources, lack of concern." In Varela's heyday, Paraguay seemed to offer all of these.

In 1954, a group was organized to smuggle cocaine from Colombia and Ecuador through Paraguay to Brazil. The principals were a Paraguayan Air Force general; his brother, an airline executive; another man; and the brother of the Minister of the Interior. Varela, according to intelligence reports, though not yet twenty became the ring's distributor. He was the transportation expert.

(The same year, General Alfredo Stroessner, a stout but handsome man whose blond hair and mustache reflected his German ancestry, attended the U.S. Army Command and Staff School at Fort Leavenworth, Kansas—and also became the President of Paraguay.)

Six years later, when a Brazilian undercover narcotics agent working in Asunción was killed with thirty people in the explosion of an Aerolineas Argentinas DC-6 twenty minutes outbound from the Paraguayan capital, the air force general was suspected of having had unusual knowledge about the incident. In 1964, when a second Brazilian operative shot a man in the Splendide Cinema in Asunción but was himself killed, the brother of the Minister of the Interior committed suicide.

By some accounts, Auguste Joseph Ricord visited Asunción about that time and set up a bar that became a hangout for *contrabandistas* and their friends, including Enio Varela. Like so many other stories about Auguste Ricord, it is disputed. But in 1968 Auguste Ricord definitely did come to Asunción.

Earlier that year, he had arranged for Lucien Sarti to be sent to Buenos Aires, where a man who was both smart and tough could be of use. Sarti, an "enforcer" for criminal elements in Europe, who had killed a policeman in Belgium—the one crime a man should not commit unless he wants to incur the hatred of all other policemen in the world—was also, as Customs agents in New York had discovered, controlling narcotics couriers. Those captured at Rouse's Point and in Grand Central Station late in 1967 were his men. Both Sarti and Francisco Chiappe—who also had joined forces with Monsieur André, alias Ricord, and like Sarti was wanted in Europe for murder—were what Latins call "pistoleros." It was not their robbery of a Buenos Aires money exchange so much as the machine guns and other arms found after their arrest that got Auguste Ricord ousted from Argentina for the second time for criminal associations.

In the late 1960s, about the time of Ricord's appearance in Asunción, Varela was in Uruguay setting up a trading company to rival Miguel Angel Napout's Paraguayan operation. That might have been considered unethical, since Varela and Napout were linked in business in Asunción. But while Varela was working his Uruguayan deal, an equally clever Napout eased him out of the Paraguayan setup. Napout had a law passed limiting the transportation of cigarettes to those who paid the government a sum that only he could afford to pay. Varela sometimes felt the world was against him.

Auguste Ricord sometimes had those feelings, too. France wanted him but only to punish him. Argentina had thrown him out twice; Uruguay once. And some of the newer, younger men in his heroin organization had strong ambitions that could conceivably affect a man's health and possibly his longevity. In 1969 Ricord was fifty-eight years old. He suffered from diabetes and more often than he cared to admit was struck by terrible weariness or bursts of ennui. The feelings became increasingly harder to shake off.

The source of his weariness with the world was not by any means Le Paris-Niza. If anything gave him pleasure it was his beloved new inn. The construction was going well. It would end up, he knew, costing more than $100,000, a major investment in labor-rich Paraguay, but it would not be simply a restaurant and a motel. It would be his Franco-Mediterranean island in this Latin American backwater.

Each day Ricord personally directed the construction workers. There was no part of the rambling property that would not bear his personal touch. At the center would be the restaurant, the small hotel, and the pool. There were six bungalows painted in gay tropical colors, and a play area for children. Ricord wanted the atmosphere of Le Paris-Niza to be as gay as the sparkle in the eyes of his pretty thirteen-year-old, Josephine Brigitte. He had even constructed a little "train" of a jeep and a tow-wagon to carry children about the play area, and he had collected a veritable zoo of animals and birds, including an anteater, a monkey, and a noisy, talkative parrot.

Most dear to his heart was the restaurant. He wanted it to be as charming and as French as he could make it. He had hired an expatriate French couple to manage it and had pressed his young friend Pierre Gahou into service to teach the waiters the Gallic manner of serving. No, it was not Le Paris-Niza that gave him disquiet. Except for a minor spat with Gahou over who should get the manager's job, Le Paris-Niza presented few problems.

It was M. Ricord's "other interests" that caused him concern. The demand for heroin in the United States was at its zenith and the market virtually cried out for the smugglers to send in bulk loads. The 1- and 2-kilo "carries" of five years before were nearly as risky as bulk shipments, and they deprived the smuggler of the massive profits now possible. Yet with the market at its all-time high Ricord, more strongly than at any time in the past, felt threats emerging from within and from outside his organization.

When he had first come to South America in 1948 it had been almost frontierlike. Governments and police were cruder, more makeshift, more open to manipulation. Well-placed *mordida* could give a man almost complete security. Now much of that had faded. One by one, the governments of the bigger countries—Argentina, Brazil, Venezuela—were moving into the twentieth century. Though they were still distinctly uninterested in crimes that did not threaten their own existence, these governments were increasingly susceptible to moral pressure from other "responsible" nations. Their corruption, Ricord knew, would now be more subtle. It would be, as in France, the corruption of power and political alliance. The simple payoff would be passé. His ouster from Argentina had convinced him that he must shift his entire operation to a more controllable environment.

Inside his own organization there was constant pressure from Lucien Sarti, Francisco "François" Chiappe, Jean-Paul Angeletti, Christian David. All had come to him from Europe as "lieutenants" fleeing police warrants. He had provided them with false documents, political safety, and assignments within his organization. But they were younger men and greedy to establish themselves. Ricord sometimes feared that his leadership was on the verge of being more honorary than real.

A third and more indefinable threat also clouded the horizon. Ricord was a careful man, an organizer and administrator, and he prided himself on planning ahead. It was his belief that his profession took as much vision as any other, if not more. He sensed that the United States would at some moment grow tired of being the principal market for the world's heroin and turn its real might to the destruction of the drug-smuggling industry. As in World War II, once the power of the mammoth state began to roll, there would be no way to stop it, and that would mean the end of the smuggling rings.

Ricord remembered clearly how confident the Germans had been entering Paris thirty years before. Collecting payoffs from Paris night clubs for the conquerers and eavesdropping on the French underworld for them, he had come to know many Germans well. They had miscalculated the Americans and the inexorable power of American planes and tanks.

When Ricord tallied these thoughts he always came out with the same conclusion. He must move swiftly. He must make a profit now, while the market was good and the trade routes open. His future was as unsure as that of a wine grower in his native France. Too much cold, too much rain, too little rain—he was at the mercy of variables he could not control.

The cardinal rule in the international heroin cartel had always been: French deal with French. Its observance had kept the narcotics trade safe from penetration on more than one occasion and from the early 1960s had made it virtually impossible for U.S. police agencies to infiltrate above the lowest levels of the heroin smuggling industry. The traffic was tightly controlled by a few families. Anyone not known for a lifetime was not trusted. The French might sell their heroin to foreigners for distribution or occasionally employ underlings and couriers of another nationality, but these men were effectively barred from the mainstream and contact was severely limited. One veteran American intelligence officer summed up the situation succinctly: "You couldn't buy an ounce of heroin in France for a million dollars unless the right people were willing to sell." The rule was enforced by a tight, rigid discipline built on centuries of French-Corsican tradition.

Auguste Joseph Ricord decided to violate this rule. He did it with full knowledge of the dangers out of what he felt was necessity. To move the bulk shipments of heroin the market demanded, he began to utilize the *contrabandista* system. It was a swift and innovative way to ship large amounts of heroin—a new method, worth millions to the smuggler. But the *contrabandistas* were almost as tightly controlled by the Paraguayans as the source of heroin was controlled by the French.

Thus Auguste Ricord must do business with the Paraguayans. The arrangement insulted his respect for security. But in all things the volatile little Corsican had a peasant's pragmatism. No planes would take off from Paraguayan soil carrying his heroin unless he cooperated with one or another of the *contrabandista* cliques.

He chose to throw in with Enio Anibal Varela-Segovia—and by doing so to gain the protection of Varela's godfather, General Patricio Colman, powerful commander of the 14th Army Regiment.

Ricord's personal feelings about the Paraguayans were mixed. Many of them were physically small, as he was, and he felt comfortable with them. Varela he did not trust. The fat, garrulous contraband impressario had a record of double-crossing partners and friends alike. But his patron, General Colman, the ruthless field officer who had become a Chaco war hero and later stamped out fledgling guerrilla movements, Ricord could not help but admire. Colman was a frequent dinner guest at Le Paris-Niza.

The mustachioed Varela, shrewd as he might be, is described by Customs intelligence officials as "a fat guy, a square. He has a retarded daughter, which has got to cost him some money, and two other daughters. He is not known to gamble. He has a couple of girl friends, but how much can you spend on a girl friend or two in Paraguay?

"He doesn't drink, he doesn't go out—so he's got a bundle of money someplace—by our count, a couple of million dollars in embezzlements. Is the money in Switzerland?

"So we can't figure out why a guy with that kind of money goes into the smuggling of junk."

But "somehow, Varela now gets tied up with Ricord," according to the Customs agents. "He's the link between Ricord, who had the heroin organization, and the method to ship it up—the *contrabandista* planes. The planes used to go up empty, but the pilots are like cab drivers or truck drivers—why deadhead if you can carry a load?"

"In defense of some of these *contrabandista* pilots, many of them wouldn't touch junk," a Bureau of Narcotics intelligence analyst said. "They're good at skimming mountain tops and dropping down into valleys—these are enormous feats. Some of them are really daredevil people—to them it's a way of making a living. They'd have a hard time giving up a lifetime of flying. It satisfies an inner need.

"No, they don't all fly junk. But this *contrabandista* system was not exploited to its maximum until heroin came along."

What most rankled Ricord was that he had to introduce Varela to the entire operation, from the receipt of the heroin from France to its delivery to the United States. Varela had become virtually an operating partner.

In late May, 1970, Ricord's "partner" held a meeting in his plush and well-furnished office over the El Nido Restaurant in downtown Asunción. Besides Varela, two men sat in the air-

conditioned comfort of the room. Aron Muravnik was a Polish
Jew of Argentine nationality whose reputation as a smuggler of
jewels and watches was well known in Latin America. He had
been associated with Enio Varela for nearly a decade. Across from
him sat a husky, black-haired Latin who used many names, among
them Cesar Bianchi. The thirty-four-year-old Bianchi was the
owner of a small air service that specialized in smuggling. He was
a typical *contrabandista*.

As he waited for Varela to speak, the pilot wore a quizzical
look. He had flown for Varela for five years, and experience had
taught him to be wary. Though he was closely associated with
the merchant—in fact Varela had financed the purchase of one
of his planes, a Cessna 210—he did not trust the Paraguayan.
Didn't Varela already owe him $38,000 for past trips?

"We want you to take another load of uranium to the United
States," Varela began bluntly. There was a long pause.

Wearily the pilot remembered the first load he had carried
on a return flight to the United States some months before.
Varela had told him the cargo was uranium dust then also. According to the merchant the bags of dust were "samples" from a
mine owned by General Colman. If they assayed well, Varela
would get a contract and "you could make a million American
dollars," he told Bianchi. My God! the pilot thought. He had
been a fool.

"Mr. Varela," he said, "it is not uranium dust that I'll be carrying."

"That is true," Varela replied smoothly, "but you have known
for a long time that it was not uranium dust and you have continued to make the flights."

"Indeed, precisely." The pilot's voice tightened. "But I have
not been paid, and there is great risk."

"Do not worry. Do not worry," Varela soothed, "I told you.
You will be paid when we are paid for the merchandise."

The pilot looked beaten. Would he ever escape these men?
Anger reddened his face, but he bit off further protests and for
the next hour joined in carefully planning the trip.

Unlike *contrabandista* missions into Latin America, there would
be no attempt to make a covert penetration of the United States.

American radar and military control were so efficient, it was agreed that as in the past Bianchi would file a flight plan and come straight into an airport like any other small private or commercial aircraft. For cover, he would depend on assimilating among the literally hundreds of Latin American aircraft that fly in and out of the Miami area with charter passengers and cargo. Miami had been the port of exit for the *contrabandistas* for two decades. Latin planes and pilots attracted little or no attention.

The load would be almost sixty kilos. Even in the privacy of the office they called it "uranium." Months later the pilot would recall: "We were a little bit ashamed to speak about it together." The "uranium" would be secreted in the backs and bottoms of the cabin seats in one of Bianchi's planes, a twin-engine Beechcraft C-50. Bianchi would fly west from Paraguay to the west coast of South America, then turn north to Panama, Jamaica, and Miami.

"Muraneek," Varela said, using the Spanish pronunciation of the name, would be Bianchi's contact and control. He would give the final instructions, help him load, and meet him in Miami. It would be simple, Varela assured the pilot, simple. "All you have to do is fly."

On June 18, 1970, a little more than two weeks after the meeting, "Muraneek" called Bianchi. "It is time to go," was his simple message. Varela had never told Bianchi the source of the "merchandise" that he had been flying, and Bianchi was surprised when Muravnik told him that they would both go to fetch it. He was even more surprised when Muravnik drove the car into the compound of Le Paris-Niza. The pilot had heard of the place as a good eating spot, and of the Frenchman who owned it, but he had never been there.

A few moments after they parked the car in front of the restaurant a small, wiry man approached the car and spoke quickly in Spanish with Muravnik. The Argentinian smuggler would later identify the man to Bianchi as "Monsieur André," and it was by this name that Bianchi would know the man until January, 1972, when he read his real name in *Newsweek* magazine.

The Frenchman disappeared inside the restaurant and reappeared a moment later with two shopping bags full of gaily wrapped packages. The bright papers, like Christmas wrapping, looked strange in June. Together the three men placed the bags in the trunk of the car. Already the pilot was feeling the tautness of stomach he felt before each flight. But this time it was worse than usual. Later he would remember that he was so nervous he paid no attention to anything at Le Paris-Niza except those shopping bags that looked like Christmas.

At the airport, the packages were carefully secreted behind and under the seats of the Beechcraft by a mechanic, and the seat frame was replaced to hide them completely. Well into the day, the pilot and his young Brazilian copilot and interpreter, Renato Balestra, took off. Balestra knew nothing of the packages.

Five days later, on June 23, 1970, the plane taxied to a stop at the General Aviation Center at Miami International Airport. Though the pilot was nervous as he filled out the Customs declaration with the awful question, "Are you carrying any narcotics or prescription drugs?," the trip had been as Varela described it: "Simple."

Following the plan, Bianchi flew the Beech the next day eight miles to Opa Locka Airport, where Muravnik was waiting. The veteran smuggler was cool and unruffled. He would take the pilot's keys, he said, and in a few hours the "merchandise" would be gone. Bianchi began to feel better at the thought of getting those damning packages out of the plane.

But he had been back at a rented apartment in Miami for less than an hour when Muravnik called. "I cannot make delivery of the merchandise today," he told the pilot matter-of-factly, "so I have put it in the trunk of your car." Bianchi winced.

"I was worried," he would recall later. "The car was registered in my name. If the drugs were found it would be a very big problem . . . it concerned me that I shouldn't leave them there." Retrieving his keys from Muravnik, he went to his car in Opa Locka's overnight parking lot and opened the trunk. There, like some macabre albatross, were the Christmas-wrapped packages. The pilot was both angry and frightened. Why should he be put at such risk? Why should his car be the one literally left holding the bags?

Hurrying from the airport parking lot, Bianchi searched until he found a used car lot a few blocks away. Swiftly he purchased an old car for $100, affixed Florida temporary license tags, and drove it back to the airport parking lot. "I took all the 'merchandise' from my car and placed it in the old car," the pilot later remembered. "Then I flew back to Asunción."

Varela and Muravnik were enraged. "They wanted to know about the drugs. Muravnik didn't find them in my car and the lock wasn't broken. I told them I had changed them. . . . They didn't quite believe me."

Varela felt sure the pilot had not double-crossed him. He had known Bianchi for five years, and he was confident that the pilot did not have the connections to hijack a load of heroin and market it. He was, nevertheless, furious. The pilot was just stupid enough, he felt, to transfer the load to an old car. Muravnik was less generous. Even later, after he returned to Miami and located the heroin, he told Varela, "This guy is insane. I don't want him to work with us any more."

But the man most put off by the incident was Auguste Joseph Ricord. Ricord had never fully trusted Varela to begin with. Their association was like that of two wary wolves growling at each other. He realized that he must take steps to protect the security of his operation. The "mislaying" of sixty kilograms of heroin decided him on much greater care in his dealings with Señor Varela. He must invoke a balance or check on an operation that he could rely upon the way he always had in his more careful past.

Early in July, 1970, Ricord called in Pierre Gahou. Though he had had his differences with the one-time waiter, he trusted him if for no other reason than that Gahou was French. Furthermore, he knew that Gahou was free from any control by Varela. Gahou had handled sensitive missions for Ricord in the past. In 1969, for instance, Ricord had chosen Gahou to go to Miami to collect a large amount of money due from a heroin shipment. Since Gahou was not wanted by a police agency he could move across international borders freely, using his own name and passport. Gahou was the only one in Paraguay, outside of his daughter and his niece Elena Ana, whom Ricord felt he could rely upon in these circumstances.

Now, with a vital mission at hand, Ricord felt compelled to have his interests directly represented. Over cups of strong coffee, he outlined the assignment to Gahou. A load of heroin—70 kilos or 154 pounds of nearly pure drug—was due to arrive from France in the next few days. It had been secreted in the body of a red and white Citroën and would come ashore at Montevideo among the possessions of a special courier from the "families" in France.

As part of his agreement with the Paraguayans, he told Gahou, Varela's organization would help him handle the pick-up of the car and its transportation across the Uruguayan border, through Argentina, and into Paraguay. Varela's connections in these countries would make this possible without hazard. But, Ricord told Gahou, he wanted the French organization to be as fully represented as Varela's was, so that there would be no tampering with the load and no hitch in its movement. Gahou must go to Montevideo, meet the car and, with the French courier, accompany it back to Asunción. It was at this meeting that Ricord also indicated to Gahou that there would be a number of future overseas assignments.

At virtually the same moment, Varela was talking on the telephone to Felix Rogelio Becker, who directed the fat Paraguayan's operations in Montevideo. They talked each day as a matter of course, but this conversation was to be more fateful than Becker would ever realize. The dour, red-haired Becker, Varela ordered, was to cooperate with Aron Muravnik in the next few days in the picking up of a red and white Citroën that must be driven back to Asunción. He, Becker, should accompany this car personally, Varela stressed. Becker must also see that there were no complications with Uruguayan authorities at the port of entry or at the border of these countries. Was that clear? No complications.

The following Friday, on schedule, the red and white car and its shepherd arrived aboard a French-flag vessel. And true to Varela's instructions, the Citroën rolled ashore with no more than a cursory nod from the Uruguayan customs men. Next morning its four occupants, the two Frenchmen guarding the product and the two Latins guiding it through the authorities of Uruguay, Argentina, and Paraguay, set out for Asunción. Again Varela's orders to Becker and Muravnik were carried out. There were no complications. The Citroën rolled smoothly across the border of Paraguay and arrived in Asunción late Friday night.

None of its occupants could see any heroin. Indeed, only the courier knew that the 154 pounds of "merchandise" had been distributed around the front bumper wells. Short of mechanical stripping, the only way anybody could pick up a telltale sign might be from a little heaviness in the steering.

As soon as the car reached Asunción, the men drove it to Varela's house. The fat merchant was clearly pleased and chit-chatted happily with the group as he dialed a telephone number. "Señor André," he said in soft Spanish to someone on the other end of the line, "Gahou has arrived."

Ricord, too, was pleased that this stage of the transport had gone smoothly. But the restaurant was crowded with guests, and he did not want the arrival of the colorful car to attract much attention. "Bring it over," he told Varela "but do not come right in. Park a few blocks away." Varela complied.

It was dusk when Ricord, accompanied by Varela, walked from Le Paris-Niza to greet the car and the men still waiting with it. None of the men at that meeting—Varela, Ricord, Gahou, Muravnik, Becker, nor the mysterious French courier—could possibly realize how fateful its hidden cargo would be.

Ricord and Varela agreed to divide the load roughly in half for delivery to the United States. The first portion, about thirty kilos, would be sent up in August. The balance, which actually measured out to some forty-two kilos, would go north later.

As, in a sense, the Latin American division manager for a world-wide organization, Ricord faced the problem that his product had to be paid for swiftly. The cost of heroin delivered in South America for transshipment was between $4,000 and $5,000 per kilogram. For a load of seventy kilos, the "front money" or advance payment could mount as high as $350,000. When the merchandise was sold in the United States, a wholesaler could double or triple that money, but Ricord still must keep the flow of cash moving. It was a business that permitted little leeway for poor money management or extension of credit. Ricord worried about keeping his operation moving at the proper pace.

Varela had to deal with more mundane problems. Though he

had cajoled Bianchi into another flight, his top lieutenant Muravnik was still reluctant to work with Bianchi because of the car-switching incident in Miami. Varela finally settled the matter by bringing Becker into the operation. From now on, he ordered, Becker would be the contact man with the pilot and would shepherd the load onto the plane heading north. Muravnik would be in charge of stashing the merchandise in the United States until delivery.

On September 2, 1970, Bianchi delivered a load of thirty kilograms (sixty-six pounds) of heroin to the United States. It was hidden aboard his Cessna 210, packed in two vinyl-leather flight bags. The transfer was made without incident on the landing strip at Opa Locka, Florida.

Bianchi's copilot, Renato Balestra, was not aware of what the two bags contained. But he remembered being suspicious when Bianchi told him as he carried them to a waiting car: "Do not lean against the load. Walk as though the bags are not heavy." The bags, the copilot would recall later, were "very heavy."

At one point in September, half this load would be delivered to a New York buyer, and the money would be returned to Paraguay via money exchange houses. Muravnik would remain in Miami with some fifteen kilos and prepare for a second delivery to New York City.

In Asunción there is a luxuriously appointed apartment building on Alberdi Street known as the Sergasa. Varela, Muravnik, and Bianchi all maintained apartments there, though none of them lived in the building full time. In early October, Pierre Gahou was borrowing Muravnik's flat for what he later called "a reason a man does not have to specify. A private reason."

Gahou felt at loose ends. He had come to Asunción hoping that Monsieur Ricord would allow him to manage Le Paris-Niza. Though the wiry Corsican had never promised him the job, there had always been an implication that it could be his. Gahou was a man alone. A man searching for something of substance. Two years in the French Army in Algeria during the war there and fifteen years at sea as a steward on commercial passenger liners had left Gahou with little he could hang onto. He had a child in Paris but no wife, and except for a minor investment with an old friend in an industrial-design and interior-decorating business in France and some paltry savings there was nothing else.

Now he found himself being used in the drug trade. It made him constantly ill at ease. Even the girl he had found at Le Paris-Niza and occasional other liaisons did not distract him. At Ricord's behest he had flown to Paris in mid-September to renew his passport and get his travel papers in order. When Ricord told Gahou he wanted to meet with him on that October weekend, Gahou knew that it would involve a hazardous smuggling assignment.

Gahou was not surprised to see Varela and Becker show up along with Ricord. The meeting at the Sergasa on October 3 was conducted in both Spanish and French. Ricord and Varela would have rapid exchanges of Spanish, and Ricord would briskly relate the conversation to Gahou in French. Then he and Gahou would have a rapid exchange of French, which Ricord would translate into Spanish for Varela and Becker.

Varela ordered Becker to go to Miami, register at the Four Ambassadors Hotel, and contact Muravnik. Both men, he said, should wait there until they had heard from Gahou. Ricord instructed Gahou to proceed directly to New York and register at the Waldorf-Astoria. Gahou and Gahou alone would know how to contact the "receiver" for this load. The shipment, fifteen kilos that had been part of the heroin flown in by Bianchi on September 2, was the first of what could be a number of deliveries. If the buyer of those fifteen kilos was prompt in accepting delivery and making payment, a larger subsequent load would be sent.

Once Gahou had made contact and set up the arrangements, Becker and Muravnik would bring the heroin to New York from Miami. A third man, Julio Rodriguez, an associate of Varela, would also be in New York. After Gahou had delivered the "merchandise" he would turn the money over to Becker and Muravnik, who in turn would be responsible for carrying it back to Paraguay.

The meeting ended jovially with the participants enjoying a drink from Muravnik's well-stocked liquor cabinet. Gahou would leave the next day, as would Becker. Though Becker had not told the others, he planned to stop off in Lima, Peru, for a brief liaison before continuing to Miami.

The next day Ricord drove his young French protégé to the airport. In the United States, he told Gahou, his contact would be a man called "Nick." He gave the Frenchman a New York City telephone number and ordered him to memorize the number and never commit it to paper.

On October 6 in Miami Becker received a cryptic telephone call at the Four Ambassadors from Gahou. "He asked me when I was coming to New York and by that I knew he was telling me he was ready." Muravnik and Becker nonchalantly flew the fifteen kilos from Miami to New York in their carry-on luggage.

When Gahou contacted his man in New York, he received odd delivery instructions. He must take the merchandise by hand—it weighed nearly thirty-five pounds—and carry it from the Waldorf to a midtown location more than two dozen blocks from the hotel, walking down Park Avenue and along side streets to the agreed-upon location. At some point, and he should not be surprised how, the merchandise would be taken from him. If the load was of the purity promised, the Spanish-speaking "Nick" told Gahou, then the money would be paid at Twenty-second Street and Broadway.

The pick-up instructions were professional and showed how wary this new buyer was of the smugglers. In the nearly 4-mile walk that he had ordered Gahou to take through midtown New York, carrying fifteen kilos of heroin, Nick would have ample time to examine whether the Frenchman was under surveillance or was some sort of plant.

At the appointed time Gahou began walking, shifting the heavy flight bag from one hand to the other to handle the weight. He was frightened, more so than he had ever been before. Here he was walking down a New York Street with a fortune in heroin in a bag, waiting for some faceless, nameless men to take it from him. The walk was excruciating torture. Forty-ninth Street, Forty-eighth Street, Forty-seventh Street. Each passing car seemed to be carrying police, each pedestrian seemed to be staring at him. Gahou felt as though he were the subject of some giant scientific experiment in which thousands of eyes had him on view.

By the time he had reached the meeting place he was so worn with carrying the 35-pound bag that his fatigue overshadowed his fear. He was glancing into one of the brightly lighted store windows when out of the corner of his eye he saw a car slow along the curb lane. Without warning a man leaped out, grabbed the suitcase from his hand, and jumped back into the still-moving car. Gahou was staggered by the force of the grab.

Glad to be relieved of the dangerous merchandise, the Frenchman stopped almost immediately in a small sidestreet bar and had a strong drink. He needed it, and he felt he had earned it.

Later in the evening he was, as ordered, standing at the corner of Twenty-second Street and Broadway on the lower fringe of New York's garment district. Though he did not feel as vulnerable as he had with the heroin, he was still uncomfortable knowing that someone knew what he looked like while he did not know them.

He had not waited long when a husky, black-haired man in his early forties approached him. "Senor Gahou?" the man said in Spanish. "I have something for you." He handed the former French Line waiter an Iberian Airlines shoulder bag. Gahou accepted the bag without comment and without opening it. The two men shook hands and Gahou immediately took a cab to the Waldorf, where Becker, Muravnik, and Rodriguez were waiting. The four eagerly crowded around as Gahou opened the bag. It was filled with U.S. currency—hundreds, fifties, twenties, and even a few ten-dollar bills.

Becker later recalled that they all sat down and counted it. "There was $107,000. I put $100,000 in a box and Muravnik took the other $7,000."

The next day, October 10, 1970, Becker left for Asunción carrying the $100,000. On October 11, Varela, several other friends, and Ricord came to Becker's Asunción home. While the others had apéritifs in the main rooms, Varela called to Ricord. "He came into the room [a side room] and Varela counted the money for him. And once more it counted to $100,000. All three of us went out into the street, Ricord got into his car, and Varela handed him the money," Becker later remembered.

Ricord was pleased. The fifteen-kilogram delivery had gone so smoothly and payment had been received so quickly and faultlessly that he felt no compunction at all about releasing the remaining forty-two kilograms for delivery.

The pilot, Cesar Bianchi, had not been at the meeting at Becker's house. Indeed, only two days before he and his copilot Renato Balestra had brought the Cessna home from Florida and landed it at a vast *estancia* 120 kilometers southeast of Asunción—the estate of General Colman. On October 9 Bianchi had left the plane and flown to Asunción with Varela by air taxi. Bianchi had spent the next two days at his home. On October 11 he had notified Varela that he had all necessary flight permits and was ready for another trip.

A few hours later Varela came to Bianchi's home. The two men lunched and Varela outlined the next mission to him. He did not tell the pilot about the delivery of the $100,000 or that the mission was "on" because Monsieur Ricord had "released" the forty-two kilograms. After lunch and the siesta period, the two men drove downtown and picked up some provisions. At one point Varela excused himself and made a telephone call.

Bianchi later recalled that after the call, "We went to the Paris-Niza restaurant. Varela stopped the car and told me to wait before going in. I said this wasn't necessary because I had already been there." But Varela entered the restaurant alone and returned a few moments later with Ricord, the man Bianchi knew only as Monsieur André. Bianchi was driving his new Alfa-Romeo that day. When it came time to load the "merchandise" he pulled the car up in front of one of the cabanas. Two suitcases fitted into the trunk. The third was put in the front of the car between the bucket seats, leaving room for Varela's bodyguard, who would accompany them on the long drive to the *estancia*.

As dusk approached, Varela, Bianchi, and the bodyguard roared south out of Asunción toward the ranch. The skies were leaden and threatening, and Bianchi had a pilot's strong sense of foreboding of bad weather. He was right. The morning of October 12 broke with high winds and rain. It was no day to fly the Andes.

Bianchi called Varela from the airstrip and told him there would be a delay. Maybe, he said, the mission could get off on the 13th. A less pragmatic man might have seen the delay as an ill omen.

# 5   Cesar and the White Horse

October 18, 1970

*Dawn came across the bay from* Key Biscayne, murky with humidity and a threat of rain. The whores meandered out of the Miami hotels in the early light, their faces bland and puffy. Along the expressways early traffic was surging in from Fort Lauderdale, Hialeah, Miami Springs, and Coral Gables.

Richard J. "Hoppy" Hopkins guided the dusty 1968 Ambassador sedan into the gravel-strewn parking lot and switched off the motor with an irritable gesture. The car had no air-conditioning, and already his shirt looked wilted and grimy.

At thirty-eight, Hopkins could have been the average office worker. Sandy-haired but balding, of middle height, husky but not musclebound, that September morning he wore the white-collar worker's 1970 summer uniform—an olive green wash-and-wear suit, inexpensive striped tie, black wing-tipped shoes.

Carefully rolling up the car windows against the almost certain rain, Hopkins lifted a cheap brown attaché case from the back seat and headed for the coffee vendor's booth at the corner of the parking lot. "Large coffee, cream, no sugar, and one of those," he ordered, pointing at a cellophane-wrapped doughnut and trying to ignore the calories.

Balancing the brown paper bag in one hand and the briefcase in the other, he headed back across the parking lot to the green six-story office building. He might have been the manager of an insurance office on his way to work. Except that an insurance manager would hardly be carrying a specially balanced, molded-grip .357 magnum revolver in his attaché case. And it was even less likely that an insurance manager's case would contain a hand-sized radio transmitter and receiver, a leather-covered blackjack, and a pair of handcuffs.

Hoppy hit the lobby of the building in full stride, made it through the fast-closing doors of an elevator, and with a curt nod to his elevator companions pushed the button for four. The irritation at no air-conditioning had given way in his mind to computation. He had worked late three nights that week and had been duty officer at Miami International Airport twice. Though the airport stints normally were on-call assignments, they had ended with four hours of overtime each night. If his arithmetic was right, he had three days of compensatory time coming. It would be good to get away for a few days.

On the fourth floor, Hoppy unlocked an unmarked brown door and entered a shabby, sparsely furnished office. Six gray metal desks with identical green blotters, clear of papers, sat in two rows. Along one wall stood four gray steel file cabinets, their drawers secured by an iron bar locked at the top and bottom. A paper card at the top of each cabinet warned that the contents were "classified." The brown panel walls were blank except for a giant map of Latin America and another of Florida. Both maps had clusters of colored pins stuck in them.

Hoppy settled down behind his desk. He was the first one in. Relishing a few moments to collect his thoughts, he was just prying the plastic top off the coffee container when the intercom buzzed and a woman's voice said crisply:

"The SAC wants to see you."

Hoppy methodically tamped down the lid of the coffee, hoping to trap its heat, locked the office door, and headed for the elevators.

The SAC was the Senior Agent in Charge of the Bureau of Customs enforcement office in Miami. When he called Hoppy upstairs it meant two things. It was important, and it was a narcotics case.

Hoppy had been some sort of cop almost all his working life. He'd started as a uniformed policeman for the Hialeah Police Department in 1959. Two years later he had become a plainclothes investigation agent for the enforcement division of the Florida Alcohol and Tax Commission. In six years he had worked every type of case: illegal stills, tax frauds, liquor violations. He'd spent hours posing as a happy customer in plush Miami Beach bars to break prostitution rings.

"You do this so long," Hoppy likes to tell friends, "you begin to look like fuzz after a while. Ten years ago I wouldn't have believed it even though the oldtimers told me so. But after a while I've got to go along. I used to be able to walk into a place over on the beach working undercover and make a prostitution case by my second drink. Now, I'm sure the first thing that bartender would think when I sat down was fuzzy, fuzzy, fuzzy."

Four years ago Hoppy had taken the examination for Customs Bureau Patrol Officer, a uniformed police job guarding ports and airports against everything from smugglers to freight hijackers. Though returning to a uniformed patrol assignment was a step down for a state tax investigator, Hoppy saw it as a chance to qualify as a special agent in Customs enforcement.

A year after joining the Customs Agency Service he was made a special agent. Six months later he was assigned to a special detail formed to deal with the growing narcotics smuggling menace.

He liked the work. His job was, in a sense, the "clean end" of the narcotics law enforcement field. Many other police agencies and the Bureau of Narcotics and Dangerous Drugs use as their main technique the undercover agent who "buys" quantities of illicit drugs and thus traps the pusher—or wiretaps to spot illegal drug operations and collect evidence for search warrants.

"BNDD agents burn out in two years. The guy gets known around, he can't make buys any more so they send him to another city. But usually it's hard for him to click there. After that he's no use at all," one critic of BNDD claims. "They don't do skilled investigative work. It's just buys and wiretaps." Furthermore, the BNDD hounded users right down to the ghetto and the gutter for what other lawmen felt were trivial amounts of narcotics. "Look at their seizures," Hoppy argues, "two ounces, one key [kilo], maybe two keys."

As the war against the narcotics smuggler heated up in the late 1960s, the Customs agent had two powerful tools to help him catch his quarry. Under Customs law, an agent may conduct a search of anyone or anything that enters the United States from abroad. He can make this search on demand, without a warrant and without showing probable cause that the person or object is carrying contraband. Furthermore, the search need not be made at the border so long as the Customs agent keeps continuous surveillance on the suspected contraband after it enters the country. Thus an agent can follow a load of drugs all over the country to find out who receives it before seizing the drugs and arresting the receiver. Since the bulk of narcotics cases that are overturned in court are overturned on the basis that lawmen made an illegal search and seizure, Customs' *carte blanche* remains a powerful weapon. "When we make a seizure on a guy, he knows it's going to stick," Hoppy points out.

Customs law also creates a system of rewards that can be paid to anyone who helps agents find or seize contraband being smuggled into the United States. The "reward" for turning in a heroin smuggling operation is $500 a kilogram. The reward system legitimizes payments to the most important investigative aid of any police agency—the informant.

The result was to make the Customs narcotics assignment one of skill and imagination and footpounding detective work. No entrapping some pathetic junkie or muscling a suspect on the street. It was, as cops say, "clean work."

Hoppy liked it. Drugs were the most serious crime menace in the country, and Hoppy as a father could put his gut into the fight against drug-smuggling. It was a crime about which the public was not at all ambivalent. It wanted drug-smuggling stopped.

On the sixth floor, Hoppy automatically adjusted his tie and stopped at the secretary's desk. "He's waiting for you. Go on in," she said, her tone and eyes indicating it was not a routine visit.

There were few agents in the Miami field office who didn't like Jim Mosley. The SAC was a quiet, low-key, hard-working career investigator who had the respect of his men because, if he asked them to do something difficult, they knew he'd probably done it himself. For agents like Hoppy, the men who had worked up in law enforcement without a college degree, Mosley presented a living example of what an up-through-the-ranks man could do.

The SAC looked up from his writing, leaned back, and lit a cigarette. He wished he had twenty more like Hopkins. When you called Hoppy up on his day off, he didn't ask you "How come?" He simply asked you "When and where do you want me?" This was an important distinction for a man who supervises a field office trying to cover eighty-three airfields, including five international airports and Puerto Rico, a thousand inlets and coves, five major ship anchorages—and who tries as well to watch for the semipros in sailboats full of duty-free booze from the Bahamas.

"The FBI sent this over," Mosley said, handing Hoppy a two-page, double-spaced, typewritten letter on blue complimentary Eastern Airlines stationery. "It's postmarked Miami and at first glance it looks interesting. If the guy who wrote that thing isn't a kook we've got something pretty important," Mosley said.

"Do we know who wrote it?" Hoppy asked, glancing at the second page.

"Yeh, it's the same guy who writes to cops all over the world— Mr. Anonymous." Mosley suddenly sounded bored.

He went back to his writing. "Keep me well posted okay?" Mosley said, without looking up. The interview was over.

Back at his desk, Hoppy ruefully discovered his coffee had gone cold. Putting the cup aside, he spread the letter's two pages and the envelope out and began to study them. The letter had been addressed to the "Federal Bureau of Investigations, Narcotics Division," which told Hoppy at once that the writer was not overly familiar with federal law enforcement. The FBI does not investigate narcotics cases, and its normal practice is to turn over all information on drug traffic either to the Bureau of Narcotics and Dangerous Drugs or to the Customs Service.

The letter was a jumbled, often misspelled, strangely typed set of allegations about narcotics smuggling operations. It listed sixteen persons and six aircraft that were allegedly involved in smuggling hard narcotics into the United States. "Dear F.B.I.:" it read,

Urgent check with American consul in Paraguay about report mailed to him about the following: aircraft argentinian registration LV-HDW, flown by Ricardo Rodrigues, alias Roberto Galluci, brought cocaine from Chile to Miami about 3 weeks ago. Check Opa Locka.

: aircraft twin bonanza american registration N-10-TS, supposed to arrive in the States, coming from Paraguay and Chile, in one week with the same stuff. This merchandise will be sent by G————— B—————,* Paraguayan, the leader of this business in Paraguay, Asuncion the capital, Address: Chile 924, A————— V—————, argentinian, owner of this aircraft, H————— D—————, argentinean. D————— was supposed to fly last monday by braniff, the 14th, from Asuncion to LaPaz Bolivia, to make arrangements to load this cargo into N-10-TS, also another aircraft DC-3 reg. N-78-V, which will be brought into the States, loaded of cocoa, and planing to unload in Opa Locka Airport.

aircraft bringing the same cargo from So. America to Panama, and in Panama transfered to others aircrafts: B-23 reg. N-1755-L. People involved: R————— B—————, owner of the ship, L————— P—————, pilot, C————— Y—————, based in Paraguay, resident of the USA, J————— V—————, pilot, M————— Z—————, American, Ft. Lauderdale, which stole a C-46 two months ago from Panama to Miami, and here the plane was stolen again out of Miami intl'l. This theft was a fake. The plane was loaded. The aircraft was flown from So. America to Panama by D————— and V—————.

The following aircrafts and persons are supposed to be involved with the same group, organization and stuff: C-46, reg. N-1846 based in Asuncion, Pilot: A————— G—————. C-46 Reg. N-5447 based in Panama. Pilot J————— H—————, yugoslavian based in Asuncion, operating under instructions of a man named Jorge Porta, argentinean, bringing this cargo from Argentina to Asuncion, then to Panama. In Panama a man named Joachim Him, working for aeronautical civil or tower comptoller at Tocumen airport. In

---

* The names, except for Rodrigues/Galluci and Joachim (Joaquim) Him, are identified only by initials because of ongoing federal investigations.

Asuncion a lawyer named L———, B———'s partner. Both are dangerous and usually are armed.

In Panama a pilot named C———, american, supposed to live in New Jersey, some place near Teteboro. Could be Richfield or Ridgefield in a Holiday Inn motel or hotel. Check at Belmar Hotel or Motel in Miami Beach the name of two argentinean fellows, together with V——— and D——— last july. At that time a drop of about 150 pounds was made by N-10-TS in Opa Locka and received by these four gentleman, staying at Belmar Hotel.

The C-46 Curtiss stolen out of Panama had the reg. N-67934. In panama check on a jew named F——— W———, at Continental Hotel. The consul in Asuncion, american consul, is supposed to have by now a good check on all this people. Do not ask any help to the regular police in Asuncion, because they are in business too. Check with interpol or get the President's help. Both can help you, thru the ambassador in Paraguay."

Hoppy read the letter through twice. It had some strong points going for its authenticity. The tone was hurried and angry, as though somebody were trying to get back at the people he was writing about. Cursory examination indicated the aircraft designations were at least the right type for private Latin American—registry airplanes.

Furthermore, the agents had suspected for a long time that some of the *contrabandista* pilots had been "turned around" and were now flying narcotics north. Indeed, Hoppy and his colleagues had already been preparing their own list of suspect aircraft. Whoever the letter writer was, Hoppy figured, he knew the *contrabandista* business well.

(It was two years before the Customs Bureau was to learn who had written the strange letter. It turned out that he did, indeed, know the *contrabandista* business well. He had been a *contrabandista* pilot. Government intelligence officers learned that Mr. Anonymous had been severely beaten with a monkey wrench in a pilot's bar in Panama by one of the men named in the letter. What had made the beating even more painful was that it had happened before a roomful of pilots, many of whom knew the victim. It had been, government agents learned, a terrible loss of face. The unknown informant, they discovered, had actually written four such letters, each naming his antagonist. One was a complaint to the Federal Aviation Administration that his attacker was the pilot of a B-26 that had mysteriously bombed Dictator Papa Doc Duvalier's palace in Port-au-Prince, Haiti. Shortly after his vengeful letter writing began, the anonymous informant was killed in an airplane crash while flying a load of contraband over the Andes.)

It was clear to Hoppy that the letter was worth pursuing and worth pursuing fast. For a moment after his second reading, he wistfully reflected that he was not going to get that "comp time" he'd been counting in the elevator.

He picked up the telephone and dialed his supervisor, Steven Csukas, to bring him up to date. "This thing has two dozen possibilities to check. Any chance of getting a little help?" Hoppy asked.

There was pained silence on the other end of the line, then weary agreement. "I'll get Tony to help you."

Special Agent Adam J. DeGaglia was known to one and all as Tony for reasons that were unclear even to him. It had been his nickname since childhood. But if no one knew why "Tony," at least they agreed it fitted him.

Tony was a New Yorker who'd come to Florida to visit his parents and stayed the next twelve years. He was as delicately built as Hoppy was husky. Slim and graceful of movement, Tony liked mod clothes, ruffled shirts, bell-bottom trousers, and jackets with almost an Edwardian cut. His slim Italian face was framed in well-groomed sideburns and, even though he hadn't lived in New York for fifteen years, he couldn't shake the hand gestures and the Manhattan accent.

Hoppy was pleased to hear it was going to be Tony. Though DeGaglia had been in Customs only two years, at thirty-four he was an ex–Fort Lauderdale cop with ten years' experience. "You've heard this before," Hoppy will tell a friend, "but when you step out of that car into something tight you want a guy behind you who doesn't faze. A guy who knows what he's doing."

After a quick conference, the two agents decided they would split the letter's leads into two parts—the aircraft and the people. Hoppy would look for the planes, Tony would look for the people.

It has been written and more often said that detective work is really boring—a painstaking following of routine which occasionally pays off on a grand scale but more often than not simply leads to more painstaking routine. Hoppy's assignment seemed of the latter variety. For the remainder of September and early October he plodded through Customs and Federal Aviation Administration records at Miami International and the international airport at Opa Locka.

It was no easy task. Hundreds of planes a day land and take off from fields around Miami, and the flight plans had to be sifted for those covering domestic flights and those covering international flights. What complicated the job even further was that Hoppy could not tell from the letter who actually piloted each plane and if any of the names was real or one of many aliases.

Meanwhile, Tony was having slightly better luck. Two names in the letter had previous criminal records in the United States, and both were for narcotics violations. The "rap sheets" on these two gave Tony an even wider pool of names to link up with those in the letter. Furthermore, the Belmar Hotel in Miami Beach had records showing that two men mentioned in the letter, V_____ and D_____, had stayed there.

The Belmar was a stroke of luck in another way. Large hotels generally use a computer-run device to feed local and long distance calls. The long-distance call goes directly to a telephone company operator and the charges for the call are relayed to the hotel as part of a general bill. This makes it a Herculean task of record-sifting to find a specific call made by a specific guest. But the Belmar was not a big hotel. Nestled on the lower end of Miami Beach's Collins Avenue facing the ocean, it was a small, beautifully appointed, family-run hotel that catered to a regular group of guests. All long-distance calls from the Belmar were placed by the hotel's operator, who carefully recorded the name of the caller, the room number, the number called, the party (if it was person-to-person) and the length of the conversation.

The operator, a shapely brunette with an eye for men, found Tony's charm and the excitement of being involved in a big government investigation irresistible. She supplied the agent with records of all the calls made by the suspected smugglers who stayed at the hotel.

Tony organized these numbers into a massive, multipage chart and began tediously running each down. Slowly the patterns began to emerge. There were calls to a known Mafia chieftain in Louisiana, to a Panamanian trading company that agents had long suspected of being deeply involved in the drug trade, and to Joaquim Him, the senior Panamanian Civil Aeronautics official mentioned in the letter. But though the tough leg work showed patterns and mysterious links between the individuals in the letter and known figures in the narcotics trade, the agents still had nothing hard to go on. They were not even convinced the letter was genuine. The only way to find out and perhaps snag one of the smugglers, they felt, was to mount a full-scale surveillance of airports. And to get the backing for this they would need something tangible.

The break came, not unexpectedly, amid the crowded disarray of Miami International's General Aviation Center. The center, which occupies the northwest corner of the busy airport, is the administration and hangar area for private aircraft and nonscheduled airlines that do not have hangar facilities at the main field. Over the past two decades it has become a landing place for every sort of nondescript aircraft coming north from Latin America. The result is a virtual museum of vintage airplanes. DC-3s, old Lockheed Lodestars, Piper Cubs, converted B-25s and B-26s in a dozen strange configurations are parked there, being worked on by Spanish-speaking ground crewmen in costumes as varied as the planes.

It was in this milieu that Hoppy got the first real break. The records of the center showed that an aircraft with Argentine registry LV-HDW had entered the United States on September 2 and cleared Customs. The plane, a single-engine, four-seater Cessna 210, had not been flown by anyone using the two names mentioned in the letter—Roberto Galluci or Ricardo Rodrigues. Instead the pilot was listed as Cesar Mendice Bianchi, who had presented Paraguayan passport Number 0730.

The Cessna had departed from the United States only a few

days before, on September 28, carrying Bianchi, a copilot identified as Renato Balestra, and Bianchi's wife Daysi. Further checking showed that the aircraft had passed through Panama on October 3, heading south.

Hoppy and Tony knew the break was a hot one. The aircraft had come into Miami and left almost to the day when the letter said it would. Coupled with the other verifications of the letter, it seemed to build a base for commandeering the extra manpower necessary to keep a watch on LV-HDW.

Mosley was impressed. His twenty years plus of experience told him this one was good. "The case now has top priority," he told Hoppy. They were to parcel out their other cases and work on the letter full time. Furthermore, he gave authority for the monitoring of aircraft arrivals at the five main fields around Miami.

Hoppy immediately put out a canvass request to every federal aviation facility and Customs office in South Florida. If anyone using the name Bianchi, Rodrigues, Galluci, or Balestra sought entry to the United States or filed a flight plan for a plane registered LV-HDW, Hoppy was to be notified immediately.

Early on the morning of October 13, 1970, Cesar Mendice Bianchi guided his single-engine Cessna from the landing strip on the private *estancia* at Saint Elena into a clear dawn. The early sunlight reflected off the flat Paraguayan countryside as it fell away to the Argentine border. Bianchi lifted the small plane in a wide bank and set his course west for Salta, Argentina. Though he sat in his usual relaxed half-slump at the controls, a furrow of concern crossed his brow. The Cessna had developed an oil leak during its return trip from the United States a week earlier, and there had been no chance to overhaul it. And the plane's radio transmitter and receiver were not working well.

As the Cessna climbed high toward the border, the copilot, young Renato Balestra, asked a question that spoke of what lay uneasily on both their minds. "Are we going to fly the Cessna back?" "No," Bianchi assured him quickly, the Cessna would be left behind in the States to be completely repaired. They would fly home in a twin-engine Beechcraft Bonanza that Bianchi was having worked on at Saint Petersburg, Florida. But they still had the northbound trip ahead. Even as they spoke, the towering Andes emerged in the distance.

Bianchi settled down to business, the business he really understood best, the business of relating man and machine. He was going to fly a worn single-engine plane from Paraguay over 3,800 miles to Miami. It was his thing—the calculating of the risks, the judging of a machine to drive it past normal safety stresses and thus to flirt with destruction and death.

A husky, well-muscled man, Bianchi stood five feet, eight inches tall and weighed 190 pounds, very little of which was fat. His curly black hair topped a pleasant, rounded face centered on a proud Pancho Villa mustache. Bianchi wore his favorite flying togs—an open-at-the-throat knit sports shirt, wide leather belt, and chino trousers. Behind him hung a worn, comfortable-looking corduroy jacket. It was as calculatingly casual a mode of attire as a pro golfer's.

Cesar Bianchi had been born in New York but had been taken to Brazil as an infant. His life there was a mystery, a secret upon which Bianchi would shed only sudden flickers of light. It was in Brazil that he had first tested himself against danger with a machine. He became a devotee of sports car racing as the owner and driver of two Alfa Romeos. Indeed, he had once driven in Brazil's Grand Prix. Using the profits from a successful construction-truck company, Cesar had also gotten into flying. By the mid-1960s he was known as a man of consequence, a man who liked plump, beautiful women, fast cars, good food. He also was known as a man with a swift and violent temper.

There are no details. Some say it was a fight. Some say it was a revenge killing. Bianchi, a man of iron discipline when it is needed, will not say. But a Brazilian was dead and in early 1965 Bianchi suddenly appeared in his native Asunción with $50,000, a pilot's license, nerve, and intimacy with machinery. It was inevitable that he would enter Paraguay's largest export business—smuggling by airplane.

The contraband business was good to Bianchi. He flew them all—perfume, watches, Levis, cigarettes. In good months he made

$8,000 and $10,000. He was again a man of consequence. He bought a workhorse Douglas DC-3, a twin-engine Beechcraft Bonanza, and a single-engine Beech. He married a Paraguayan girl, Daysi, and the couple had a daughter.

Along with his wife, child, and airplanes, Bianchi had other signs of Latin affluence. He kept an apartment he later rented to his copilot where he brought a succession of mistresses—an indiscreet but not unusual practice in Asunción.

It was through flying contraband cigarettes that Bianchi met the enigmatic Enio Varela, who was to turn him from the profits of the tobacco leaf to the profits of the opium poppy. In the spring of 1970, Varela helped Bianchi buy the Cessna. Bianchi had made other runs for Varela, but only one previous major flight in LV-HDW, the month before to the United States. That time he had sent for his wife, Daysi, to join him, and with Balestra they had vacationed in Miami for three weeks.

The worry over the oil leak affected young Renato Balestra far more than it did Bianchi. The lanky twenty-five-year-old Brazilian copilot loved machinery. But he did not share Bianchi's thirst for pushing machines to their limit, seeking danger. Danger to him was a working reality, not a heady narcotic.

Balestra's love affair with machinery had begun in Waterloo, Iowa, where he had lived in the early 'sixties. From Waterloo in 1966 he enlisted in the U.S. Navy. He had been trained as an engineman and had ended up fighting the Vietcong in the swamps and rivers of the Mekong Delta from the deck of a Navy patrol boat. Wounded in 1968, he ended his tour with a Purple Heart and citations from the President of South Vietnam.

Balestra had always wanted to fly, and in 1969 he obtained single-engine and multiengine pilot's licenses and sank his Navy mustering-out pay into a used Piper two-seater. He headed homeward to South America to see if he could make a living as a peaceful charter pilot.

Six months later, in early 1970, he ended up in Asunción—broke, discouraged, and ready to sell his beloved airplane. There he met Bianchi hanging around the Paraguayan capital's airport. Bianchi the *contrabandista* took a liking to the young Brazilian, giving him a job, room, and board. Bianchi also helped him sell his Piper to an American living in Asunción.

For Renato Balestra, the older Bianchi became an idol. The tough smuggler had qualities of coolness and command that Balestra admired to the point of worship, flying skills and a race driver's daring that Balestra yearned to copy.

Balestra knew that Bianchi flew ordinary contraband—cigarettes, whiskey, electronic equipment—in and out of Latin America, and this in the young Vietnam vet's mind was quasi-crime. It did not disturb him. But smuggling narcotics, particularly to the United States where Balestra had friends and hoped to return to live, was something else again.

Balestra had become suspicious on their September flight to Miami when he discovered that Bianchi had secreted two suitcases on board. His fears had been allayed when Bianchi told him the suitcases contained uranium sand to be assayed secretly in the United States. He believed his idol, but he was worried, and he told Bianchi earnestly that he wanted no part of any further smuggling missions to the United States.

As the Cessna headed across the 20,000-foot Andes that October morning, Balestra was trying to figure out for himself if the plane was again carrying contraband. Much later he was to recall: "I looked in the baggage compartment to see if the lid of the fuselage and the fuel tank in front of it was any different from the position I had seen them last and noticed no difference. Another way I thought I could detect if there was weight in the rear of the plane was by the attitude of the aircraft in relation to the ground. It looked normal to me at the time but Bianchi could have drained some air out of the nose-strut shock-absorbing system.

"There were other reasons why I didn't think he'd have contraband on the aircraft. One of them is that as an experienced smuggler he couldn't do the very same thing twice, in a pattern-like fashion, and expect to succeed."

The trip north was to follow the established route of the *contrabandistas*. It was a route dictated by the limitations of small, short-range planes and the hazards of the Amazon jungle. It was safer to move west, cross the towering Andes, and hedge-hop northward up the coastline cities than to risk disappearing on the long flight across the vast, uncharted wasteland of Brazil.

The first day the Cessna flew to Salta, refueled, and made the 300-mile-plus jump to Antofagasta, Chile. Then it turned north to Arica, Arica to Lima, Peru; Lima to Guayaquil, Ecuador; Guayaquil to Panama.

As the hours and days throbbed onward, the two men became more and more concerned about the oil leak. The oil pressure gauge continued to flirt above the danger level, and the anxious Balestra at one point vowed he would never go aloft in the Cessna again until it was repaired. Still, LV-HDW seemed to know its destiny.

It arrived in Panama on October 17, and on Sunday morning, October 18, Bianchi walked into the operations room at Tecumen Airport in Panama and filed a flight plan for Miami via Kingston, Jamaica. He estimated his time of arrival in the United States as after 6 P.M. the same day.

The phone in Hoppy Hopkins's apartment rang at an indecent hour on Sunday morning. He cursed as he stumbled to stifle its intrusion. The voice of the duty officer at the Customs communications center was teasingly informative: "They've got a report on your Cessna, baby. If the flight plan's correct it oughta be coming into Miami International today."

Hoppy was suddenly totally awake. He suggested to the duty officer that the boss be notified and sprinted to the bedroom to get dressed.

The problems were enormous. There was no reason that the Cessna had to land at Miami International. Indeed the flight plan could be just to mislead anyone watching for a plane. The Cessna could put down at any of the eighty or so other airports if it was carrying contraband. Or it could unload the junk by air drop without ever landing. Hoppy ticked off the unpleasant possibilities as he shaved. The Cessna might not be carrying any contraband this trip—or maybe it had never been involved in the drug traffic at all. Maybe Mr. Anonymous and his letter were wrong about LV-HDW.

But Hoppy's instincts told him different—this was a good one.

The letter checked out in every other respect. The plane, the pilot, the routes were all right—right for a *contrabandista.*

At Customs headquarters a few minutes later, a hastily assembled team agreed to increase the stakeouts. By stretching the men thin they would at least be able to cover Miami International Airport, Opa Locka International, Broward International, Tamiami Airport, North Perry, and the executive plane strip in Broward County. If the Cessna came in anywhere else—

There is a special adrenalin that courses through the men in a police organization as a case "goes down," and it was running hot that Sunday. "It's not just wanting to be in on an arrest for glory. It's not that simple. It's confronting people face to face, dealing with the very core of what you are supposed to be doing. I suppose it's partly because it's physical and otherwise the job's so much on paper," Hoppy says.

By midafternoon twenty men were on duty in cars or airport runways surrounding Miami, and backup teams of men stood by.

At 6:50 P.M. a single-engine Cessna of Argentine registry touched down at Miami International, taxied to the General Aviation Center at the northwest end of the runway, and parked for the night. Hoppy stood quietly in the corner of the GAC waiting room and watched the two Latin pilots walk in.

The excruciating process of following the bait was beginning. If there was any single prerequisite for the game it was patience. The Customs men all knew that, yet they had to restrain themselves from ripping the plane apart that night for fear of alarming their quarry. Often, they had learned, someone from the smuggling ring itself was assigned to quietly watch the plane to ensure that the contraband was not discovered.

The purpose of the agents' caution is to enlarge the net. In the training classes the investigator is taught that the contraband is the bait that can lead him to the receiver, to the senders, and to the wholesalers—all the important links in the chain—as well as to the actual smugglers. A mistake, a premature arrest, a clumsy surveillance can leave the agent with only the narcotics and the arrest of low-level members of the conspiracy.

But in the one-story GAC building on the night of the 18th, it was no training class, and Hoppy had also to face the agonizing reality that while the agents watched, a smuggler might already be completing his mission.

Bianchi and Balestra checked quickly through Customs and walked to where Bianchi kept his Pinto. It was the same car that had briefly held the Christmas-wrapped packages in its trunk on an earlier trip, though Balestra had not known about that bit of business.

Both pilots were tired from the grueling day in the air, and when they reached the Towne Motel in Miami they went immediately to bed. Neither of them noticed the 1968 Ambassador sedan that had followed them from the airport—nor the other one that had taken up a station across from their motel.

Early on Monday the 19th, the two Latins drove the Pinto to Merlin's Car Rental on Biscayne Boulevard, picked up a Chevrolet Malibu, and drove back to Miami where they checked out of the motel. They then drove both cars to North Perry Airport, a small private field for executive and private aircraft near Hollywood, parked Bianchi's Pinto, and used the rental car to get back to Miami International.

It was when they rented the second car that Balestra began to get bad feelings about the trip. "I understood then what was happening and why the extra car," he recalled later. He was sure now that he and Bianchi had brought in contraband, but he did not know how to extricate himself.

At the Miami airport the pilots gassed up the Cessna, paid the parking fees, and took off, ostensibly for Saint Petersburg. A few moments after the Cessna cleared the runway an unmarked Skymaster roared off into the clear, bright Florida sky. At its controls were two Customs agents.

For an hour the two planes played a subtle game of tag over Dade and Broward counties. "We didn't know it then, but that's when Bianchi made us," Hoppy recalls. "We knew there was something wrong, though, because he kept trying different kinds of evasive action, course changes, sudden turns."

Finally Bianchi landed the Cessna at North Perry and arranged to park it overnight. Then, briskly, he and Balestra left the field in the Pinto, taking nothing from the plane.

By late afternoon the agents were disconsolate. They had lost the trail of Bianchi and Balestra in Miami traffic, and the pair had never reapproached the plane. "So all we had was the plane and no suspects," Hoppy remembered.

The only thing left to do now was to search the aircraft, and, for the moment, forget the human quarry.

The Cessna 210 is not a big plane, but to the searchers that night it presented an infinite number of hiding places. First they checked the obvious, accessible spots—the cabin, chart pouches, seats, dashboard. Then with the aid of a Federal Aviation Administration mechanic (responsible for seeing that the plane was restored to its original safe condition in case it wasn't carrying contraband), the agents began to tear the plane apart section by section.

They removed panels covering the wing tanks, checked the engine housing, and traced along the fuel lines. Nearly three hours went by. Hoppy had a growing fear that maybe, somehow, the pilots had dumped the contraband on their way in, although heroin was almost never delivered that way.

He was removing the back seats, examining the auxiliary fuel tank when he suddenly realized that behind the fuel tank was another panel—a removable panel. Pulling the tank out, he unscrewed the bolts holding the metal plate.

There they were—three cheap plastic "flight bag"-style suitcases, stacked tightly in a little compartment leading to the tail section. Hoppy pulled the first one out and opened it. The bag contained dozens of little plastic-wrapped pouches of white powder.

"I was shaking all over . . . Goddamn! I kept thinking, Goddamn!" Hoppy tells it.

All together, the suitcases contained what later tested out as ninety-four pounds of almost pure heroin. Even by conservative estimates its "street" value was about $10 million. It was one of the largest seizures of heroin ever made.

For a moment the agents just sat staring at the load. Then Hoppy ran to the small airport's tower building and called in. "It's skag, all right. We just ripped off three suitcases," he reported.

It was then that Hoppy got the bad news. "We can't find the pilot and the other guy. We don't know where they are."

There was only one move that could be made: replace the heroin in the aircraft and stake it out for the night in the hopes that Bianchi and Balestra might return to the bait. Hoppy and the mechanic furiously began to put the plane back together.

In downtown Miami, Cesar Bianchi was running scared. His nerve endings tingled with fear. It was like the tight turn in a Grand Prix.

He knew that they had been made. Somebody was on to them. The tip-off had come flying over the Everglades that morning. He had just asked the kid to take the suitcases out of the back so they could make a quick transfer to the car at North Perry when he saw the Skymaster out of the corner of his eye. It was too far away to see the pilots, but he knew it was the same Skymaster he'd seen earlier. It could not be a coincidence. "Put the bags back," he had ordered Balestra, "put them back." Maybe he could shake the Skymaster. Bianchi dipped the Cessna into a tight left bank and headed for the clouds, but even as he completed the maneuver he knew it would be no good. The sleek P-38-like Skymaster had no trouble staying near a Cessna. Despite all the twists and turns the shadowing Skymaster seemed to hang back there, far enough so that Bianchi couldn't see the pilots but close enough for him to know it was the same plane.

Still there was doubt. Maybe it was a coincidence. Maybe it was just some wise guys in the Skymaster. But his instincts told him this was not so. Something was going wrong. Yet they'd been allowed to take off from Miami International and no fighter planes had been sent up. Maybe it meant the government agents weren't sure. Maybe it meant they had only planned to follow him out of suspicion.

Bianchi made his decision. He would land at North Perry as though nothing were wrong. But he would not try to transfer the bags to his car. He would just get away from the plane quickly. He must get away from the plane.

On the ground Bianchi felt as if he were trapped in a bad dream. Arranging for the plane's parking and walking to the car seemed interminable. Any moment he expected men to move in, flash their identity cards, and arrest him.

On the drive downtown, Bianchi had constantly scanned the rearview mirror for a tail car. Every car seemed to be driven by agents, every car that drew alongside seemed about to pull them over. The Paraguayan pilot wove his Pinto in and out of traffic, suddenly driving very fast, suddenly slowing, making lights at the last second and turns without signaling.

By the time they reached the motel he felt he'd temporarily lost any surveillance. Alternative plans raced through his mind. If he was wrong, if the Skymaster hadn't been flown by government agents, then he was leaving $10 million worth of heroin and a valuable aircraft parked out in the middle of nowhere. Somehow he had to find out if their plan had been compromised. Maybe he could send Balestra.

First he told Balestra he would let the young copilot fly the Cessna to Waterloo, Iowa, alone the next day. Balestra seemed eager. He gave the kid $20 to go out and buy the charts he would need. Later Bianchi changed his mind. If the load got tagged in Iowa, even by accident, it would blow the whole thing anyway. He tried to persuade Balestra to fly the plane back out of the country to South America alone. But Balestra refused because the trip over water was too dangerous. Bianchi lapsed into silence.

During the afternoon, still running scared, they had driven around haphazardly. First they had picked up the rental car at the General Aviation Center at Miami International and transferred their belongings from its trunk to the Pinto. Then they had turned the rental car in. Finally, in mid-evening, they had checked into a small beachfront hotel on Collins Avenue in Miami Beach, the Georgian, where Bianchi had stayed before.

Bianchi still did not have a firm plan and seemed deep in thought through dinner. After dinner they walked a few blocks north and caught a movie. When they got back to the Georgian, Bianchi gave Balestra a $100 bill. "He said he wanted me to have it in my pocket," Balestra recounted later. "This was unusual . . . he never gives me any more than the necessary amount of money for whatever I have to do. That night, he burned some papers in the bathroom." When Balestra awoke the next morning he found a message by the telephone. "Don't leave this room until I come back or you get a phone call. Eat your breakfast up here." Bianchi was gone.

At North Perry, Hoppy and the other agents had spent a long, cramped night in the small, darkened tower building watching the plane. The night had passed but no one had approached the Cessna. In the early morning hours he and Tony DeGaglia talked by phone. There was one possibility left.

In his early investigation of the letter, Hoppy had learned from an aircraft supply company that Bianchi had mentioned having an account in a bank on Biscayne Boulevard. The Customs agents decided to stake out the bank the next morning in the hope that Bianchi might go for his money. Somehow, possibly as a result of fatigue—he had been on duty with little sleep since Sunday and it was Tuesday morning—Hoppy made a slip. He gave Tony the name of the wrong bank.

"We went to this one bank. It was right next to the bank we should have been in. By the time I found out Bianchi didn't have an account there it was 9:30 or 9:45," Tony recalled, "I called in and we finally got the name of the right bank.

"We raced up the street and into the First National. The guy was very nice. 'Yes, Mr. Bianchi had an account. As a matter of fact he's just been in and drawn out $26,000. Too bad, but you fellows just missed him.'"

"I just stood there," Tony said later, "and thought a whole string of very bad thoughts."

The only thing now was to try to seal the escape routes to South America as fast as possible. Rousting everyone they could, including communications and desk personnel, the Customs officers tried to blanket the airports and shipping offices. It was like trying to close off holes in a sieve.

Pan American Airways flew a 12:30 P.M. flight direct from Miami to Asunción, Paraguay. Shortly after 11 A.M., a Customs agent hurried toward Pan Am's ticket counter to see whether a certain Cesar Mendice Bianchi might have a reservation. There had been no time to circulate a mug shot of the suspect and the agent had only a cursory, telephone description to work with. In the front of the line was a short, husky, black-haired man in a corduroy flight jacket. The agent wasn't sure. He edged his way to the front as the man presented his passport to the ticket agent. There it was: "Cesar Mendice Bianchi."

"I'm a federal officer and you're under arrest."

For a moment Bianchi looked confused, frightened. "No Bandito! No Bandito! You got me but I'm no Bandito!"

Nearly thirty-five hours of continuous surveillance, miles of tailing, two hotels, two airports, and a break at last.

Bianchi was taken to a Customs interrogation room on the parking level of the airport, informed of his legal rights, booked, and charged with smuggling illegal narcotics into the United States. Bianchi flatly denied smuggling—but he agreed to tell the agents where Balestra was.

"At this point we don't know what to expect when we get to the hotel," Hoppy recalls, "Bianchi had sort of said be careful of Balestra so we go charging in ready for anything. We find Balestra as docile as a Koala bear. What Bianchi meant we later figured out was that he, Bianchi, should be careful of Balestra. After what Bianchi tried, maybe he was right.

"He was using Balestra throughout. You know what Bianchi had done before the kid got up? He set the clock in the room back an hour so by the time the kid realized what was happening, Bianchi's flight would have been long gone for Asunción. Even when we showed Balestra the clock, he wouldn't believe us.

"Later, we told Balestra what we found in the plane and he wouldn't believe that either. He claimed Bianchi told him it was uranium sand. He worshipped Bianchi. He worshipped the ground he walked on."

Though the agents now had ninety-four pounds of heroin, the smuggling plane and the two pilots, they knew they had only scratched the surface of the kind of organization that had set this up. They had no inkling as to the receiver or who had amassed the capital to get a shipment this large together. The next twenty-four hours would be far more crucial than even the first thirty-five.

The agents began the pressure as soon as they had taken their prisoner back to Customs headquarters in downtown Miami. They told Bianchi he was in deep trouble. He was going to take the fall for smuggling ninety-four pounds of heroin into a nation that was damned tired of its kids getting hooked on drugs, and when he next saw light outside a federal prison he wouldn't be able to get a date in an old ladies' home. "Your Daysi and your kid are going to be down there in Asunción all alone and you're not going to be one goddamn whit of help to them for twenty years."

Bianchi, as one agent later put it, was a "pisser."

"I used to sit and talk to him for three hours to get three paragraphs of information. His was a typical South American attitude —I was his superior, so he was going to be real polite but he wasn't going to be very helpful."

Slowly, as the day passed, the agents tried to "flip" Bianchi, to get him to lead them to the others. Under Customs law the government is entitled to seize everything that is used to further a smuggling operation, such as Bianchi's car and plane, and any fruits of an illegal operation. The agents could tie up Bianchi's $26,000 for years in court and ultimately might be able to confiscate the money. They began to use his own money to try to persuade him. They told him that, for full cooperation, they might be willing to ask the U.S. Attorney to release part of the $26,000 so it could be sent to Bianchi's wife Daysi in Asunción.

All day they couldn't make a deal. Bianchi would walk right up to the idea, then retreat. "At times," one of his interrogators said, "he was a wheeler-dealer, a hot-shot-pilot type, a show-off." The cool but frightened *contrabandista* knew if he cooperated he could never go back to Asunción, that he could never be sure the organization wouldn't take revenge. On the other hand, he knew enough about arrests of other drug smugglers to know that the agents weren't kidding. A U.S. court would deal harshly with him.

The interrogation went on into Tuesday evening, but the agents seemed to be coming up against the same blank wall time and time again. Bianchi was concerned about his wife and daughter, but he wasn't yet sure that going over to the side of the agents was the best course.

"You know when he came around? It was when we were taking him to Dade County Jail. He took one look at the bars and said he'd help us," Hoppy said.

But it was still touch-and-go. The agents had no way to be sure that Bianchi was telling the truth or that he might not try co-operation as an opportunity to escape. Moreover, they didn't know whether his arrest had been spotted by the smuggling organization. In many cases, the actual smuggler was never left alone with the narcotics. Instead the organization sent along steel-eyed "shotguns" to be sure the smuggler made his delivery without deviation or arrest—and to tip off the organization if anything went wrong.

Bianchi told the agents he had cabled his contact in Panama of his safe arrival when he first reached Miami and that, as far as he knew, the plan was moving forward without a hitch. He said he knew no more about the ultimate destination than the agents now knew. He had simply been ordered to fly to Miami, transfer the contraband to the trunk of his car and wait, making periodic calls to the Four Ambassadors Hotel, until his contact arrived. If a movie set was needed for big-time smuggling it would be the Four Ambassadors. It had originally been built in the mid-sixties as condominium apartments, and its four twenty-story towers rose like giant rocket-launchers on the Miami side of Biscayne Bay.

The Four Ambassadors attracts that brand of *nouveau riche* which feels compelled to press ten dollar bills into the hands of headwaiters and honk for service at the main door from a Cadillac. It is very popular with Latins, and on most nights the pub off the main lobby is noisier with Spanish than with English. The Margaritas are potent, the women well polished by sun and beauty parlor, the room rents extravagant, and the clientele a pot-pourri often including, ironically, members of the White House staff. The hotel is press headquarters for President Nixon when he is staying across the causeway in Key Biscayne.

At 7:30 P.M. on Tuesday, October 20, while Bianchi was still being interrogated by agents, two Latin American businessmen checked into the hotel. One, a tall, balding man of thirty-five with an almost Germanic appearance and well-dressed confidence, signed the register as Felix Rogelio Becker of 3677 Mariscal Estigarribia Street, Asunción, Paraguay. His traveling companion, a nervous-looking man in his late forties, registered as Juan de Dios Rodriguez Benitez, also of Asunción.

In midevening Becker came downstairs and strolled out of the hotel toward downtown Miami, a few blocks away. His mind was not on narcotics or American police. He failed to notice the men stationed in the lobby and the plain sedan with the two men in it parked near the hotel's sloping, half-moon driveway. All he saw were the two black prostitutes who stationed themselves a few hundred feet from the hotel. With confident swagger Becker approached, and after a brief conversation the two busty, booted women followed him toward the hotel. He avoided the main bank of elevators to circumvent the hotel desk and, with the women, disappeared into his room. It was nearly midnight.

Becker and Benitez were Bianchi's long-awaited contacts. The pilot had told the agents that Becker was the man who had shepherded his last narcotic smuggling trip a month before. He said the man with Becker, who had registered as Benitez, was actually an Argentinian name Aron Muravnik who was connected with the organization. As the time approached to make his first contact and get his first instructions, Bianchi's nervousness grew. But finally, about midnight, he made the call.

Becker sounded angry when he answered. Sure they'd meet that night. Okay. Just wait there and Becker would come by. Bianchi hung up. He wasn't sure whether Becker's anger was because he was suspicious or because a liaison had been interrupted. But a few moments after the call was made, agents staked out in the Four Ambassadors lobby saw the two black women leaving the building looking bewildered. "I'll bet he was mighty pissed off when that damn phone rang," one agent speculated, "not getting laid and having to pay for it anyway."

About 1 A.M. Becker came out of the Four Ambassadors and got into his rental car. He drove in a leisurely fashion toward Miami Beach. His mind was still not on narcotics. Just as he turned on the causeway he saw a young blonde hippie thumbing a ride. He picked her up and drove again toward the beach, turned off, parked for a while, then later dropped the girl off.

"He was the coolest guy I've ever seen," said one agent who

had been in the trailing car. "He's going to make a deal for 10 million bucks' worth of pure heroin and he stops and tries to make it with a hippie. You'd have never thought a drug deal was going down that night anywhere in the world."

But nonchalant as he had been, Becker was a pro. The first time he approached Bianchi's Georgian Hotel he never slowed, never gave the slightest inkling that this was his destination. Collins Avenue, crowded during the early evening with strollers and night club hoppers, was now empty, and Becker would have an easy time spotting a tail. Twice Becker drove back and forth in front of the hotel without stopping. The time lapse was so great that Tony DeGaglia, hidden across the street in an alley, was almost convinced that something had gone wrong. Finally Becker pulled the car into the driveway, parked, and ran into the hotel.

He went to Bianchi's room (agents were posted in rooms on both sides), but refused to discuss the plans in front of Balestra. He invited Bianchi "for a ride." If Bianchi was nervous it wasn't anything like what the agents felt. To allow their prime suspect to walk out of the hotel and get into a car could leave them with egg on their faces.

They had to keep up with the pair. "The next twenty minutes was the toughest surveillance I've ever had to handle," Hoppy said. "It was a twenty minute hopscotch game." Becker drove north on Collins Avenue, sometimes hitting speeds as high as sixty-five miles an hour, then dropping back to fifteen or twenty. If a tail car had kept the same pattern it would have been an immediate tip-off.

"We criss-crossed to keep up with him, using our radios. One car would follow him for a while, then drop, race over two streets and get ahead and pick up Becker's car at the next intersection."

In the car, Bianchi's cool was fading fast. He was tired and afraid. It was one thing to agree to work with the government, another to get into a car with a key member of the organization and not show nervousness. Becker, too, appeared wary. He constantly glanced through the rearview mirror and seldom looked at Bianchi.

He gave his instructions in staccato Spanish. The pilot was to put the ninety-four pounds of heroin into his Pinto and drive it to New York. He was to register under his own name at either the Sheraton–St. Regis at Fifth Avenue and Fifty-fifth Street or the Sheraton-Russell at Park Avenue and Thirty-seventh. He must arrive no later than Friday, October 23, and contact Becker at the Sheraton Motor Inn at Forty-second Street and the West Side Highway. He would receive further instructions then.

Bianchi did not press for other details or names. He knew that any sign of trying to learn more than necessary would alarm Becker. As the two talked, Becker doubled back and headed south toward the Georgian, at one point nearly shaking the tail cars. He dropped Bianchi at the Georgian Hotel with a final warning to be careful and a curt goodnight.

At 8:30 the next morning Bianchi was awakened by a telephone call in the room. Startled, he picked up the receiver only to hear Becker's guttural Spanish. "Why haven't you left yet?" the contact man asked suspiciously. Bianchi explained he was just getting ready to. Becker said he and Muravnik would fly to New York that same day.

Bianchi was mystified by the call. Could Becker be getting suspicious? It was a tired, nervous group that drank coffee and ate sweet rolls in the Georgian Hotel room that morning. Hoppy and Tony knew they had made a crack in a major drug-smuggling syndicate, but they also knew that they had only identified the peripheral characters in what was obviously a vast and complex organization. They wearily wondered if the New York agents would be able to follow Bianchi to other key figures. The Customs men had decided to take Bianchi to New York by air. They would use the license tags from his Pinto and put them on an identical rental car to make it appear as though the Paraguayan had driven. They would also substitute milk sugar for all but a tiny fraction of the heroin.

If Bianchi's credibility and nerve would only hold out in New York. New York was the jewel. It was there they might tag the receiver.

For Bianchi, the morning's coffee was bitter. Twenty-four hours before he had almost been a free man on his way back to Daysi.

Now he was trapped in the terrifying role of a government informer, an unwilling double agent in a very lethal battle. He could not even be sure the Customs men would keep their part of the bargain.

# 6    *A Case Goes Down*

*October 20–27, 1970*

          *Felix Becker and Aron Muravnik* crossed the main concourse at John F. Kennedy International Airport at a brisk pace, the skycap hurrying to keep the baggage cart up with them. The temperature was at least twenty degrees cooler in New York than it had been in Miami, and the anticipation of seeing the city again made them eager to get downtown. Becker was relaxed. The assignment was going faultlessly. The trepidation he had felt briefly in Miami had vanished.

    For the dozenth time he mentally checked off his security list. It was habit, this constant mental rechecking, and Becker nurtured it as some men finger a Saint Christopher's medal. The habit had kept him from harm on more than one occasion.

    He had made contact with his "carrier" four times, once in Panama, three times in Miami. Three times by telephone, once face to face. He had kept the telephone contacts short and cryptic, and few wiretappers could have made head or tail of the hurried

Spanish. Besides, there was no crime, Becker told himself, in calling an acquaintance to chat about a trip to New York.

The personal contact had been as carefully handled. Nothing had been said in a hotel room or lobby where a bugging device might have been hidden. Nothing had been said in front of the copilot Balestra. The conversation had been limited to a drive in a car, his rental car, a car he could be sure had not been fitted with a transmitter. The whole thing had been smooth, professional. Even to the flight from Miami, Eastern Airlines Flight 16, chosen at the last minute so their names would not be listed on the manifest hours ahead of time.

Indeed, the flight seemed to be the few moments he could let down his guard. Nothing ever happened on airplanes. Becker relaxed on the flight, sipping Chivas Regal and soda and lazily watching the tanned thighs of the stewardess as she bent to wait on passengers. If Bianchi followed instructions, Becker mused, it would be a piece of cake.

Like a good omen a cab was waiting as the two men stepped out of the main airport building. After the baggage man had stowed their luggage, Becker passed two crumpled dollar bills into his hand and stepped into the cab. "The Sheraton Inn," he told the driver. The cab swung out onto Van Wyck Expressway, and Becker and Muravnik sank back into the black vinyl seats and silently watched Queens whisk by.

The driver, a friendly young Italian-looking man, attempted conversation once by yelling something about the weather back through the partition, but neither passenger heard him or, if they did, responded. The remainder of the ride passed in silence as the cab sped across the Triborough Bridge, down the East Side Highway and west along Forty-second through the elegant shop-corridors of the East Side and the tawdry glamour of Times Square.

The Sheraton Inn had been built in the early 'sixties to attract a growing number of tourists who balked at driving their cars into the cauldron of New York traffic and were giving their business to New Jersey motels across the river. It rose hard by the viaduct of New York's West Side Highway, a few hundred feet from the wharves of the Hudson River and only a block from the Lincoln

Tunnel leading to New Jersey. Though much of this part of the
West Side was now squalid and deserted, on that brisk fall day
the area took on a certain brightness. A swift breeze kicked up
tiny white caps on the nearby Hudson. Becker, his eyes shadowed
by dark aviator sunglasses, paused for a moment to survey the
scene as he got out of the cab.

He could not know that this pose, like many others he would
take in the next few days, would be immortalized on film—film
being shot by U.S. Customs agents. Reaching into his pocket
Becker drew out a wad of bills and leaned back into the cab to
pay his fare. He smiled briefly as he pressed a two-dollar tip into
the driver's palm. "Thank you, sir," the man responded warmly,
smiling as he pulled the cab away. He would not be able to keep
the tip. The driver was a special agent of U.S. Customs, and New
York hack number 019348 was owned and operated by the U.S.
Customs Service.

As Becker and Muravnik entered the hotel they failed to notice
the plump, curly-haired man sitting a few hundred feet away in a
plain American Motors Ambassador sedan. The man was not
very noteworthy. Conservatively dressed, mid-thirties, he could
have been a musician, teacher, young executive, salesman. His
face was pleasant enough, rounded, faintly Gallic, faintly Near-
Eastern. At this moment it wore a slightly acquisitive expression,
rather like a collector viewing a new collectible. Would it prove
authentic?

Paul Boulad was indeed a collector. He was a collector of facts;
of tiny pieces of information and large chunks of information; of
data and rumor; of hearsay and truth. From his collections Paul
Boulad wove patterns. Only in his business patterns were called
"conspiracies." He shifted his position in the car and watched the
two men disappear into the Sheraton Inn. Where did they fit?
Were they big? Were they small? Was the man with the glasses
the leader? Or was he simply a follower? In the next few hours
and days Boulad would find out.

Special Agent Paul Boulad was no stereotype policeman. Indeed
he was a strange admixture of strains and qualities deceptive to
friend and quarry alike. Boulad had been born in Cairo of a
French family and had come to the United States when he was

twelve. He spoke fluent French, some Arabic and, more important, had a sense for Latin and Mediterranean people that many
of his colleagues lacked. He had not trained to be a cop. After the
army he had taken education courses at Nassau College and had
taught briefly in a public school. But always there had been something missing. His life had not seemed complete until he had become a Customs patrol officer. His timing was good. Boulad
joined the Customs service when a college degree was more the
exception than the rule, and his degree coupled with his language
ability marked him early as a comer. In a matter of months he was
made a special agent handling complex smuggling cases.

Assigned to the American Embassy in Paris for two years as a
Treasury Department attaché, Boulad became acquainted with
French narcotics and customs officers as well as intelligence officers of the Sûreté. Though he was not working on narcotics cases
at that time, it was from what these sources told him that he came
to view heroin smuggling as a single carefully woven tapestry instead of a hundred separate incidents. The same sources convinced him, long before the notion was popular in his own
government, that the bulk of heroin entering the United States
came from a relatively small group of French-Corsicans and that
thus most major smuggling routes must have one common de-
nominator—the point of origin.

In Paris Boulad had begun the painstaking cataloguing of
names, pictures, nicknames, family connections, and dates that
would later take shape on the worn blackboards of the Customs
Intelligence Unit at 201 Varick Street in New York. So it was not
with the glance of a policeman nor the glare of the antagonist that
Boulad surveyed Becker and Muravnik that October afternoon. It
was with the careful eye of the archaeologist evaluating two new
artifacts. They were, the eyes said, of the right shape, age, and
design—but where did they fit?

Becker and Muravnik checked into the hotel without flurry and
headed for the elevator. Their room had been selected with far
more care than they would ever realize. A Customs agent occupied the room next door and through his door could hear all the
comings and going of his neighbors. The set-up was not entirely

ideal. Though the agent could hear everything that went on, he couldn't see the people going in and out of Becker's room without opening his door. The resourceful undercover man assigned to the room decked himself out in Bermuda shorts and a T-shirt and each time he heard a noise he would grab the ice bucket in his room and head down the hall as if going to fetch ice cubes. "There was such a lot of activity one night," Boulad said, "our man was flushing ice cubes down the toilet."

The agents had also quietly arranged for a monitoring of incoming and outgoing calls and for a constant surveillance both in the lobby and across the street. The set-up across the street was to prove troublesome, too. In order to keep a full view of the Sheraton's doorway, the agents had to pull their cars under the West Side Highway's viaduct, which coincidentally was a favorite place for the local police patrols to "coop" (cop slang for sleeping or goofing off). Despite frequent efforts to get some working liaison through the local precinct, including calls from Customs Senior Agent in Charge John Fallon and from Al Seeley, both former New York Police Department detectives, the police took to routinely "tossing" (asking for identification from) the federal men. "To add insult to injury," Boulad said, "the NYPD towed away three of our cars while they were empty."

Yet at this point the physical act of surveillance became virtually the crux of the entire case. If the surveillance was clumsy or inept the entire prosecution would be forfeit. On October 21, the day before Becker, Muravnik, and Bianchi arrived, Seeley held what he called a "pregame session" with the same care a pro football coach uses to plot a bowl game. His team: the men who were going to conduct the surveillance. The team had three advantages. It knew where both sets of principles would live—the St. Regis at Fifty-fifth Street and Fifth Avenue, and the Sheraton Inn. It knew the physical descriptions and would soon have photographs of Becker and Muravnik. And of course it had Bianchi.

But the liabilities were legion. New York's crowded sidewalks and car-clogged streets were a maze that could mislead the most adroit tail, and the men in this country waiting for the heroin might spot the Customs men before contact was ever made. "The hardest part is the first three days," Seeley warned his men. "We have no idea whether this deal is going to go down immediately or at all.

"During the first twenty-four to forty-eight hours expect anything. This is the time for everybody to see and know who the actors are and who will play the parts."

The Customs car teams would be linked by radio, but Seeley warned his men to use them sparingly and always speak in code. "There's been more than one case where the smugglers were monitoring our band," he said.

It was at this meeting that he had ordered the immediate taking of photographs of Becker and Muravnik both at the airport and the Sheraton. "There's nothing worse than sitting on a hotel looking for a guy with only a description. I don't care if he's wearing a yellow shirt and a red tie," Seeley argues.

Among the enemies that Seeley knew he would face would be the fatigue of his men. He had divided the team into two shifts, 11 A.M. to 11 P.M. and 11 P.M. to 11 A.M. Boulad would head the night team, Bob Nunnery the day team. In the next five days the case would eat up energies and man hours at an appalling rate. An average of fifteen men on each shift would be required to keep track of the "actors" in Seeley's theater.

There was no need to use the meeting to talk of danger. The shirtsleeved young men all carried pistols—some in "sky marshal clips" slipped unobtrusively into their belts, others in short leather holsters sitting tight by hip, and others clipped into shoulder holsters, the guns suspended literally upside down for quick draw.

The danger, the men knew, was far more real from the "receivers" than from the smugglers. The smuggler relied upon his brains, wit, and the ability to jump bond after arrest to protect him.

"The foreigner who comes in is going to come in as clean as possible," Boulad points out. "Why should he get caught on a gun rap before he does his thing?" But the receiver, Boulad and his colleagues knew, has none of these restraints and facing long drug sentences can be a terrible impetus to violence. The night before Becker arrived Boulad took a few moments to prepare. The quiet former school teacher carried a standard .357 magnum with sky marshal clip and what he called his "surprise," a tiny 9 mm. Walther parabellum automatic so small that it appeared no larger than a pack of cigarettes in his shirt pocket. "This pistol was issued to German pilots to hide in their boots," Boulad relates, resting it in the palm of his hand. "You can see why." It is lethal.

Bianchi and Florida Customs agents flew into New York on the night of October 22, a few hours after Becker and Muravnik. They registered at the Penn Gardens Motel in midtown to pre-brief themselves and await the signal to move into position at the St. Regis. A highly skilled Spanish-speaking special agent was assigned to Bianchi.

Virtually as Bianchi was arriving, however, the case began to move. "The subjects have left their room and are proceeding from the hotel," came the message from the stakeout team at the Sheraton Inn. Immediately, the first of Seeley's tricky street operations swung into gear.

Becker and Muravnik went by cab through New York's deepening dusk to the glittering Hilton Hotel a few blocks north of Rockefeller Center on what to tourists is the Avenue of the Americas but to New Yorkers will always be Sixth Avenue. The tailing agents groaned as they saw the pair enter the Hilton. It was a surveillance nightmare. The massive hotel had sides on three different streets and an alley. The lobby could be entered or exited through doors from all three sides—not to mention through several bars, restaurants, and shops.

Puffing hard, Boulad entered the hotel a few minutes after the pair, worried that he had already lost them, only to find himself face to face with his quarry a few steps into the lobby. "I passed by them as close as I am to you," he later told a friend. "They paid no attention to me."

Becker, Muravnik in tow, went to the house phones and spoke hurriedly with someone in an upstairs room. A Customs agent nearby was able to hear the room number, 3456, but little else. The two Latin Americans then left the hotel and walked east toward Fifth Avenue, pausing occasionally to window shop. Their leisurely walk ended at a French bookstore between Forty-ninth and Fiftieth streets on Fifth.

The man they met—agents later learned he was the occupant of

Room 3456—was slim, of medium build with light brown hair and brown eyes. His clothes were well tailored, indeed quite stylish and cut with a European flair, and he had about him a delicate, almost effeminate grace that made every step and gesture dramatic.

Pierre Gahou, at thirty-nine, had spent more than half his adult life at sea. Not in the rough atmosphere of the forecastle nor the crew's quarters of tramp steamers but as a steward aboard some of the finest liners launched by the French merchant marine. It was serving the passengers in these salons that had given him his very grand, very Gallic manner.

A decade before the October meeting on Fifth Avenue, Gahou had first sailed the Latin American run. Like Frenchmen abroad anywhere in the world, he had sought out his native language and native food in every port. In Buenos Aires this desire for French companionship had led him to the Bar el Sol. Gahou had no criminal record. Indeed in many ways he was a quiet and unassuming man who, when he was in Paris, still stayed with his mother at 143 Rue Oberkamph. But somehow he hit it off with the rough-hewn Corsicans at the Bar el Sol and particularly with its proprietor, "Monsieur André," or Auguste Joseph Ricord. By the late 'sixties, the two men had become so friendly that when Ricord left Argentina for Paraguay he invited Gahou along. The steward, whose livelihood was threatened by the decrease in sea travel, went gladly. His friend Monsieur André presented a comfortable source of income with Le Paris-Niza and with other "special" assignments. Not that he liked the present job much.

When the three men from Asunción—Becker, Muravnik, and Gahou—met on Fifth Avenue they barely acknowledged one another. To a disinterested observer it would seem as though the three men were simply walking in the same direction. Turning off Fifth, they headed for Danny's Bar and Restaurant, a small boozery a block away.

The meeting was brief. The bar was jammed with the after-work crowd, and the three men sipping apéritifs blended into the bustle and the noise. Becker told Gahou all systems were go. The stuff was on its way north from Miami in Bianchi's car and would arrive in two days. Yes, Becker stressed, the light was green, Gahou could now make contact.

Gahou surveyed his two companions at the bar without showing emotion, but inwardly he could hardly contain his distaste for them. He was French enough and conspiratorial enough to appreciate the intricate security measures of "Le Organization," but occasionally, at moments like this, he despaired of his companions.

"Becker, the lover," he thought, and "Muravnik, the Jew." In Paraguay Becker was another functionary in the system of *contrabandistas*; another hanger-on, wheeling and dealing. Muravnik, a Polish Jew, Gahou had to grudgingly admit, was indeed a smuggler of professional stature. Like a Corsican, Muravnik had the blood of smugglers going back three centuries flowing in his veins.

Sitting at the bar that night, though, Gahou could not help but admire Ricord's system. It was a subtle combination of the age-old traditions of the Union Corse and the rigid rules of German and Allied intelligence services born in World War II and sharpened through the cold war. Bianchi and Balestra, who actually had the heroin, flew a plane to an appointed place and waited for instructions. They did not know the buyer of the cargo and without this "connection" were nearly powerless to hijack the load even if they had wanted to double-cross the system. Becker and Muravnik, who did not have the heroin, were sent to shepherd Bianchi to delivery. They knew where the heroin was but the only contact they had in New York was Gahou at the Hilton.

And he himself, Gahou, alone knew who the buyer was and was authorized to collect the agreed-upon price. But he did not know where Bianchi was or how to make contact directly with the heroin. Auguste Ricord's system, like a jigsaw puzzle, worked only when all the pieces fell into place. No single person had enough information to make the system work without the other parts. Momentarily, Gahou wondered who had been assigned to watch him.

While the three conspirators were meeting at Danny's Bar, Bianchi and Balestra were going over their story for the thousandth time in a stuffy room at the Penn Gardens Motel with Customs agents while other agents were scouring rental car agencies to find a car that exactly matched Bianchi's Pinto. Despite the constant questions, Bianchi stuck to what he had said to the agents in Miami. He was told to go to New York, told to register at the St. Regis or the Sheraton and to wait for instructions. He was to call Becker only in an emergency.

Standing in the darkening evening out in front of Danny's Bar, Boulad was growing deeply concerned while he and the other agents waited for their quarry. As the number of characters in the plot increased, the ability of the Customs agents to keep pace with them grew more strained. They would have to watch Gahou at the Hilton, Becker and Muravnik at the Sheraton Inn, and Bianchi and Balestra at the St. Regis. "Why in God's name couldn't these people all stay in one hotel?" Boulad wondered out loud.

He knew that as the number of surveillance targets increased it would stretch the agents thinner and thinner, resulting in longer and longer hours for each man. "If a guy is really tired . . . worn out," Boulad explained later, "he makes mistakes. A case this complex means the agent has to think on his feet and he has to be able to stay ahead of the game. After a point you just can't do it without sleep." Facing these same concerns, Seeley later that evening made a command decision.

Only one team of Customs men would follow Gahou as a "target of opportunity," and not attempt to keep full coverage on the massive Hilton Hotel. "We controlled the heroin and we controlled what we knew were two key men at the Sheraton," Seeley later pointed out. "It was a risk, obviously, but it was better than trying to cover all three locations and possibly making a mistake."

The meeting in Danny's Bar broke up shortly before 7 P.M. and Becker and Muravnik returned to the Sheraton by cab. Gahou, obviously relishing his stay in the city, walked back to the Hilton at an easy pace. Two agents were behind him.

Shortly after 8 P.M., the same night, Gahou again left his room at the Hilton and walked south along Sixth Avenue. It was chilly now and he was wearing a light raincoat as he ambled along. At the corner of Fifty-third Street he turned east and eventually stopped in front of the Brasserie, a popular French restaurant. The street was crowded with diners, moviegoers, and tourists heading in both directions.

Suddenly, as Gahou paced up and down before the restaurant, another man, a man the agents did not recognize, fell into step with him. The man was tall, dark-haired, dark-eyed with a Latin or Italian visage. He was husky and walked with the agility of an athlete. He was dressed modishly with his hair styled long, almost to his collar, and a dark suit and dark green car coat.

The two men never entered the restaurant. Instead they walked around the block—for fifty-five minutes, one agent recalled—deep in conversation. As they walked one or the other seemed constantly to study passersby, and occasionally they would pause as if to see who might be behind them. Gahou could be seen gesturing, the other man nodding.

Then, as suddenly as it had begun, the interview was over. The mysterious new figure hurried down a darkened sidestreet to a blue Volkswagen parked with its motor running. The car drove away so swiftly that the agents were barely able to keep it in sight. As it made a turn north onto Park Avenue the street lights revealed the car's driver—a beautiful dark-haired woman.

The car went north nearly nine blocks and then pulled off into a parking lot near Fifty-ninth Street. The agents followed the couple to the Baronet Theater a half block away. "Do you know what the movie was?" one of the men on the team later recalled, "It was *The Great White Hope*. It struck me funny later. That's what they were dealing in—the Great White Hope."

One of the two agents entered the movie behind the couple and sat down a few seats away. He could not help but admire the woman. "She was five-four or five-five and she was wearing a pair of tight toreador pants. Her figure was terrific and her face was softly beautiful. Large brown eyes and a sort of olive complexion, you know, sort of Spanish-looking. Her clothes were mod—like a Spanish dancer's costume."

From the movie the agents followed the couple to a motel on Queens Boulevard in the Corona section. A swift check of the registration revealed the man had booked the room as "Nick Russo." It was now midnight and the agents settled down across from the motel to wait. Well before dawn, about 3 A.M., the couple hurried out. "I don't think they were trying to beat us," one agent recalled, "I don't think they knew we were there, for that matter. I think they were just getting laid and the party was over."

But the agents faced the same problem their colleagues had a few days before in Miami. In the predawn hours there were so few cars that the surveillance team could not follow too closely without tipping their hand. "We lost them on Queens Boulevard. We were hanging back and the VW hooked a U-turn. We just couldn't follow. By the time we got onto a side street the Volkswagen was gone," one of the agents said.

In the half-light of that dawn the Customs men weren't sure what they had or didn't have. The man and woman in the Volkswagen could simply have been personal acquaintances of Pierre Gahou. Indeed Gahou himself might not be linked to the heroin. They didn't know. But they did have some starting places—the license of the VW, New York 8058ML, the name "Nick Russo" on the registry, and descriptions of the man and girl.

For the Customs men the next hours and days became interminable. Becker and Muravnik again met with Gahou, but the trio acted like tourists; walked about, ate meals at the Market Diner at Twelfth Avenue and Forty-third, and went on seemingly endless window-shopping tours.

October 24 was little different. The three met for drinks at Jack Dempsey's Restaurant on Broadway, later walked over to the Cattleman's Restaurant off of Seventh Avenue for dinner. October 25 was drearily the same. Lunch at the Market Diner at 1 P.M. and a brief foray to Madison Square Garden, where they bought tickets for the closed circuit television showing of the Muhammad Ali–Joe Frazier fight the next evening.

On October 26 Becker and Muravnik stayed in their room until 3 P.M., then began another of their rambling shopping tours. They bought Stetson hats at a store near Times Square, looked at the "peep shows" along New York's pornography alley on West Forty-second Street, and made a brief visit to a small export company.

It all seemed routine until midevening, when the agents ran into bone-chilling trouble.

Becker and Muravnik had met Gahou at Madison Square Garden for the fight show. The trio entered through Gate 24 and took seats ringed on three sides by agents. But midway through the show one of the giant screens blacked out and the audience shifted to new seats in the dark. "When the lights came on all three of them were gone," one agent ruefully recalls.

"For all we knew we had been completely had. The darkened Garden was a perfect place to ditch a tail." The team at the Garden immediately radioed the men stationed at the Sheraton Inn and dispatched units to the Hilton. One hour and many near-ulcers later, Becker and Muravnik nonchalantly appeared. But the agents had no way of knowing what the men had done in that hour.

It had now been nearly nine days since Bianchi's little Cessna landed in Miami. The Customs men were becoming increasingly edgy. To keep up the multipoint, round-the-clock surveillance many of the agents had put in extended overtime and the fatigue was beginning to show. Some of the agents did not trust Bianchi and began to wonder whether the husky Paraguayan had somehow passed a warning signal to his colleagues. Could the whole New York scenario be a sophisticated charade?

Seeley and Boulad remained firm. They pointed out that the Customs men had successfully strung out a tricky subterfuge for more than a week. To date, Bianchi and the heroin had led them to Becker, Muravnik, Gahou, and the still unidentified mystery man at the Brasserie restaurant. Furthermore, Seeley told his men, the waiting and watching would, at a minimum, establish evidence for a conspiracy charge.

The dispute centered on two points. If the agents continued the operation they stood to net the receiver of the heroin shipment an enormously important objective since it effectively amputated one end of the smuggling operation. Moreover, by piecing together the smuggling apparatus as it entered the United States the lawmen hoped to have enough evidence to indict the overseas shippers as a part of the conspiracy. Admittedly, the extension of U.S. conspiracy laws to persons living abroad was new and tricky. Essentially it meant that the United States was charging persons who may never have entered the country with plotting to violate

U.S. laws. If the arrests in New York could lead the Customs men to the shippers of the heroin it would be the most auspicious indictment under the new law yet handed down. It would also provide a base for the United States to extradite the kingpins in Latin America.

On the negative side, the points were also strong. "The risk is simply too great. If we sit tight and lose the whole ball game we're taking an unacceptable chance," one veteran agent pointed out. "It's better to pull in what we have now. Maybe we can squeeze a conspiracy indictment on the receiver out of the statements of one of these guys."

The final decision was partly made on guts and instinct and partly overtaken by events. A series of overseas calls from Muravnik to Asunción led agents to believe that another operative was arriving from Paraguay. His arrival, Seeley and his team decided, might be the signal that the deal was going down. They would continue the operation for at least one more day.

For Cesar Mendice Bianchi the days, even hours, were becoming excruciating. Virtually a prisoner in the plush confines of Room 629 at the St. Regis, he had been in suspended animation for more than a week. He could feel the distrust of the agents, and his fear of his colleagues from Paraguay was growing with each minute.

October 27 dawned chill and overcast, adding to Bianchi's sense of despair. In late morning the room telephone jangled. The noise made Bianchi and the agent with him jump. Hesitatingly, Bianchi answered. "It's Becker," he whispered "he's in the lobby." Swiftly the agent went next door and closed the doors between the two rooms. Bianchi was alone.

The knock at the door came a few moments later. The Customs men heard only the first part of the hurried Spanish.

"How are you?" Becker asked as the door opened.

"Fine," Bianchi answered.

"You were supposed to call me at the hotel," Becker interjected heatedly. "I arrived here Friday night."

"I am tired of waiting here," was Bianchi's evasive reply.

"You might leave today," Becker's voice said, "if it is not possible, you're going to have to wait a couple of days more. You stay at the hotel. Do not visit me." The door closed on the pair.

Becker was in the room for five minutes as the agents strained to hear the conversation through the connecting doors. They were partially stymied by external noise and by the fact that the two speakers often slipped into Guarani, a Paraguayan dialect with many Indian words and phrases. As abruptly as Becker had come he left, hurrying toward the elevator and the street.

"What happened?," the Spanish-speaking agent asked Bianchi.

"I told Becker that I was tired of waiting; that I arrived six days ago, and that I have waited since Friday in this hotel without being called or knowing anything. Becker told me that I have to wait a few more days and I told him that I am tired of waiting and that I did not have a single peso in my pockets. Becker told me he will be seeing me again in one hour."

The case was going down. It was unspoken, but it was clear. The case was going down. By noon on the 27th Al Seeley knew that today would be the day. It was more than just the changes in the surveillance reports, it was something that his many years as a New York police detective and his nearly ten years as a senior Customs special agent had taught him. It was part of the mystique.

"When something is going to happen, you know its going to happen by the way they act—doing something tight, nervous. There is a change in attitudes. When things are beginning to move the physical outward appearances of the suspects change. It is a distinct behavior pattern, you might say. As soon as you can see this change—expect something. Keep on them tight."

Seeley's men were ordered to do just that. First because the case was moving but second because the sharp ears of the Spanish-speaking special agent had detected that Bianchi was lying to them. He had spun them around.

"When Becker came to the door of that room," one agent later explained "one of the first things he asks Cesar is, 'Why didn't you call me?' Yet all the time little Cesar is telling us that it's Becker who was supposed to call. It was subtle. Bianchi didn't have the guts to refuse to work with us or to try to warn them in an obvious way so he just forgot a key part of his orders. It was enough to put Becker on his guard."

It was going to be a tricky and nervous set of maneuvers. The Customs men had identified the operative coming from Paraguay as Enio Anibal Varela and his destination as the Americana Hotel at Fifty-fourth Street and Seventh Avenue.

Shortly before Becker made his late-morning trip to see Bianchi at the St. Regis the agents began surveillance on Varela, who had arrived at the Americana. With the help of the hotel's management the Treasury men had obtained a room that allowed them a view of the elevator bank and the hall to Varela's room.

It was the closest and best-located available room on such short notice. The only hitch was that in order to see the elevators and hall without opening the door the agents had to lie flat on the floor and watch from underneath the door. There was a space of about two inches. "I don't know if you've ever tried anything like that," Boulad wryly points out, "but the draft on your eyeballs can be excruciating." For ten hours over that day, Boulad and other agents were to use that strange method to keep track of Varela.

While Becker was out, Muravnik went to the Americana Hotel to meet with Varela. Then, with the secret entourage of agents in tow, the two men walked over to the Radio City Music Hall. It was a Tuesday and the busy throng of shoppers and secretaries hardly noticed the street-corner meeting of the four men. Varela and Muravnik arrived first and were soon joined by Gahou and later by Becker.

The deal, Gahou assured the group, was ready. The New York receiver had agreed to the price and conditions—Gahou did not reveal the price to the others—and the exchange would be made that very day.

The arrangement, Gahou said, was for the heroin to be placed in the trunk of Bianchi's car and driven to a parking lot at the corner of Forty-ninth Street and Tenth Avenue. Becker and Bianchi would handle the delivery. All they had to do was leave the car there with the keys, and when they returned the bags containing the heroin would be gone.

The money would be paid to Gahou, who would bring it to

Becker's room at the Sheraton. Thus none of the Latins would ever know the name or the identity of the receiver. Once the exchange had been made, Gahou said, he, Becker, Muravnik, and Varela would be responsible for carrying the money out of the country.

The safe movement of the money was almost as tricky a part of the operation as had been the smuggling of the heroin. Anyone attempting to deposit large amounts of cash for foreign transfer in a New York bank was immediately suspect—and as much suspicion could be caused by an airport search turning up a suitcase full of cash. One well-known smuggler, for instance, had had to abandon $287,000 when he panicked during a skyjack check as he was about to leave the country.

Thus Varela had come prepared with two letters from an established Latin American money exchange house that introduced him to a New York bank and an exchange house and explained that he had brought a large amount of U.S. cash for deposit in accounts held by Latins. It was Varela's plan to avoid having to try to carry the cash out of the country. With these letters he could send it through normal banking channels without suspicion.

Though Gahou never revealed the sale price of the Cessna's cargo, the others in the little group at Rockefeller Center that day knew it must exceed $500,000.

The meeting lasted only a few minutes. The operation was go. It would be executed after dark. On the way back to the Sheraton from the meeting something kept nagging at Becker's subconscious. He had not told the others because he was not sure and, of course, because he did not want to seem the "old woman," the worrier. But there was something about Bianchi's behavior that morning that had bothered Becker.

The slim, red-haired Paraguayan sat moodily through the afternoon staring out of the hotel window at the gray unfriendly waters of the Hudson River. He thought of his wife Marta and the two girls, and he found himself wishing he had not come to New York this time.

It was not like Bianchi to have forgotten to call him at the hotel. Bianchi was precise for a Latin and, as a pilot and a man of mechanical things, was careful and punctual. Why should Bianchi suddenly have such a lapse? Twice Becker almost told Muravnik of his fears, once he thought of calling Varela. He did not like Gahou. The Frenchman was too close to Monsieur André and he was not Paraguayan. But Varela or Muravnik, they would listen.

Each time he thought of telling the others he could not. It was he who had been sent to ensure the delivery. It was his o.k. that had brought the others into it, and it was his o.k. that had resulted in Varela's coming to clinch the deal. How would it look if he now said "Everybody go home. I think something's wrong." Becker shook off the feeling. It was nerves. Everything was going to be okay.

At dusk Becker and Varela went to the St. Regis Hotel to brief Bianchi on the final details of the transfer. Varela had some mail for Bianchi from Paraguay and word from Daysi. They called from the lobby, and again the Spanish-speaking agent went to the adjoining room. But before he left he warned Bianchi: "Do not try to escape." Bianchi became very emotional. "No, no. I will not. I am risking everything on this deal. Don't worry, I will stay in the room. I swear by God that I could have escaped last night and I did not want to do it." The agent left.

As in the first meeting the agents in the adjoining room could not hear the entire conversation, and again the participants would occasionally slip into the Guarani dialect. What they could hear was this:

BECKER: Mr. Varela, is it possible to do this in one hour?

VARELA: Let's wait two hours.

BIANCHI: I am tired of waiting. Let's try to solve this problem today. I am tired of all this.

BECKER: You have to wait.

BIANCHI: I am tired. I want to take the car out of here and dispose of the stuff that is contained in it. Follow your instructions, do whatever you must do, but do not fail me.

BECKER: I'll see you in two hours.

BIANCHI: Okay, Solon.

The pair left. Bianchi watched them walk down the hall almost mournfully. He had called Becker "solon," a slang term of comrades, and what was happening saddened him.

The agents now knew the precise time and complexion of the exchange. They had been ready for days but they again checked the set-up. Bianchi's Florida license plates were now affixed to a rental car exactly like his. The milk sugar had been placed in the very same plastic bags that had carried the original heroin and arranged in the suitcases in exactly the same order. On the top of the first bag that one would normally open in the trunk was the one package of real heroin needed to make the case.

The Pinto with its vital load had been parked in the hotel's garage since Bianchi had registered. There was no apparent guard around it. The Customs men had considered the possibility that someone from the gang might "check" the car out without telling Bianchi.

Shortly before 9 P.M. Becker returned to the St. Regis for the third time. He was still anxious about the deal and, though he had begun to chalk Bianchi's actions up to nerves, was still worried. When Bianchi met him at the room door, Becker tried to stall.

This is what the agents could hear:

BIANCHI: Well what do we have? I am at your service, sir. I go with you, if you want. I have the car parked at the hotel.
BECKER: No, do not go with me. I wait for you downstairs, outside. Everything is okay now.
BIANCHI: What time are you leaving?
BECKER: At 10 or 11.

Bianchi became very upset and in hurried Spanish told Becker: "I have not moved from here; I have eaten here and I have slept here all the time; and I do not understand the television programs. I am afraid to become sick."

Becker sought to calm him down. "Okay, okay, Solon I wait for you outside."

Calmer, Bianchi answered: "Okay. I'll meet you there."

Less than thirty seconds later the agents broke radio silence and alerted the entire network, "Be advised the package is moving."

Bianchi put on his flying jacket and hurried to the lobby. Though he knew the agents were following him he felt a momentary sense of relief that he was free of their custody. Using a lobby telephone, Bianchi called the St. Regis garage and asked that his

Pinto be brought around front. He paced up and down as he waited for the car, anxiously looking about to see if he recognized any of the men lounging in the lobby. "Which ones are my watchdogs?" he later remembered thinking.

When the car pulled up in front of the hotel's awning-covered Fifty-fifth Street entrance, neither Bianchi nor Becker, who had swiftly joined him, noticed the nondescript garage man who delivered the car. He was one of the watchdogs.

The Pinto began moving west in midevening traffic. A dozen blocks away Albert Seeley sat in his car listening as the cryptic surveillance messages flowed in over the radio. "Package passing Sixth. . . . Package passing Seventh . . . passing Eighth."

In the Pinto Becker was getting more and more jumpy. Every warning light in his nervous system was on. Something just wasn't right. He had told Bianchi to drive west on Fifty-fifth Street, but the husky little Paraguayan kept asking for further directions.

Becker lied at first. He told Bianchi to turn downtown on Tenth Avenue. "We're going around Forty-second Street, just follow my directions." When the car reached Forty-second Becker ordered Bianchi, "Just circle the block." Four times they circled the block while Becker anxiously looked out of the rear window.

On the fourth round at Eighth Avenue, Becker ordered Bianchi to go north again. "Go to Forty-ninth Street and Tenth Avenue." All the time Becker kept a watchful eye out of the rear window. At a red light at Forty-fifth Street he suddenly screamed. "We are being followed. You have betrayed us." The slim Paraguayan's right hand was already on the door handle.

For ten minutes Seeley had been on the brink. The radio pacing reports were bad. His instinct told him that either Bianchi had screwed them or Becker had made the tail. Either way he and his men could lose all. He had told his men time and time again, "In New York traffic don't take anything for granted. One light goes against you, one car double-parked and, brother, you've had it. When you lose control of that car, you lose control of the case."

It was time to listen to his own lectures. "Okay, bust 'em," he growled into the radio.

At the precise moment Becker opened the door he found himself facing the muzzle of a .357 magnum. "Out of the car slowly. Put your hands behind your head," the agent told him. As he reached standing position, the agent swung him around and threw him face down over the front of the car, kicking his legs apart as he pinioned one arm. Becker could feel swift, efficient, insinuating hands moving over his body, under his armpits, along his waist, and delving painfully into his crotch.

"He's clean," the agent called out. "Okay, give him his rights," a voice whose owner Becker couldn't see ordered. Tonelessly, in hurried phrases the agent began the litany. "You have a right to remain silent . . ."

Becker lay staring at the metal of the car. Yes, he wished he had not come to New York this time. He could hear the same litany of American justice being delivered to Bianchi, who was slammed against the back of the car.

In the back of the cramped Ambassador sedan, the agents swiftly interrogated Becker. "Where was the transfer to be made? Where were you to get the word the money had been paid? What were the signals?"

Becker was confused. To be arrested so suddenly in a strange country. It momentarily seemed very important to protect the others. The smuggling operation was his plan, he told the agents. The car was to be left at a parking lot at Forty-second Street and Tenth Avenue. Bianchi angrily interjected. "He's lying, the parking lot was Forty-ninth Street and Tenth Avenue." There was a swift exchange of Spanish, quickly silenced by the agents.

Becker then told the agents. "I was to be contacted, and my contact was to bring the money to my hotel room."

The Customs men decided to give it a whirl.

Gloom hung over Seeley and the agents in the command car. They had been pressured into moving sooner than they wanted and the handover had been blown. The only hope now was to sit on Becker for a few minutes at the Sheraton Inn and see if he was contacted. It was shortly after 9:30 P.M.

For nearly thirty minutes the agents kept Becker at the Sheraton, staring glumly first at the telephone and then at the lights on the dark river. The black telephone sat silently, almost mockingly. It did not ring.

"Fuck all," one agent finally burst out. "Nobody's going to call." The others did not disagree. At 10 P.M. Seeley put out the order to pull the others in.

Pierre Gahou was arrested in the lobby of the New York Hilton by an agent with a flair for the dramatic, who introduced himself with this line: "Monsieur Gahou, I presume?"

The team at the Americana was less gallant but as efficient. It pulled in Varela and Muravnik with little fanfare.

By shortly after 10 P.M. on October 27, the agents had under arrest six members of what appeared to be a massive heroin smuggling operation and nincty-four pounds of 98 per cent pure heroin. It was a major drug haul, indeed at that moment it was one of the largest single drug hauls ever made by United States agents.

But the pros—Seeley and Boulad and the men of the hard narcotics unit—knew that they had only torn out the connecting wires of the system. They must locate and convict the two ends.

# 7 The Girl in the Toreador Pants

*Carla Pilar was by any standards a* smashing-looking girl. Five feet, five inches tall, she was endowed with a gently plump, voluptuous figure, a soft olive complexion, deep brown eyes, and shining black hair. She spoke English with a heavy Spanish accent and the sometimes jumbled syntax and occasional "how do you say—?" made her conversation as alluring as her figure.

New York, for Carla, was the crystallization of a thousand girl hood dreams spun out in the darkened rows of a Quito movie theater or over glamour magazines from the United States. The affluence, the skyscrapers, the crowded shops were all heady wine for the twenty-five-year-old Ecuadorian. Like thousands of girls before them, Carla and her sister had come to the great metropolis to find their destiny, to live a different life from their parents'.

Jobs and men came easily in the big city. Carla sold cosmetics,

155

worked as a waitress at a coffee shop in Kennedy International Airport, and worked behind a counter at a department store in Manhasset. She had lost weight since she had come from Ecuador and had begun to follow the fast-changing fashions in the New York stores. In late 1969 her shapely legs, exciting accent, and with-it air won her a cocktail hostess job in one of Kennedy Airport's plush lounges.

Each evening brought her good tips, an occasional pinch, and a constant stream of "social proposals" that she fended off with the agility of a fencing master. Only one proposition seriously intrigued her. It came from a dark-haired, husky "regular customer" Carla then knew only as "Nick."

From the few minutes of conversation they had from time to time, she had learned that he was an Argentinian, a onetime professional "footballist" with a Bogotá, Colombia, soccer team, and a most charming man. It did not take many dinner invitations from him before she accepted.

Nick was like no other man she had ever known. Though he was forty-three years old he seemed half his age, his physical condition as trim and disciplined as it had been when he was on the soccer fields. Like many Latin men he talked little to Carla about his business, and like many Latin women she asked little. She knew he was in some sort of real estate business, and she knew he must do very well. He spent money with the ease of a man who no longer has to count his pennies, with sure taste.

Life was suddenly very exciting. Nick had acquaintances from all over the world and would often take Carla along on business meetings as his "chauffeur." They would wind up an evening with a pleasant dinner or drink or at El Quixote, a small bar and restaurant in lower Manhattan frequented by Latin Americans. As the months passed Carla learned that Nick was trapped in what he said was an unhappy marriage but one from which he saw no escape. The pretty Ecuadorian came to accept this and to cherish what moments the two could have together.

Driving Nick to business meetings had become so routine that Carla paid little attention to the meeting she dropped Nick at a few days before she left for a home visit to Ecuador. She was to remember the evening later mostly because the movie *The Great*

*White Hope* had been good and she had had one more opportunity to be with Nick.

What Carla did not know that October night was that her blue Volkswagen with New York license plate 8058ML was the only lead Treasury agents could follow to the possible buyer of the ninety-four pounds of heroin. Indeed Carla had left the country a few days after the meeting near the Brasserie restaurant oblivious to the hurricane forming about her.

Customs Special Agent Robert Nunnery looked more the college man than the narc. Slender, sandy-haired, handsome, and serious, he did not affect the mod clothes of many of his colleagues and was instead more at home in tweed jackets or gray suits. He had been one of the hard narcotics unit's shift leaders in October. And he was one of the agents who followed Carla Pilar and her mysterious boyfriend to *The Great White Hope*.

In the weeks of early November, Nunnery set about trying to find the blue Volks and the girl in the toreador pants. A check with the New York Department of Motor Vehicles revealed that the VW belonged to an Ecuadorian girl and listed an address in Lefrak City, Queens. "No," the resident manager at the Lefrak City apartments said, "Miss Pilar and her sister don't live here any more, but I have a forwarding address."

Painstakingly, from residence to residence and job to job, Nunnery traced the girl. She had lived at six different places during her stay in the United States and had worked in nearly as many jobs. The trail was distinct until nine months before the October meeting, when Carla almost disappeared from the records.

Finally he found one of the Ecuadorian's girl friends and work chums. "Oh, Carla is not here any more. She's gone back to Ecuador, I think maybe for a couple of months," the woman recalled. She also confirmed that Carla's steady boyfriend was a man named Nick. The woman did not know, however, exactly how long Carla had been gone or where she might be located in Quito.

Now Nunnery began the tedious business of surveying the various airlines that provide flight service between New York and Quito, hoping against hope that Carla had not traveled somewhere else first. He struck gold at a German Lufthansa Airline reservation office. "Our computer shows a passenger by that name holds a return ticket from Quito to New York, but no return reservation has been made," the pretty reservation clerk told Nunnery.

After much cajoling, Lufthansa agreed to notify the Treasury agent if Miss Pilar used their airline to leave Ecuador. The agents did not know enough about Carla's role in the plot, if any, to authorize any criminal proceeding or to ask the Ecuadorian police to locate her. They would simply have to sit and wait. Routinely they alerted the Immigration and Naturalization Service and Customs agents at all points of entry to be on the lookout for Carla. "Try not to arouse her suspicion but do not readmit her to the country without notifying us," were Nunnery's instructions as he activated the so-called Soundex lookout. Finding Carla and talking to her would probably provide only a thin thread of connection, but in the weeks after the bust of the smuggling ring it became one of the most important threads Customs had.

Although the Customs men had made a startling seizure and set of arrests, they fought desperately to keep any mention of the bust out of the newspapers. Silence would be one of their most valuable weapons. The longer the Latin cartel was unsure what had happened and who had informed, the better chance the Customs men had to drive a wedge into its operation. To the unsophisticated the arrest and seizures might appear a major victory. The federal agents knew they still had a vital task ahead: to snip one or both ends of the conspiracy.

Seeley and Boulad estimated there were three good possibilities: the investigation of Carla Pilar would lead them to the mystery man of the Brasserie and he would somehow be a link to the buyer; one of the four men arrested in New York would talk; or Cesar Bianchi knew more than he had said and could be persuaded to tell it.

Quietly, so as not to puncture the news blackout, the arrested men were brought before a U.S. Commissioner and held on $250,000 bail each. The bail was extraordinarily high because experience had taught that in the multimillion-dollar illicit narcotics business, suspects could easily afford to post bails of $50,000 and even $100,000 and simply walk out on them. The practice had become so routine that the smuggling organizations marked down these expenditures as a cost of doing business.

This time none of the suspects made bail. They were all held in the Federal House of Detention at 427 West Street in New York, the main federal jail for the Southern District of New York. It was an overcrowded and poorly designed facility left over from the government building boom of the early 'thirties and had held such famous guests as Ethel and Julius Rosenberg, top Mafia leaders, and even the antiwar priest Philip Berrigan.

The interrogations had begun within hours of the arrests and were to continue relentlessly for the next three months.

"I think this method of interrogation is brutal," one top Treasury agent privately concedes. "I don't mean in a physical sense. No agent in his right mind is going to jeopardize a major drug prosecution by laying a hand on a suspect. But they are mentally exhausting. The method varies. Quite often it's the bad guy–good guy routine. One agent screams and berates the suspect, constantly threatening him with every conceivable torture, real and imagined. The other comes on all sweetness and light. He only wants to help the poor suspect."

In the shabby interrogation rooms at 201 Varick Street or the West Street prison, the alternatives must have seemed bleak indeed to the suspects. They were caught in a strange country, being interrogated by men who spoke a language not their own, accused of committing a crime for which it was common knowledge the courts handed out harsh sentences. The agents played upon this last fact constantly, over and over again.

The stimulus to confession was by no means all negative. It was, in a sense, Pavlovian. The government investigators and lawyers had enormous power to "make deals." Thus they could reward a suspect for a correct attitude and cooperation or punish him even before trial for failing to cooperate. They could promise to help get the suspect's sentence reduced, see that he was assigned to a lenient rather than harsh prison, or, if he was a really vital witness, stave off trial and keep him under special custody outside of a jail. The government has even been known to supply an informer with women, special food, liquor, and other amenities—not the least of which might simply be the use of his own money, as in the Bianchi case.

The suspect, if the agents hold him on substantial charges, really has few trump cards. He must depend largely on faith that the promises whispered to him in the stuffy interrogation room will be carried out in open court. To "burn" an informant, in the parlance of the trade, is to renege on these promises or to reveal his name and endanger his life. Once the suspect has cooperated a little bit, as in the case of Bianchi, there is always the implied threat that the agents will by a gesture or an unwise word reveal his role and thus put his life in danger.

The justification for these sometimes sordid out-of-court maneuverings is that the goal—the goal of smashing a powerful criminal organization—is more important than obtaining a long sentence for an underling. It has been a justification liberally used in all Mafia and other organized crime prosecutions—that strange world where civil liberties seem to fade away.

What complicated the case for Seeley, Boulad, and the U.S. Attorney's Office was that in addition to information they needed testimony. They had to persuade two or more of the suspects to take the stand and testify against the receiver and the sender of the drugs. For three months after the October arrests this was the tense game being played by agents and suspects alike.

Utilizing Bianchi's initial cooperation as a wedge, the agents and Assistant U.S. Attorney Charles Updike brought enormous pressure to bear to persuade Bianchi to testify and name the source of the drugs.

"At the time of his arrest and on numerous subsequent discussions," Updike was later to write in a government memorandum, "Bianchi was informed that in exchange for full cooperation the government would consider a tax count in lieu of the more serious charge." Over the next two years this "deal" was offered again and again to Bianchi, his wife, his sister, and his lawyers. It was strong pressure. The tax charge carried a two- to ten-year sentence, whereas smuggling narcotics carried a mandatory five- to twenty-year sentence and the defendant could not be paroled for the first five years. Furthermore, in Bianchi's case there was always his $26,000. The government was ultimately to dole this money out to him in various amounts over nearly two years.

The Treasury men had worked hard to keep the suspects from guessing about one another. Although they knew that Becker suspected Bianchi was the informant, they treated Bianchi so scrupulously as a hostile suspect that Becker's mind was filled with doubt. Even the night the car was stopped on Eighth Avenue, Becker could have found no sign in the way Bianchi was handled to suggest that the agents had ever seen him before.

Nevertheless, Bianchi in the first weeks was clearly frightened. He knew the men he was dealing with, and he knew the stakes of the game. Many of his fears were groundless, the result of the paranoia induced by his position. But in late December, Bianchi received a warning that even the Treasury men felt could not be ignored. During a recreation session at West Street, Enio Varela was able to reach his side for a few moments of whispered conversation. "If you should talk," Varela told Bianchi, "our lives would not be worth a single cent. The merchandise you carried belonged to the Mafia. Hold out. Hold out."

Terror seized Bianchi. He knew of the pilots who had "disappeared" and of the planes that had been mysteriously blown up. Though undoubtedly assassination was easier in Paraguay than it was in an American prison, Bianchi was convinced that if he was marked for death there was nothing the guards or the bars at West Street could do to protect him. Realizing his growing trepidation, Agent Boulad arranged for Bianchi to be secretly moved from West Street to the jail in Nassau County, Long Island. This move would be the first in a series of "safe houses" and hideaways in which Customs men would stash key informants in the case.

Despite the importance of Bianchi's information, the pilot did not hold the key to the entire case. Agents were convinced that though Bianchi might know the name and identity of the real source of the heroin he did not know the name of the ultimate receiver. Thus the men of the narcotics unit began a careful evaluation of the other suspects to see who could supply the link.

Varela was very important. It was clear to the agents that only his presence in New York would have permitted the deal to go through. It was clear he knew the source of the heroin and more than likely might be able to identify the buyer. Furthermore, Varela appeared vulnerable. He had been very frightened when the agents arrested him at the Americana, anxiously chattering "yo no hablo el ingles," or "que pasa?" as they handcuffed him. But as the interrogations got under way in the following weeks and months Varela proved a tough nut to crack. Though fat and soft-looking, he proved self-assured during the questioning, often sneering at his captors and answering their questions with rambling, unimportant conversation.

Part of Varela's composure turned out to be based on the circumstance that, unlike his compatriots who were at a loss to find a lawyer to defend them, Varela was immediately and mysteriously represented by a well-known Fifth Avenue law firm. "These guys weren't the usual drug lawyers," one Treasury man recalled, "they were well hung financially, pillars of society—you know, the Sands Point type." The firm had apparently been retained through Varela's cigarette company connections in New York. To the agents it was clear the portly Paraguayan had powerful friends in New York as well as Asunción.

Muravnik also seemed oblivious to pressure. After only a few days of interrogation the agents knew that Muravnik and Varela were somehow more closely linked than the others and that Muravnik also did not appear at all willing to cooperate.

Gahou was far less secure. The slim Frenchman with the engaging manner was confused and dismayed by his predicament. He found the vicious atmosphere of the West Street jail demoralizing and the realization that he faced twenty years in prison mind-blowing. Gahou had $1,700 in U.S. currency and a Varig airlines ticket to Brazil with him when he was arrested. These seemed to be his only resources and no one in New York stepped forward on his behalf. Like so many of the confused who end up behind bars, Gahou obtained a lawyer on the recommendation of another prisoner. The lawyer told the frightened Frenchman not to cooperate with the Treasury men, and collected Gahou's $1,700 as a legal fee.

Not knowing what to do, Gahou remained mum on important information during interrogations in November, December, and

January. But his idle conversation, unlike Varela's, led the Customs men to believe he might help them. Boulad, utilizing his fluent French and lively taste for Gallic chitchat, had painstakingly probed the seagoing waiter's background and had come to believe that Gahou was not like the other suspects. He evaluated Gahou as a passive, unaggressive man who had been lured into the role of liaison in a heroin smuggling ring because his years at sea had inured him to smuggling of all kinds and increased his tolerance for this form of criminal endeavor.

It was Gahou, incidentally, who underscored for Boulad a personality factor that has confounded all U.S. agents in their investigations and interrogations of members of foreign narcotic smuggling rings. The smugglers rarely if ever used narcotics themselves and indeed had relatively little contact with a society where its use was widespread. They seemed remarkably unmindful of the repugnance that heroin's effects had created in American minds. To these smugglers heroin was still just a commodity—like tobacco, whisky, gold, or precious jewels. Smuggling it was a crime, but not a mortal sin. A man could still go to confession.

Nevertheless, Boulad sensed that Gahou had a growing anxiety about the seriousness of the crime he had become involved in and a realization that he was virtually isolated. The Treasury agent carefully pressed the advantage.

Becker was another matter. Though Becker was no longer sure that it was Bianchi who had betrayed them, the ladies' man was still convinced somebody had talked. Moreover he knew his personal predicament was far greater than anyone's except Bianchi's. He had been arrested in the car carrying the heroin. There was literally no defense. He would have to make a deal.

It was with these thoughts in mind that Becker faced each interrogation. Behind a quizzical half-smile, he doled out his cooperation with the care of a Beirut street merchant, trying to sell each revelation for the best possible price. His stories were not always true. At one point he told the agents that he had come to New York to borrow $10,000 from Gahou for a business venture; at another point he denied all knowledge of this transaction.

Two years later he was to admit on a witness stand that at first he had lied and later changed his story. He had decided to tell the truth, he later said, "when I decided to cooperate with the Government of the United States." And he had decided to co-operate with the United States, he said, after he understood the charge he faced carried a mandatory five- to twenty-year sentence.

But even when Becker decided to cooperate he was not always candid. As he later recalled: "I told the truth in a great part of the statements, but I was confused at this time. I did not have a lawyer to explain to me the laws of this country." In other words, the agents suspected, he held out hoping he could make a better deal.

While the interrogations were going on, outside investigations and Balestra's more candid answers had revealed some intriguing information. The flight of the Cessna 210 was clearly not the first smuggling mission. There was in fact an indication of two or more earlier "deliveries." Moreover, a careful study of the passports of the principals indicated that a number of them may have been in on the earlier trips.

Relentlessly the agents pressed Bianchi and Becker. "Were you carrying an earlier load? How much? Who sent it? Who received it? Where was it delivered?"

Yes, there had been a load. Maybe two loads. Bianchi held fast to the story that he thought it was "uranium," and Becker also colored his version. But the two men did confirm the trips. Bianchi admitted that he had carried part of one load in his personal suitcase. That's right. The one he was using for his own clothes on October 18.

Becker was even more helpful, if not more accurate. The previous load had been far smaller than the cargo on the Cessna's final trip. The delivery mechanism had been almost exactly the same. The load was carried to New York, held briefly, and then delivered in a "blind pickup" system. He did not know who the buyer was or what he looked like, but he knew it was the same person slated to receive the ninety-four pounds. And, more important, he knew the deal had gone through. Had he not been assigned to carry $100,000 in U.S. money back to Paraguay? The man who gave him the money? Why, Gahou, of course.

The revelation was vital. First, because it gave the narcs a real case against the receiver. Whoever Mr. X was, he had not received the last load because the arrests had come before the delivery. It would be a near impossibility to try him as part of a conspiracy case since he had not actually received any heroin. But as the intended receiver of ninety-four pounds, with testimony showing he was the actual receiver of an earlier load? The odds on that case were better. The agents now had an additional and powerful lever to pry cooperation out of Gahou and Varela.

Boulad and his colleagues had been scouring the documents of the suspects for other levers. A man not overwhelmingly frightened by a lone smuggling charge might be far more cooperative if he faced a multitude of other federal raps. And these "side" charges, though appearing innocuous and technical, carried five-year sentences. When added one upon the other they could end in a devastating total of years behind bars. As the agents carefully told each suspect—if a federal judge were to levy the sentences on each charge consecutively—well, it was a long time.

For instance. Aron Muravnik had not entered the country under his own name. Instead he had come in carrying papers identifying him as Juan de Dios Rodriguez-Benitez of Argentina. An exhausting and painful tracing of his papers through fingerprints had revealed the subterfuge and put Muravnik in jeopardy of a charge of falsifying immigration forms. Bianchi also carried two aliases—Roberto Magalenes Galluci (he was later to claim this was indeed his real name) of Paraguay and Ricardo Rodrigues of Brazil. Varela was carrying fake documents in the name of Aladio Rojas.

"These guys change passports and identities the way we change clothes," Boulad suggests. "Even when you're finished checking them out you're not really sure which identity is the real one." What further complicated the tracing of identities was that the passports themselves were often genuine—that is, they were not forgeries. The smugglers by chicanery or bribes were able to obtain genuine national passports made up for their false identities.

On November 19 and 20, 1970, a grand jury met in a stuffy jury room in the Federal Court building of the Southern District of New York off Foley Square in lower Manhattan. Secretly and with no fanfare, Bianchi and Becker were brought in unmarked Customs cars to testify. On November 23, the jury handed down a multicount indictment charging the six men with conspiring to smuggle $10 million in heroin. The cat was out of the bag. The next morning both the *New York Times* and the *New York Daily News* reported the story. "CITE SIX AS SMUGGLERS OF $10M IN HEROIN" trumpeted the *Daily News* headline.

The main charge, of course, was a violation of the federal conspiracy law carrying a five-year prison sentence and a $10,000 fine. But Gahou, Becker, Varela, and Muravnik were also charged with possession of heroin. The total package meant those four men each faced sentences of up to twenty years in prison and $20,000 fines. The pressure on the defendants was building. By Christmastime they would have been behind bars for nearly two months. Legal efforts to have the bail reduced had failed, and even the least bright among them knew that the case against them was virtually airtight.


Early in January a prominent Paraguayan attorney, Juan Cecilion "Boobi" Fleitas, came to New York to consult with Varela's American lawyers. During his conversations with the members of the U.S. Attorney's office, it appeared as though his mission was to evaluate just how much trouble his client, Enio Varela, was really in. Of course the government attorneys painted a bleak and frightening picture of Varela's predicament. Despite Senior Varela's prominence in Paraguay, they pointed out, he had been caught red-handed smuggling heroin.

More important than the evaluation made by the government lawyers was the private view of Varela's own U.S. defense: There was little chance of getting bail reduced and even with the most imaginative defense, Varela faced almost certain conviction on a conspiracy charge. Fleitas was duly impressed. He would contact those in Paraguay interested in Varela's welfare and explain the situation. A decision would be made, he promised. But the Paraguayan left New York a few days later, never really explaining what that decision was.

Shortly before dawn on Sunday, January 24, 1971, eight men

escaped from the federal house of detention at West Street. It was a neat, professional exercise. Congregating surreptitiously in a third floor cell, the prisoners cut their way with tin shears into a ventilating shaft leading from the cellblock to the outer wall. Where or how they obtained the tin shears has never been explained.

They crawled along the ventilator shaft until its junction with the wall where a series of half-inch steel bars had been placed to prevent just such an escape. There they sawed their way through the steel bars with a hacksaw blade. Where they obtained the hacksaw blade has never been discovered.

Then, using bedsheets to make a rope, the men lowered themselves onto the roof of a warehouse below. The warehouse was abandoned, and on an icy Sunday morning there was no one around to hear or see the escape. Seven of the escapees had jumped to safety when the rope of bedsheets broke. The eighth was left at the end of the ventilator shaft, abandoned immediately by his companions, and later apprehended.

At 7:30 A.M. that Sunday morning, Senior Customs Special Agent Seeley received a call from the New York field office of the FBI. "Seven men escaped from West Street early today and when we checked we found some of them are apparently Customs defendants. We need 'pedigrees' [criminal background and identity records] to get the search started. Let me read you the names."

With sinking heart, Seeley sat on the edge of his bed and listened to the FBI man's crisp monotone: "Emilio Diaz-Gonzalez, Guiliarmo Hernandez, Miguel Angel Valencia, Enio Anibal Varela, Aron Muravnik, Paul Padilla, David Stanley Jacobinis."

"Have you got any of those?," the agent pressed.

"Unfortunately," Seeley answered wryly, "I do."

Customs had been badly burned. Five of the seven escapees were suspects in major narcotic smuggling cases. Most damaging was the loss of Muravnik and Varela. One intriguing angle in the otherwise devastating break was the linking of Muravnik and Varela's names with that of Emilio Diaz-Gonzalez, a key figure in the "Chilean wine bottle" caper of December, 1969, and husband of the known drug-trafficker Yolanda Sarmiento, who had operated a drug ring from the Concord Village apartments in Brooklyn.

For the next week there was hope that the massive federal drag-net would snag the escapees boarding a plane or holed up in some remote apartment. But as the days passed, the mood at 201 Varick Street turned gloomy. Over the coming months some of the escapees were picked up, usually by accident in other arrests. Diaz-Gonzalez was critically wounded in a gun battle with Argentinian police on December 2, 1972, in Buenos Aires, where his wife, Mrs. Sarmiento, was then running a high-fashion wig shop across the street from the U.S. Embassy. When police closed in to serve a U.S. warrant Diaz-Gonzalez decided to shoot it out. Many residents of the area believed terrorists or bandits were involved, and in a few moments a tremendous gun battle was raging.

Varela is still at large. For nearly two years there was seldom an accurate report of Muravnik's whereabouts, though he has allegedly been sighted at different times in Uruguay, Argentina, and Paraguay. But federal law-enforcement and intelligence agencies were more successful in tracing Varela and in reconstructing how the break from West Street was engineered.

From the start investigators knew that neither Varela nor Muravnik had contacts in New York to set up a well-engineered jailbreak. But Diaz-Gonzalez, then forty-two, and another of the January escapees, Paul Padilla, twenty-seven, had made a break from the same jail on June 29 of that same year. Federal agents believed the pair still possessed the "connections" in the West Street guard force to buy such items as the tin shears and the hacksaw blade and the deliberate inattention of at least one of the guards on duty that Sunday morning.

Federal investigators theorize that when Varela's lawyers ascertained that the case against him in the United States was airtight, powerful associates of his in Paraguay, including his former business partner Army General Patricio Colman, sought ways to free him. The effort was not entirely altruistic. Varela, these agents suggest, was in a position to embarrass people at the highest levels of the Paraguayan Government. He could have laid bare far more than the heroin-smuggling apparatus, they claim.

Had he chosen to, the thirty-four-year-old businessman could have divulged information extremely detrimental to certain U.S. cigarette companies, major money exchange houses, and other Latin governments as well as Paraguay's.

Federal intelligence reports indicate that a colleague brought a vast amount of money to New York and that this money—possibly as much as $350,000—was later used to effect Varela's freedom. "The money was turned over to contacts of Diaz and Padilla at the Abbey Victoria Hotel in New York a few weeks before the break," one agent reported to the authors.

"The two key men were Emilio Diaz-Gonzalez and Padilla. With Varela's money and Diaz-Gonzalez's connections the break was set," claims one federal officer. "They brought along the others in the breakout for cover and because they probably knew the break was planned. Muravnik, of course, was included because he was as important in many ways as Varela."

For two years since the break, informants have rendered splendid scenarios about how Varela fled the country. One version suggests he boarded a private yacht somewhere along the East Coast and was carried to the Bahamas where he was picked up by *contrabandistas* in a Cessna 182 and flown to Puerto Rico. In Puerto Rico, this version goes, Varela obtained a new set of false documents and continued on to Paraguay as a regular passenger aboard Chilean Airways.

The version that federal investigators suggest is more likely is that Padilla, Hernandez, Muravnik, and Varela stuck together after the break. They hid out for two days in New York City in an apartment arranged for by Padilla and Gonzalez and then, one by one, went to Miami on Trailways buses. The group stayed in Miami's sprawling Cuban community for more than a month waiting for false documents. Varela, investigators believe, flew from Miami aboard a Latin American airline after having been brought false documents by Uraguayan *contrabandistas*.

Whichever version of the escape story is true, U.S. Treasury agents were to learn for sure from an ironic source that Varela had returned to his native Paraguay. Like many wealthy Paraguayans, Varela sent his daughter to an expensive private "American" school in Asunción also favored by the families of senior

U.S. diplomats. Shortly after the law-enforcement agencies alerted the embassy that an escaped heroin smuggling suspect might turn up in Paraguay, an embassy attaché saw Varela at a coffeeklatch of the school's Parent-Teachers Association. Despite the numerous requests for cooperation, however, the Paraguayan Government has never officially acknowledged that Varela is in the country.

At first glance, the West Street jailbreak appeared to be a disaster for the men who had carefully put together the Bianchi smuggling conspiracy case. It had deprived the United States of the two most important figures arrested in October and put at large men who undoubtedly were in a position to send more loads of heroin to the streets of North America. Furthermore, it eliminated one opportunity to learn the origins of the heroin and the name of the buyer in the United States.

The atmosphere at the Customs narcotics squad headquarters at 201 Varick Street for some weeks after the break was one of despondency and anger. The agents had successfully made a difficult and complex case only to have the best of it snatched from them. But as January passed into February the men working the interrogations began to notice a subtle change in the attitudes of the suspects who had not escaped. It was as though some weight had been lifted from them, some concern removed. The agents could only guess at the reasons but it appeared as though Varela's escape meant two things to the remaining men: first, everyone was now apparently "on his own," as this was the only help the organization was planning to give, and second, with Varela gone also gone was the discipline of the organization.

It was on February 8, 1971, that the turning point in the case came. The day broke chill with little hint of what lay only hours ahead. Since Gahou had failed to cooperate, his case on narcotics conspiracy charges had been set for that day before District Court Judge John M. Cannella in a sterile, wood-paneled courtroom at the gray and grim Federal Court House in lower Manhattan. Cannella, a hulking former New York Giants professional football player and one of the most learned judges in the Southern District of New York, had experience in narcotics law dating back nearly thirty years to his own service as a prosecutor in that court.

When the French waiter stepped into the courtroom that day, he seemed at his lowest ebb. His money was all gone, eaten up by legal fees, and although he was willing to plead guilty he seemed confused and ambivalent about what his role actually would be. Until that day he had steadfastly refused to cooperate with the government agents. Indeed they had almost written him off.

The session did not go well. Gahou, through an interpreter, told the court that he would plead guilty but persisted in saying he thought what he was carrying was "aspirin" powder. Angered, Cannella told Gahou's lawyer that he had "never sentenced an innocent man in his twenty years on the bench" and suggested the lawyer take the defendant into the hall and "explain" the charge to him again. It was afternoon when Gahou finally pleaded guilty to heroin smuggling, and it was afternoon when he suddenly agreed to cooperate with Treasury agents.

He would tell them what they wanted to know if only they would help him get leniency. In a stuffy room in the court building, the Frenchman began to pour out the facts. His contact in New York he knew only as "Nick." He had a telephone number where he had reached this Nick on two occasions. While Gahou talked, agents hurried out to trace the number. It was registered to the Buenos Aires Realty Company. Further checking revealed that among the realty company's salesmen was a Nicholas Giannattasio, an Argentinian of Italian descent who was living in the United States on an alien's visa.

At the exact moment when Gahou was telling his story at the Federal Court House, Special Agent Bob Nunnery was at the wheel of a government car roaring out the parkway toward Kennedy International Airport. In the growing dusk of the winter evening his mind was entirely on Carla Pilar. It had been over three months ago that he had caught the fleeting glimpses of her and her mysterious companion and now, if everything went right, he might have a chance to talk to her. Earlier the same day Nunnery had received an alert from Lufthansa indicating that the ticket-holder Carla Pilar, about whom he had inquired, had boarded Lufthansa's Quito-to-New York flight. The flight was due at Kennedy at 6:30 P.M. Nervously, Nunnery eyed the growing traffic ahead. He was going to be late.

The weary-looking Immigration Service officer read the Ecuadorian passport with the studied indifference born of years behind the little booth. The only indication that he recognized the name Carla Pilar on a page of his Soundex alert was a tiny flickering of the left eyelid. By the pretty brunette across the counter the flicker went undetected.

Carefully following instructions, the inspector passed Carla through Immigration while sounding an alarm in the nearby Customs office with a touch of his knee. A few seconds after Carla stepped toward the Customs inspection line, a man in a neat business suit made an unobtrusive visit to the Immigration booth. "I've got a live one for you," the Immigration inspector whispered. "She's the girl in the traveling suit in that far line. Your lookout identifies her as Carla Pilar."

The plainclothes Customs man nodded and briskly walked across the room to the Customs chief inspector on duty.

"Slow line seven as long as you can and don't let a woman carrying a passport in the name of Carla Pilar through until you check with me. But try not to make her suspicious."

By ordering his inspectors to check virtually every inch of every suitcase or handbag coming through Customs that day, the arrivals chief delayed processing nearly forty-five minutes. Carla's bags were just being opened as Nunnery came puffing into the arrivals area.

It was the same girl, all right. Even though she had a new hairdo, Nunnery recognized her face and figure immediately.

"What do you want to do with her?" the plainclothes customs officer asked.

"Let's wait until she gets through the line. I want to question her and I've got a subpoena for a grand jury, but it will be just as easy to approach her quietly when she's in the terminal," Nunnery answered.

In 1970 the Kennedy Airport International Arrivals Building

was nicknamed the "fishbowl" because the main floor was surrounded by a glass-enclosed mezzanine where visitors, friends, and waiting travelers could watch passengers going through the Customs search. As the last lock clicked shut on her bag, Carla began searching the faces of the crowd around the windows above her. Suddenly with a happy little gesture she waved to someone behind the glass. Nunnery followed her gaze almost automatically. He froze. For a moment he felt as if his heart had stopped. Waving back from the window was the man he had seen with Gahou in front of the Brasserie restaurant.

Grabbing the other Customs officer, Nunnery pointed to the man on the balcony. "See that guy with the black hair who's waving? Get upstairs and stay with him. Don't let him out of your sight."

While Carla was gathering up her bags, Nunnery made a hurried call to 201 Varick Street. "Remember the suspect we saw meet Gahou that night in front of the Brasserie?" Nunnery reported to Seeley in hurried tones, "Well, he's here at the airport meeting the girl."

"Bust him," was Seeley's crisp reply. "He's been fingered by Gahou."

Eight minutes later in a dark portion of the airport's sprawling parking lot, Nunnery's nearly four-month quest came to an end. He stepped forward and holding open his leather identity case, said: "I'm a federal officer, and you're under arrest."

Though shaking with rage, Nick Giannattasio submitted quietly to arrest. Carla, fighting to keep back tears, accepted the summons to appear before the federal grand jury.

Through hours of questioning, the husky Giannattasio would only identify himself and say little else. He denied having any contact with heroin and denied knowing anyone by the name or description of Pierre Gahou. By carefully piecing together papers in his possession, however, agents were able to link him to figures in an earlier cocaine smuggling case and a major drug seizure made by the New York police in March, 1970. Even these revelations failed to shake the tough Italian. Giannattasio fell into complete silence after his arrest. He would only see his lawyer and his wife. When Carla made an attempt to visit him in prison he passed out the word: "I really don't want to see you any more."

Giannattasio's reticence notwithstanding, the Customs and Bureau of Narcotics and Dangerous Drugs agents knew they had made a major score. They could identify Giannattasio as the receiver of at least two of the loads that Bianchi had flown in and as probable receiver for at least two other smuggling missions by other teams. Though he was undoubtedly only one of the figures in the receiving group, he was a key contact man.

As important as the arrest of Giannattasio, however, was the fact that a dam had broken among the October suspects. Gahou's talking enabled agents to confront Becker and Bianchi with some apparent inconsistencies in their stories, and in the next five weeks a wholly different plot began to emerge. The smuggling attempt had not been the hit-or-miss occasional thing that its participants had first admitted to. It had been a carefully engineered conspiracy beginning early in 1970 that had seen wholesale amounts of French heroin move from the port of Montevideo over a tortuous route to Miami and New York.

Becker, Gahou, and Bianchi still tried to reduce their own roles in the affair. But they gave strong evidence of a clear-cut criminal conspiracy, and their independent stories checked out in most of the important details.

Gahou was further drawn into the role of an informant as the government's key witness against Giannattasio. Faced with Gahou's potential testimony, Giannattasio pleaded guilty, was sentenced to seven years in prison, and was sent to the federal penitentiary at Lewisburg, Pennsylvania. Gahou by that time was also at Lewisburg. "We found out about it and had to get Giannattasio transferred to Terre Haute, Indiana," Boulad recalled later, "but God it was close."

In March, 1971, a second federal grand jury in the Southern District of New York began to consider new testimony in the smuggling case. This time evidence solidly implicated a new figure in the case, an "André Ricord," also known as "Monsieur André." Though the first name on the indictment, "André," was not the suspect's real first name, the rest of the document was legal and lethal. Four years to the month after the Oscilloscope Case the U.S. Government had finally amassed enough evidence to seek the extradition of Auguste Joseph Ricord as a top, if not the topmost, leader of the Latin American narcotics-smuggling cartel.

# 8　Heroin Diplomacy

*The cardboard chart hanging in* Paul Boulad's office at 201 Varick Street was showing signs of wear. As big as a desk top, it had been tacked to the wooden frame of the blackboard, taken down, worked on, and put back until its upper edge bore endless staple scars the way a heroin addict's arms bear the tracks of too many needles.

Each time a new scar was added, so was critical new information. Boulad, weaver of patterns, evaluator of artifacts, used the policeman's eye and the scholar's patience as he penciled in names, dates, cases, relationships—the connections that reveal conspiracies.

At the end of a long case, when the grueling hours of surveillance were over, filling in the blanks was therapeutic. It was like a hobby that was related to work but pleasantly different from it. But Boulad always cautioned that to dwell too long on any one section of the chart was to look at the trees and "miss the forest primeval." The trees were all there—Oscilloscope, Grosby, TWA,

Luccarotti, Grand Central, Bonsignour, wine bottles, "Domingo," "Marcelo," and many more.

In July, 1970, six months after Boulad had started the chart, Customs agents held a briefing for agents of the Bureau of Narcotics and Dangerous Drugs. It was based on bits and pieces pulled together in more than forty months of probing into the smuggling of heroin. It was to have repercussions in the White House, the Department of State, the Central Intelligence Agency, and many embassies and chancelleries abroad.

Customs had the unenviable job of trying to pinch off the heroin flow at 294 international ports of entry and anywhere else a smuggler might choose to penetrate the country's 20,000 miles of coastlines and land borders. More than 220 million people and more than 60 million aircraft, ships, trucks, and autos move in and out of the United States in a single year. Each is a potential carrier of contraband.

The heroin always came from somewhere else—starting in "countries of origin," passing through "transit countries," ending up in what law-enforcement men called "victim countries," including the United States. The smugglers had representatives all along these routes, but Customs did not. Not only did it lack overseas narcotics agents; it was not even permitted to follow the flow of heroin past the borders and into the United States unless continuous surveillance of the contraband was maintained.

Partially offsetting this awesome task of watching open and seemingly limitless borders, the Customs men had certain equally awesome powers. The most important was the right to search virtually anyone and anything they saw moving across a borderline. More than one Customs inspector had offered an irate traveler Judge Learned Hand's observation that "the man stands naked seeking readmittance" when he journeys into another's country or returns to his own.

The Bureau of Narcotics, which could operate anywhere within the United States, could also send agents abroad. Its men did not have powers of arrest, but they could gather invaluable intelligence. This function was becoming more and more important— an addition to the "street-cleaner" role of making undercover buys from pushers and then trying to trace the heroin backward up the chain of distribution. As skirmishes escalate into wars the need for intelligence becomes more critical.

For too many years, Customs had been limited to the borders and the Narcotics Bureau had concentrated on the streets. No one had systematically pursued the rich, cleverly organized, and far-flung networks that brought the heroin problem to North American shores in the first place. But by 1970, with the help of some valuable information from Narcotics Bureau agents overseas and much more from talkative defendants in Miami and New York, the Customs narcotics intelligence unit had offset its lack of field men in Marseilles and Asunción. It was piecing the puzzle together without leaving home.

The essence of the mid-1970 briefing was a single sentence:

"South America has evolved as the principal hub of the international heroin traffic."

On the basis of this briefing, the Bureau of Narcotics established a systematized, computerized attack on the Latin American heroin-traffickers. A major part of the campaign, aimed at Auguste Joseph Ricord and the *contrabandistas*, was appropriately named "Operation Condor" after the great, bare-necked vulture found in the highest Andes. ("The name 'condor' evokes both the geography and air operations," a Bureau man said grandly.) Inevitably, Boulad's smudged and dog-eared piece of white cardboard acquired the nickname "Condor Chart."

Much of the intelligence that the two agencies swapped was specific and intimately detailed, down to physical descriptions, arrest records, favorite hangouts, and sexual peccadillos of suspected traffickers. But some of it was general enough to be revealed publicly, as Al Seeley and other Customs and Narcotics agents did before the hearing in New York of the U.S. House of Representatives Select Committee on Crime a few days before the Condor briefing.

The agents complained about bail-jumping, specifically mentioning Jack Grosby. ("We made whatever pleas we could to the court, telling them that because of a previous pattern of the South American couriers, we were afraid he would jump. However, nobody listened to us. They put him out on bail and he is now a fugitive.")

They disclosed new details about Grosby's TWA smuggling scheme, which had been even more profitable than they had first thought. ("There was $1 million a month going into a secret Swiss bank account and there was 100 kilos of heroin being smuggled into the United States in this manner each month.")

They complained bitterly about the lack of cooperation from other countries. The Fish Can and Paella cases, in which heroin was smuggled in commercial shipments of canned foods from Spain, had grown out of the Grosby investigation. Sixteen defendants had been arrested in Spain, France, Italy, and Switzerland on the basis of information supplied by the United States. Yet "to this day, we in the Customs Service have no idea of what happened to any of them as far as sentences, what happened to them in the courts," Seeley's partner testified. "We have no information from the foreign governments."

Seeley, boldly offering a correction to a Narcotics Bureau map of smuggling routes, even told the congressmen in general terms about the Latin connection.

"In the past couple of years, this solid line [showing the flow of heroin] is now running from the source of supply in Europe straight into South America and then being shot back up through the southern part of the United States and into the northeast quadrant . . . by an organization in South America, predominantly South Americans, who have established themselves with a source of supply in Europe. . . . The French have picked up a tremendous amount of customers here [in South America] that they are feeding this stuff to, who in turn are now shooting it in from South America."

Representative Claude Pepper, a Democrat from Florida, was the committee chairman. He cautiously asked Seeley: "Does any come in from Miami, Tampa?"

Seeley reached deep into his reserves of diplomacy and said simply: "I don't like to be a bearer of bad news—"

These and other disclosures, growing concern over the deaths of teen-age addicts in New York, and persistent rumors of heroin addiction among young American soldiers in South Vietnam were increasing public awareness of the heroin problem. Internal governmental pressures for action also were building rapidly.

Late in May, 1971, two months after Auguste Ricord's indictment by a federal grand jury in New York, the lid threatened to blow completely off the heroin issue. Two members of the House Foreign Affairs Committee published a report entitled "The World Heroin Problem," in which they estimated that "as many as 10 to 15 per cent of our servicemen (in South Vietnam) are addicted to heroin in one form or another." That meant literally thousands of young addicts who would bring their habits home with them.

It was a sensational charge, dropped into the midst of an already thunderous debate over why the United States did not end its participation in the Vietnam War. In many minds, the additional risk of heroin addiction by GIs was one more strong argument for bringing American troops home as soon as possible.

The report made one damaging accusation after another of "very little action" at home and very little cooperation abroad in the struggle against heroin. Its nineteen recommendations (beginning with "the President should take personal command . . .") skillfully pre-empted a number of initiatives that the Nixon Administration was planning to take but had not announced.

Since the report had been prepared by Representatives Morgan F. Murphy, an Illinois Democrat, and Robert H. Steele, a young Connecticut Republican, it was considered a bipartisan effort. Steele had served five years with the Central Intelligence Agency in Washington and Latin America. Both his CIA background and the fact that he was a Republican criticizing a Republican Administration tended to lend credibility and impact to the charges. But ironically, the report did not deal with Latin America—Murphy and Steele had toured only European, Middle Eastern, and Asian countries.

On June 17, 1971, culminating efforts that had begun long before the Murphy-Steele report, President Nixon again declared heroin addiction "Public Enemy No. 1" and told the Congress in a message requesting more drug-control funds:

America has the largest number of heroin addicts of any nation in the world. And yet, America does not grow opium—of which heroin is a derivative—nor does it manufacture heroin, which is a laboratory process carried out abroad. This deadly poison in the American lifestream is, in other words, a foreign import.

Three days earlier, the President had met with his ambassadors to all the countries that grew opium poppies, converted opium gum to morphine and morphine to heroin, or played major roles in the transshipment of heroin. He had called them home to impress upon them the seriousness of the situation and to order each of them to make heroin a daily, personal, and official concern. His "war" on heroin was assuming global proportions. Foreign visits by John E. Ingersoll, director of the Narcotics Bureau; Myles Ambrose, the Customs director; and even Attorney General John Mitchell and White House aide Egil Krogh had not brought about the desired results from other governments. They tended to treat heroin addiction as a wholly American problem.

"Because each country must be taken on its own," a White House aide explained, "the ambassadors must lead. In a sense, we are shifting our focus from police efforts to the ambassadors. It allows us to penetrate at the high levels of government and make the point that we are deadly serious about this heroin business.

"We are not saying to other countries, 'You have to do this.' It has been proposed that we boycott French goods unless they increase their cooperation on narcotics, for example. That is nonsense. We export $400 to $500 million more to France than we import. We cannot possibly drive a government to its knees."

Nevertheless, some countries would see the forthcoming diplomatic push as a kind of heroin imperialism, with the White House offering financial and technical aid to fight the growers and smugglers while the Congress threatened an end to financial aid and severe trade restrictions unless other countries cooperated. Particularly in areas where the working of the U.S. Government was not fully understood, this smacked of the carrot and the stick—which, in fact, it was.

In September, 1971, a newly created Cabinet Committee on International Narcotics Control held its first formal meeting at the White House. It was chaired by the Secretary of State and included the President's close friend and adviser, Attorney General

Mitchell; the secretaries of Defense, Treasury, and Agriculture; and the Director of the Central Intelligence Agency. The vast resources of the CIA had been added to the international anti-heroin effort, and it was not long before outsiders were suggesting that poppy fields would be fire-bombed and smugglers quietly hunted down and "terminated."

But that was not the approach. The Cabinet committee's mission was to serve as a strategy board for the international war on heroin-trafficking—and to hold the feet of U.S. ambassadors to the fire until they convinced heads of state that President Nixon was a determined commander-in-chief.

At least one ambassador—J. Raymond Ylitalo, the U.S. representative to Paraguay—would come to regret the President's zeal in this matter.

The diplomatic front was not the only one active in the summer of 1971. On June 8, Jacob Grodnitzky, alias Jack Grosby, appeared before the Federal Court for the Southern District of New York in Manhattan. On the same day, he also went before the Federal Court for the Eastern District in Brooklyn. Each placed him under $500,000-bond. Not even Grosby the bail-jumper was prepared to post another $1 million in cash.

Gentleman Jack Grosby had been missing from the United States since September 6, 1968, when he fled to Buenos Aires. Two years later, in August, 1970, he had been indicted *in absentia* for another narcotics violation in Brooklyn. This time, Swiss police had located him in Geneva, arrested him, and held him for extradition.

For a year, Grosby had sat in a Swiss jail before Customs Special Agent Al Seeley and Narcotics Bureau Special Agent Morti mer Benjamin went to Europe after him.

As so often happens when the stakes are high, a deal was made. The government would consolidate the two cases into one in the Southern District and Grosby would plead guilty to both. This would mean years in prison but not as many as if he put the government through the time and expense of conducting two full-fledged trials. In return, Grosby would talk.

Customs agents seldom disclose what information comes from

which informant. But before the end of the summer of 1971, with some help from Jack Grosby, they had collected a vast amount of knowledge on the operations of Auguste Joseph Ricord.

*Excerpt from a narcotics intelligence report of that period:*

[The Ricord group] does in fact represent the singularly most important heroin smuggling [organization] in existence. It is our evaluation that this organization has been directly responsible for smuggling the major portion of heroin into the United States for at least the last six to seven years.

In addition it is believed that most European heroin cases, both courier and bulk shipments, detected by the United States Customs and the Bureau of Narcotics and Dangerous Drugs since 1966, are directly attributable to this organization.

The report stated that these conclusions were well documented. It went on to identify the case of *contrabandista* pilot Cesar Bianchi and his codefendants as perhaps the most important in a decade. The Bianchi case had finally made possible the indictment of Ricord, further demonstrated the "magnitude of the French-Corsican operation," and produced an extremely important new development—clear insight into the intricate manipulations by which the ring moved its money through legal and illegal channels.

"The magnitude of this investigation is so great," the report concluded, "that it has become necessary to computerize the financial data in order to properly coordinate it."

Auguste Ricord remained in his Tacumbu Penitentiary cell in Asunción through the summer of 1971, but he did not languish. There was no loss of strength or vitality, no withering away. Posters of the French countryside, the Eiffel Tower, and Paris at night brightened the walls of his cell, alongside photographs of his niece and daughter and his own oil painting of a Marseilles street scene, done in jail.

The little Frenchman who had enjoyed the use of Paraguay's *contrabandista* system now enjoyed its right of refuge, and the Paraguayan courts seemed in no hurry to turn him over to the

Americans. His meals were brought in—from Le Paris-Niza—and his orders went out. The Ricord organization, still in the hands of trusted subordinates, continued to function.

Directly below Ricord in the chain of command were two men known to narcotics agents then only as "Jean-Paul" and "François." The public had not yet heard of them, even by nickname. In fact it did not hear of Auguste Ricord until *Newsweek* magazine wrote about him early in 1972.

French-Corsican heroin suppliers in France, including Ricord's old friend Joe Orsini, pushed a minimum consignment of 1,000 kilograms a year to Ricord's Latin organization—a whole metric ton. At the relatively modest price that the smugglers charged the receivers in New York, a thousand kilograms was worth $12 million. At the street level it would bring $220 million. But narcotics agents believed that the organization actually moved as much as two tons or more in its better years.

To handle this volume, Ricord needed lieutenants like Jean-Paul and François. Beneath them, the organization was divided into five subgroups, each responsible for one-fifth of the heroin and each headed by a French-Corsican. By mid-1971, four of the five group leaders and six of their ten main subordinates were known to U.S. agents at least by a nickname.

Whether Ricord was present or not, Jean-Paul and François spoke and acted with great authority over the five group leaders. It was Ricord's role to know men and recruit them, suggest methods and techniques, find safe places from which to operate, and provide the European ties of blood and criminality that would make "the firm" a success. He was an executive, and Jean-Paul and François were his special assistants.

Jean-Paul, only thirty in the summer of 1971, was fairly tall for a Corsican, a thin man with a thin face and dark, straight hair. The heavy bags under his eyes were put there by nature, but they added to his reputation as a swinger, a man who lived it up at the Carnival in Rio every year and frequented the gambling casinos in Argentina, Brazil, Paraguay, and Uruguay. The agents would learn much later that his real name was Jean-Paul Angeletti and that his criminal record was extensive.

François would have been recognized by Paris police as Francisco Chiappe, under sentence of death for two murders there. A burly six-footer who weighed 210 pounds, he towered over his diminutive boss, Ricord, and several of the others. He had been present at both of Jack Grosby's attempts to raise bail money for Felipe Spadaro/Louis Bonsignour and he had helped Grosby celebrate Grosby's own bail-jumping late in 1968.

Customs agents had never had a crack at Jean-Paul or François. It was likely that the two never handled heroin directly. But Al Seeley had arrested another key Ricord assistant in New York on March 21, 1968, for possession of false documents—without at the time realizing his importance. To the Ricord organization, this man was "Raniers," head of the first of the five subgroups. When Seeley arrested him, Raniers appeared to be Miguel dos Santos. It had a nice Spanish ring to it. At other times, he was known as Abraham Goldman. Whatever his real name, he jumped $50,000 bail and fled to Buenos Aires—where he would later warmly welcome Jack Grosby as a fellow fugitive.

A short forty-year-old, Raniers typified the headaches of chasing narcotics smugglers as far as Seeley's young assistant, Frankie, was concerned.

"It's fantastic," Frankie DeSantis said, chopping the air with both hands. "These people are not jerks. We've ripped off a thousand of their couriers and this group doesn't founder. It perseveres." (Raniers's only known assistant, Michel Russo, had in fact been arrested by Customs in Miami as a heroin courier but was now free. Born in Naples, he was one of the few Italians in the organization.)

"They change identities like we change shirts," Frankie said. "Take Raniers, who is Miguel dos Santos—we get six countries telling us he's six different people. Bust him, and he doesn't give you just a passport—he gives you documents *like this!*" DeSantis indicated a stack six inches high. "Driver's license, BankAmericard, the works. The people in junk—everybody knows about complexity, but the phony identification you wouldn't believe!" The techniques Ricord had learned from the wartime French Gestapo were indeed useful in the postwar world of crime. (Frankie would find Raniers/dos Santos/Goldman even harder to believe a year later when Brazilian police arrested him and discovered that his real name was Michel Nicole.)

Seeley had lectured his assistant many times on identification —how there were only two sure things, identity by someone who knows the suspect, or real documentary evidence—meaning photographs or fingerprints and not faked passports. For an example he always uses the Frenchman, headed out of the country with $287,000, who dropped the bag of cash and ran when a Customs inspector challenged his passport.

"Now we know he's a phony, but we have his photo," Seeley says. "He can come back in as Hairbreadth Harry or Tom Mix or Hoot Gibson and no matter what his name is, we've got him. He can change his name but he can't change his photo or his prints . . ."

Despite all the intelligence they had gathered, the Customs men knew virtually nothing in mid-1971 about the second subgroup—only that it was headed by "Marcelo." Informants had said that Marcelo was a tall young Corsican with straight, dark brown hair, a light complexion, and "striking, beautiful green eyes." He was a neat dresser, possessed the mind of a businessman, and was a close friend of Raniers, but the striking green eyes kept their own council.

The third group was headed by "Jean-Pierre"—in reality the short, stocky Corsican whose genuine name was Christian David. Auguste Ricord's bodyguard, he always carried a pistol and was believed to have stepped into the leadership of the group after Ricord's nephew Spadaro/Bousignour was jailed in France.

Jean-Pierre, like Raniers, had many aliases. For a long time his true identity was unknown. And like Jean-Paul, he was a gambler who loved the casinos in Buenos Aires, Asunción, Rio, and Montevideo. He was also a talker, who once disclosed to Grosby that the smugglers had been forced to switch to a pay-on-delivery system because some New York receivers had been too slow at coming up with the cash.

It was Jean-Pierre who bragged that in 1969 the organization had moved 1,000 kilograms of heroin into the United States all in one massive load. The heroin had been concealed in bags of money, placed in an armored truck, driven from Mexico to Houston, Texas, and warehoused there until it could be distributed to customers in Los Angeles, Chicago, Cleveland, and New York. Maybe Jean-Pierre was a liar as well as a talker. But he was Ricord's trusted bodyguard, and he might know. Stranger things had happened—heroin had been hidden in ski poles, picture frames, tigers' heads, crucifixes, and even the dead bodies of soldiers being returned for burial.

Jean-Pierre, like Raniers, would end up talking to Brazilian police—but only after the most hideous of tortures.

Like the other group leaders, Jean-Pierre had two main deputies. One was William Perrin, a pasty-faced man who was always at his side and spoke only French. The other was known only as "Michel," the quiet, white-faced man with the toupée badly covering his straight, dark hair who had been at the "board of directors" meeting when Jack Grosby finally raised Spadaro/Bonsignour's bail.

The chieftain of the fourth subgroup went by the nickname "Raymundo." Once Al Seeley heard his description—French-Corsican, about forty, five feet ten, dark hair, light complexion, blue eyes—he recognized Raymundo immediately as Mario Deniz, whom he had once investigated in New York. Deniz had been photographed by police in Switzerland and had been seen both in New York and at a racetrack in France by a Customs informant. Much later, Raymundo was to escape American justice by suffering a far harsher justice imposed by his own fellow criminals.

Raymundo's subordinates were Joannas ("Peluquitas," or "Wigsy") Muñoz, who had been on the same plane with Ange Luccarotti as a monitor in 1967, and René Santamaria, who had been arrested on a narcotics conspiracy charge by Seeley in New York in May, 1968. Charges against Santamaria had been dismissed. But he was a man whose name kept popping up in many cases and, like several others, he had had the address of Ricord's Bar el Sol, at 380 Marconi Street in a Buenos Aires suburb, with him when he was caught.

"Wigsy" Muñoz, true to the form of the high-rolling traffickers, was a world traveler. While Grosby was still free in Geneva, a "customer" had entrusted him with $40,000, which he was to hand over to Muñoz in the bar of the Grand Hotel in Paris.

Grosby obliged and was rewarded by Muñoz's story of a fellow trafficker who found his wife in bed with another man. The trafficker became so infuriated that he compelled his wife to become a prostitute and the trafficker became her procurer.

"Domingo," the heavy-set man with dark, unruly hair who headed the fifth smuggling group, had the distinction of being the only "official" actually born on the island of Corsica. His real name was Dominique Orsini. A cigar always jutted from his full, round face. He had an Argentine wife and two small children, and he was connected with the shipping of cocaine from Bolivia and Chile. Domingo worked closely with Raymundo, the leader of the fourth group, whereas Raniers, Marcelo, and Jean-Pierre were just as closely associated.

Domingo had been seen at the New York Hilton with the lawyer in whose Buenos Aires office the matter of Spadaro/Bonsignour's bail had been discussed. He had also been seen with other French and Latin traffickers in La Totarina Restaurant in New York—proving once again that smugglers had little fear of visiting the very city where they were most wanted by police, the heroin capital of the world.

The only known subordinate of Domingo was an Argentine—a rarity in the upper and middle ranks of the Corsican-dominated organization. To the best of Customs' ability to determine his real name, it was Luis Calabrese-Carignano—or "Luis the Argentine" of the Oscilloscope Case.

As the agents had come to understand much more about Ricord's organization, they had also come to know why the South American climate let it flourish.

Paraguay—small, poor, surrounded by the hungry consumer appetites of Argentina, Brazil, and Uruguay—simply chose the most logical way to compete with its neighbors. It welcomed the flying *contrabandistas* of the 'fifties and 'sixties and 'seventies, and it also welcomed, when he needed refuge, the super-smuggler Auguste Ricord. A declining demand for the most profitable contraband commodities, whisky and cigarettes, undoubtedly helped create the official willingness to let hard narcotics trickle in behind the marijuana that already flowed through the contraband channels. After all, the cocaine and heroin were only passing through. There was even a certain David-and-Goliath satisfaction in seeing the North American giant so agitated about a crisis that was caused as much by its own affluence and social upheaval as by the smugglers who fed the addicts' appetites.

It was easy for a North American columnist like Jack Anderson to accuse virtually every official in Paraguay with involvement in the narcotics trade. But it was not so easy to prove. "Paraguay is a warehousing point, a safe haven," a State Department official said. "It is a practically uninhabited country—two and a half million people, all bunched around Asunción. The Chaco Boreal is two-thirds of the land area but only 100,000 people live out there, and it is dotted with landing fields. Who would be there to control it?

"You hear all about General Colman's *estancia* and General Rodriguez's control of the Hernandarias airstrip, but where is the hard evidence? All you can do is draw a circle around the top of the government and say, 'Someone in there knows a lot about narcotics.' "

U.S. intelligence agents had learned by now that Ricord's organization was primarily a "transporting company" but that it also provided "services," including bribery. Bulk heroin that once moved slowly by sea from Europe to Buenos Aires or Montevideo now often came by air, boldly carried in suitcases through customs checks at Rio and again at Buenos Aires by high-ranking "family" members who once would not have run such a risk.

"The only conclusion you can draw is that they had things so well greased they were not afraid," a Bureau of Narcotics official said. "We are finding now that there are people in the organization who do nothing but bribe—keep certain officials on the hook. It is a rather new revelation. It has led us to a new respect for their sophistication."

Discoveries like these helped explain the glacial pace with which some governments moved in their "cooperative" efforts to stamp out the heroin trade.

"Talking about bribery raises nationalistic hackles," the intelligence official said. "But it is a fact, without being an accusation or a moral judgment, that there is bribery that facilitates the movement of heroin in virtually every country of Latin America. And this organization utilizes virtually every country."

Some men offered *mordida*. Other specialists provided only authentic-looking documentation. Still others did nothing but transport money and documents—bring bail-jumpers new identities and travel fare home, for example. Others, including some former Swiss bankers, specialized in the "legal" movement of millions of dollars in illegal profits.

"Money movement is very important," Seeley says. "They take it out in suitcases, in women's girdles—all the same ways that they smuggle the junk in. One million dollars will go into the linings of two Samsonite suitcases," he says accusingly (as if the suitcase manufacturer had planned it that way) "and $10,000 in one-hundreds is only a quarter-inch thick.

"They use foreign money exchanges, where it's harder to trace. They'll have an account with a foreign money exchange and move the money out to it through a bank with a foreign-accounts division. It goes through two or three channels before it gets to the ultimate receiver. And the money always goes overseas even if it's meant for somebody here in the States. Finding out who the receiver is is very difficult."

The narcotics intelligence men, who admitted that they had been case oriented for far too long, were now learning what they called "the dynamics of smuggling." As they began to add up all the "mules" (couriers), idea men, bribers, document specialists, controllers, bodyguards, bankers, and executives, they were amazed.

"It is much, much bigger than the Ricord organization as it was originally thought to be," one intelligence official said. "It's very frightening. If there's more than one this size, we're in trouble.

"We were thinking in terms of maybe twenty people. But now we've got it up in terms of more than a hundred. That's a guess—not a head count, much less a body count." The total included couriers, who stayed active until they got caught, got too hot, got scared, or got enough money to get out.

One surprising discovery that narcotics agents were reluctant to believe for some time was the intermixture of French-Corsicans, Italians, Spanish-speaking Latins, and a scattering of Chinese making up the South American smuggling picture. "Where these ethnic groups don't mix too well in Europe," an official said, "they seem to amalgamate a little more effectively in Latin America." It was not the simple old Corsican-to-Corsican relationship any longer.

The earlier thinking on heroin-smuggling rings had been: "If the cultural pattern of Corsicans is a close family relationship, the cultural pattern of Corsican criminals is an even closer one." Now heroin had truly gone international; Corsicans were still the key, but their control could not be as tight as it was before.

As the Latin tapestry unfolded, four amazingly intricate smuggling patterns were discerned. Each was complex enough to add considerably to overhead costs, but each had been successful enough to keep being used.

At first, the French-Corsicans had recruited pimps, pickpockets, and other minor figures from the Latin underworld, sent them to France and Spain to pick up "body carries," and then had them flown directly from Europe into Canada or the United States.

Then, as the Marseilles heroin masters forged tighter links with the Latin cocaine chiefs, Latin couriers began taking cocaine to Europe, swapping it for heroin, and taking the heroin direct from Europe into the United States.

As a variation, Latin couriers also began taking small amounts of heroin from Buenos Aires back to Europe and catching planes from there to the North American gateways. It was as if they thought the farther heroin traveled, the less likely it was to be seized.

The most common pattern of all, however, had become the Latin connection: Move heroin South from Europe by ship or plane, concealed in suitcases, cargo, or automobiles, to Buenos Aires and Montevideo and Asunción. Then ship it north by every method conceivable, including false-bottomed wine bottles and *contrabandistas'* planes.

Added to the other complications of understanding modern smuggling patterns was a growing realization that groups such as Ricord's were not rigid but flexible. The organization chart was not as fixed as that of an army or a government or a corporation. Groups cooperated while it was to their benefit. But neophytes became sophisticates and moved up or branched out on their own; gang warfare resulted when tensions ran too high. Loyal lieutenants, or sometimes greedy, ambitious outsiders, stood ready to take advantage of a Grosby or a Ricord who stayed too long in jail. The dynamics of once fairly static smuggling rings meant that it would take more than the arrests of a Bianchi and a Varela and a Ricord to bring down the heroin house of cards.

As the computers of Operation Condor began to sift the data on the complicated marriage between the heroin- and cocaine-smuggling cartels and the *contrabandista* system, federal agents discovered what pilots like Cesar Bianchi had known for years: The pivot point for the flow of smuggled goods North or South was the strategic Republic of Panama. Both navigationally and politically, the country that surrounds the U.S. Panama Canal Zone had for two decades or more been hospitable to the tough pilots and tiny planes of the *contrabandistas*.

Furthermore, intelligence agents for the Narcotics Bureau soon discovered, the pivot point within Panama was a forty-two-year-old Chinese-Panamanian named Joaquim Him Gonzales—nicknamed "Chino." The slight Panamanian with the Oriental features was, as one federal intelligence agent put it, "the man everybody had to know in Panama." As Chief of Air Traffic Control and Deputy Inspector General of Civil Aviation, he was Panama's equivalent of the number-two man in the U.S. Federal Aviation Administration. He had in fact been trained by the FAA.

No plane legally entered or left the busy Tecumen International Airport or other subsidiary airports in the country without Him's stamp of approval. And, as the *contrabandistas* knew, Him's stamp came high. Chino had a well-known flair for the gambling tables, and except for caring for his ten-year-old after his separation from his wife in the 1960s, he had few personal responsibilities to slow him down. Him's "extracurricular" air traffic routing had begun in the days when the bulk of the smuggling had gone from North to South; in the days when 20,000 pairs of Levi trousers bought for $4 in the United States could be flown to Paraguay and smuggled into nearby countries for sale at $12 a pair.

The *contrabandista* who did not work through Him or who did not have an arrangement with a large Panamanian trading company with offices in New York and Panama City might find his aircraft searched, seized, or seriously delayed. At the very least, he might discover at his next landing in South America that someone had tipped off the local customs authorities.

When the *contrabandista* system expanded into carrying drugs in the late 1960s, Him understandably followed the trend. He became known as a traffic manager for the busy heroin and cocaine schedules, a man who could put a buyer in touch with a seller. It was clear to top narcotics agents that Him's "removal" would seriously crimp if not halt the transshipment of coke and horse. Though they knew his switchplate activities had support from Panamanian officials even within the President's Palace, they also knew that it was a business he carried in his head and that his disappearance would be a hefty blow at the trade.

By the spring of 1970, Him was an important target for Operation Condor. What no one knew at that time was that Him's case would trigger a major diplomatic storm that would still be raging when Auguste Joseph Ricord was jailed in Paraguay—one that would intimately affect the treatment of Ricord. Him was no easy case. He was a prominent official of a friendly government, and he had never committed a crime within the United States. He seemed to all intents and purposes to be invulnerable to U.S. law-enforcement officers.

But while Him was pursuing his pivotal work in Panama and Bianchi was making his first drug flights from Paraguay, a thirty-nine-year-old former federal convict was beginning an undercover assignment for the U.S. Government that would affect both men. Ronald David Watkins, a wiry and articulate private pilot and owner of a Dallas aircraft equipment firm, had once served time for fraud. For nearly a decade he had been out of prison and developing a profitable business selling liquid-nitrogen air-conditioners for airplanes.

His work kept him in close touch with the private and small commercial air-transport industry in the Dallas and East Texas area, and his prison record gave him an entrée to the strange world of airborne smuggling that was actively pursued along the U.S.–Mexican border. Watkins later told Dallas *Morning News* reporter Earl Golz that he learned that many of the airborne smugglers "had three ports of entry to fly narcotics from South America." The primary one, he said, was Brownsville, Texas, a tough little flatlands city a few miles north of the Mexican border.

"They had two alternatives at Brownsville. They would hide it on the plane and hope Customs agents wouldn't find it, or they would first fly from Panama City to an isolated landing strip just over the border in Mexico. They would unload the stuff there, then go on to Customs at Brownsville for clearance. They would then circle back over the border, pick up the narcotics at the landing strip, and fly low returning to this country. The next stop would be Denton, where the pilot carrying the narcotics would not have to worry about Customs," Watkins said.

One principal figure in this smuggling system seemed to be a forty-eight-year-old former World War II Air Corps pilot named Robert Louis Robertson III. Robertson was a mysterious man. He was president of the Robertson Aircraft Company of Dallas and had been an executive of a major international airline for eleven years. But there were many in Dallas who suggested that Robertson may have been something more—an operative for the Central Intelligence Agency. This was never established. But in Dallas aviation circles, it was observed that Robertson and the two or three companies he had formed in recent years flew some strange trips into Latin America.

It was Robertson's alleged smuggling operation that Watkins was asked to infiltrate. The case had mysterious overtones from the beginning. Watkins, for instance, was able to enter Robertson's employ only after one of the Texan's pilots had died in an airport motel on June 20, 1970, leaving a suitcase filled with twenty-three and one-half pounds of cocaine. The death of the pilot, Hobart Higgins, has never been fully explained.

Watkins gained Robertson's confidence by posing as a tough underworld figure with Mafia connections in the East and in Chicago. Over the summer of 1970 he was to introduce Robertson and another defendant, a forty-one-year-old man known as J. D. Vicars, of Hurst, Texas, to a string of tough-appearing men he identified as Mafia figures. They were in fact agents of the Bureau of Narcotics and Dangerous Drugs. The "Mafia" men told Robertson and Vicars they were prepared to purchase large amounts of cocaine; Robertson promised them he could supply 200 milligrams each month for $200,000. At one point the federal agents showed the smugglers a quarter of a million dollars in U.S. taxpayers' money as a "flash roll" to prove that they were ready to deal.

On December 2, 1970, Robertson flew to Panama City with a narcotics agent he believed to be a Mafia bigwig. In reality the man was a special agent named Victor Maria. Within hours after landing, Robertson, Watkins, and Maria made contact with a man Robertson described as his connection in Panama—the Narcotics Bureau's target, Joaquim Him Gonzales.

Him was instantly wary of the set-up. Though he was later to admit that he had "witnessed" Robertson's receipt of three suitcases of cocaine, each weighing twenty-three and one-half pounds, in an earlier transaction, he claimed that on the December 2 meeting he did not help the Texan and his two friends obtain narcotics.

Nevertheless, thirty days later the U.S. Government felt it had a case. Under pressure, they knew, Robertson would admit his part in the case because Watkins would testify that he had obtained cocaine from the mysterious Texan. Furthermore, despite the fact that Gonzales would later deny it, the U.S. Attorney's office had the testimony of Robertson and two agents that Gonzales had promised them one hundred kilos of cocaine in that Panama City hotel room on December 2 and that he indeed did come up with a "sample" of the narcotic. It was enough for a Dallas federal grand jury, which handed up a conspiracy indictment in mid-January.

To have such an indictment naming a top official of the Panamanian Government wasn't really having very much. First it developed that Panama did not have a conspiracy law and was less than willing to extradite a well-known citizen on some strange North American charge. Though the crime had taken place on Panamanian soil, it was also clear to U.S. narcotics agents and State Department officials that Panama was unlikely to arrest and try Joaquim Him there.

A daring plot was then developed that some in the U.S. Government would like to forget and others point to with pride. Joaquim Him Gonzales was among other things an avid softball player. His

time in the United States as an FAA student had left him with a
good throwing arm and a deep affection for the game. He particularly liked to arrange games between Panamanian aviation employees and FAA officials stationed in the Canal Zone, that strip
of U.S. territory along the Canal that so rankles the people of
Panama. The strip is virtually U.S. soil. It is administered solely
by the American Government, from governor down to the police.
The Panamanian Government has no authority within its bound-
aries, where U.S. military garrisons serve to remind the small
country how powerless it really is.

On Saturday, February 6, Him had arranged a softball game
with his U.S. counterparts. It was warm, of course, but not the
heavy tropical swelter, and Him was looking forward to a fast-
moving game. He drove into the zone as he always did, a baseball
cap jauntily perched on his head and his favorite glove and bat
on the seat beside him. He was just closing the door to his car
when he heard the steely voice: "Joaquim Him Gonzales, you are
on United States territory and we are putting you under arrest on
a charge of conspiring to smuggle narcotics."

Him's rapid Spanish and facial expression revealed the anger,
fear, and confusion that flooded over him. They could not do this
to him. Not more than a few yards from the country of his birth.

The resulting diplomatic explosion tore an enormous gash in
U.S.–Panamanian relations. The government-controlled press of
Panama began a violent anti–North American campaign, charging
that U.S. pirates had literally kidnapped a prominent citizen. The
Republic's foreign ministry fired off a sharp and angry note to the
State Department protesting both the arrest and the fact that two
U.S. agents had been allowed to come to Panama and pose as
cocaine purchasers.

Coming in the spring of 1971, the diplomatic fire-fight had more
serious repercussions than immediately met the eye. There were
those within the State Department and the executive branch who
believed that the narcotics war was at best an unwanted adjunct
to the main business of government—and that the acts of policemen should by no means be allowed to interfere with larger national interests. Since the renegotiation of the Panama Canal
Treaty (the document that spells out U.S. control) was under

way, these veteran diplomats pointed out that a relatively minor arrest might now jeopardize a far more important international effort.

The lawmen, of course, were not helpless. Through Jack Anderson's news column friends, and on Capitol Hill, they worked to stave off attempts to limit their activities drastically. But it was clear to even the most hard-nosed narcs that their methods in the future had to be a little more subtle.

When the Ricord arrest in Paraguay came less than two months later, it was the lessons of the Panama experience that guided American hands. Quietly the lawmen were coming to work with, and better respect, some of the State Department's cookie-pushers. Crediting their support, one top agent admitted later: "The State Department has had to put up with some fairly kinky activities from us."

Him had been quietly whisked out of the Canal Zone to the United States by air. In mid-April of 1971, he went on trial in the Federal Court in Dallas, along with Robertson and Vicars. It was a strange trial. One by one, the agents who had posed as Mafia leaders took the stand and wove their case. But strangest of all seemed to be the effect of the trial on Robertson.

On Friday, April 23, the husky former pilot broke down on the witness stand and stormed from his seat screaming, "I can't tell the truth under these conditions." Federal Judge Sarah T. Hughes was not impressed. "No! You get back on the stand," she told him, "you are just putting on a show for the jury. Now you collect yourself and get back up here on the stand." She later ordered Robertson to undergo a psychiatric examination, which found him competent to stand trial.

The following Monday Robertson appeared even more irrational, muttering over and over again, "I am Judge Sarah T. Hughes . . . I am John F. Kennedy. I was assassinated in Dallas, Judge Sarah T. Hughes, on November 23, 1963 . . . I am a sinner, I am a sinner."

Despite the outbursts, the jury found the trio—Robertson, Him-Gonzalez, and Vicars—guilty two days later. Him was later sentenced to two five-year terms, running concurrently, for his part in the plot. "I beg you, Your Honor," he pleaded on the day he was sentenced, "back in Panama, a ten-year-old girl waits for her father." His voice broke at this point, "And she still doesn't know where I am."

Robertson was never sentenced. Four days after he was convicted, he died in his cell at the Dallas County jail. His death, as his life had been, was mysterious. A deputy marshal gave sworn testimony that on April 26 the pilot had told him, "I will be dead in five days." Robertson was pronounced dead on arrival at Parkland Memorial Hospital of pulmonary embolism on May 2. His prediction of death had been wrong by one day.

The fact that Joaquim Him had ultimately been convicted by no means sheltered the narcotics agents from the growing storm of criticism in Washington. Ricord's arrest, even though the lawmen had restrained themselves from trying to snatch him away from the Paraguayan Government, had served to heat up the debate once again. Like so many of the capital's most vicious battles, the issues were argued out behind closed doors of meeting rooms, through newspaper leaks, and in the restaurants and cocktail lounges of the city on the Potomac. As in many such battles, the opposing sides were never clearly drawn.

In the simplest form, this was what was happening: The White House, ever mindful of the President's political future, was pressing forward on a number of drug fronts. The law-enforcement agencies, Customs and the Bureau of Narcotics, had accepted this as a mandate for action and believed that the United States should ignore some international niceties in order to smash the Latin drug rings. At the same time, of course, the two agencies feuded between themselves on what methods were best and who should carry them out.

The Narcotics Bureau's director, Jack Ingersoll, the husky former Charlotte, North Carolina, police chief, bit his pipe stem and decided to take the direct approach. He went around Washington briefing key Capitol Hill and executive branch leaders on what he felt was the controlling issue in South America: Two countries were largely responsible for much of the narcotics traffic, and their governments were corrupt to the highest levels. Even though he presented his intelligence reports and evidence in private, the names and allegations continually leaked into the press.

The result was badly strained relations with both Panama and Paraguay, though the Panama situation was by far the worse.

The lawmen continually pressed the point of view that the support these two Latin governments gave the *contrabandistas* and the narcotics cartels was by no means accidental or insignificant. Indeed, the federal agents charged that these two governments were routinely supplying the smugglers with passports and safe havens, and extending them the safety of their diplomatic immunity in countries throughout the world. The critics at the Department of State and in other parts of the executive branch were skeptical. They would accept the idea that a few low-level officials might be corrupt and might give individual support to the *contrabandistas*. They would not accept the idea that this might literally be national policy.

In early July, 1971, an incident in New York's John F. Kennedy International Airport was to remove much of this doubt.

On July 8, Braniff's flight 906 from Panama City touched down a few seconds after 7 P.M., almost exactly according to the airline's advertised schedule. Among the passengers who deplaned was a pale, anemic-looking young Panamanian named Rafael Gonzalez Richard. At twenty-four, Richard was a product of Panama's upper classes. His father was Panama's Ambassador to the Chinese Nationalist Government in Taiwan, and his uncle Guillermo Gonzalez was a *compadre* and long-time business associate of the Panamanian Ambassador to Spain, one of the country's most important diplomatic posts. His uncle also had top contacts within Panama's National Guard, which was both the country's military force and its police agency. The young man was married to the attractive daughter of an American Army colonel who had been stationed in the Canal Zone. He and his wife lived a soft and comfortable life of advantage.

Richard was ticketed through from Panama City to Madrid. But instead of moving through the international traveler's "in transit" room, he ended up in the Customs line as though he planned to deplane at New York. Furthermore, his four Samsonite suitcases and attaché case were all tagged "JFK" instead of being marked for through-shipment to Madrid.

A few steps ahead of Richard was another Panamanian, Nicholas Polanco, thirty. If Richard appeared pale and aristocratic, Polanco was a marked contrast. Swarthy, tough-featured, and husky, Polanco appeared to be what he was—a former Panamanian secret police officer.

Polanco was processed through Customs and Immigration quickly and without halt and left the arrivals area. Behind him, Richard seemed more and more nervous. Though he claimed the five bags for which he had baggage checks, he seemed unsure which ones were his. He presented the Customs inspector a diplomatic passport, which normally would have excluded him from baggage search, but something about it caught the inspector's eye. Though it was indeed a Panamanian diplomatic passport, the visa for the United States was of the type issued to regular travelers and did not entitle Richard to any diplomatic protections at the border. The Customs man said he wanted to inspect the luggage.

"I don't have any keys," Richard said lamely. "We do," the inspector assured him as he drew forth a huge set of standard luggage keys.

Inside the luggage the customs men found 156 pounds of heroin in plastic bags—"nothing else, no shorts, no bathing suit, no anything." Richard appeared nearly in tears as other passengers craned their heads to see what was happening. "I think you'd better step in here," the Customs man said gently, motioning to a small office off the inspections area.

There, Richard broke down and immediately agreed to cooperate. Terror and tears made his face seem even more pale and puffy than it had when he had landed. He had been sent on this mission, he said, by his uncle Guillermo. It was, he admitted, not the first trip of this kind he had made. He knew he was being watched by a "shotgun" and that even at this moment the chaperon might be informing Panama that he had been apprehended.

The Customs men from 201 Varick Street, many of the same team that had worked on the Bianchi case six months before, immediately went into action. Since Richard had no idea of where his "shotgun" was going in New York or even what he looked like, the Customs men knew they had only one chance to snare the man before he could report that Richard had been caught.

They even suspected, though, that the "shotgun" might have missed the arrest, since most of the passengers had been processed through by the time Richard was pulled out of the line.

Agents called the security office of New York Bell telephone office and asked that they be notified of the source of any overseas calls to Panama City. At the same time, other agents took Richard to the McAlpin Hotel at Thirty-second Street and Broadway, a favorite hangout of Latin American visitors and the place where Richard said he had been told to register. With agents at his elbow, he booked into a room.

Less than three hours after the Braniff plane had touched down, an overseas telephone operator reported that she was at that moment processing a call to Panama City from a phone booth at Forty-second Street and Eighth Avenue. "Hold him on the line as long as you can" an agent pleaded. Before it was over, the resourceful woman operator had kept the caller on the line for forty minutes with skillful small talk and not a little flirting.

"I took him right out of the phone booth," the customs agent who arrested him recalled. "It was a hot night and he'd been trying to get his call through for nearly an hour, so he's standing sort of half in and half out of the booth trying to keep cool, with change lying all over the place."

The man was Nicholas Polanco. Unlike Richard, Polanco was not enormously perturbed by his arrest. "The first thing he did was fall asleep on us," one interrogator said. But Polanco finally agreed to call his contact in Panama City, "Uncle" Guillermo Gonzalez, and pretend that the load had arrived safely.

It was only a few moments after Polanco had completed his call that the telephone rang in Richard's room at the McAlpin. It was Gonzalez. "I'll be in New York about 10 A.M.," he told his nephew. Richard was so frightened he could hardly control his voice to answer. "The kid never slept," recalled one of the agents assigned to guard him. "He was ready to jump out of the window."

The next morning, Gonzalez arrived from Panama City shortly after 7 A.M. Under surveillance by Customs agents, he went directly to the McAlpin. Richard was alone in his room, his guards now listening from adjoining rooms. They had told him that if he could not go on or if he felt his uncle was becoming suspicious, he should try to slip the name of his wife, Marilyn, into the conversation.

"Pretty soon after Gonzalez arrived the kid is practically yelling 'Marilyn,' 'Marilyn,' " one agent remembered. The agents held off long enough to allow Gonzalez to contact someone by telephone, then broke in and arrested him.

Using the 156 pounds as bait, and with the cooperation of Richard and his uncle, the Customs men were able to nab one of the receivers of the heroin load literally within twenty-four hours of its entering the country. It was, of course, an outstandingly successful and well-publicized case. What was not well publicized, though far more important, was what it had revealed to critics within the American Government about Panama.

Richard had not obtained his passport by being the son of a diplomat. His father, in fact, was in Taiwan and had no knowledge that he was making those trips. He was deeply shocked. Furthermore, Richard was too old to continue to share his father's status and should not even have had a diplomatic passport. Yet the passport was genuine and had been issued in his name in Panama City.

Richard, his uncle, and his father, as well as intelligence data from Panama, indicated that the passport had been obtained through the good offices of the Ambassador to Spain and the top official of the National Guard and had been given to Richard for the express purpose of smuggling. Panama made no diplomatic protest after Richard's arrest and fell strangely silent about the earlier arrest of Him.

Equally important, federal intelligence agents later traced the route of the 156 pounds of heroin. It had come from France via the system and apparatus of Auguste Joseph Ricord.

At a White House reception soon after Richard Nixon took office, his old friend and fellow Republican Senator Karl Mundt observed that the United States did not have a single ambassador who was from Mundt's home state of South Dakota.

J. Raymond Ylitalo had been an FBI man at the time of World War II and had since become a good consular officer. One of the difficult jobs that he had done well was to operate the State Department's visa section. Ylitalo also happened to be from South Dakota.

Career foreign service officers at the State Department, hoping for ambassadorships themselves, deplore the White House practice of frequently selecting ambassadors from among men who have made large political contributions or have political influence. But it is a fact of life. The question became, where could the new Ambassador Ylitalo be assigned that there would be no real diplomatic hot potatoes to handle. The answer came up Paraguay.

"He did very well there and everybody was happy until the drug thing blew up," a State Department official said. "I gather he was just unable to handle the situation. He was a very nice guy, but the Ricord problem called for someone to go in there and pound the desk with President Stroessner. Ray never did."

In fairness to Ylitalo, it would have taken the patience of a saint and the firmness of a field general to stir much action in the matter of Auguste Joseph Ricord. As far as the lawmen were concerned, the real opportunity had been missed on March 26, 1971, the day after his arrest, when the indecision of the Americans and caution on the part of the Paraguayans had let the C-141 jet transport leave Asunción without Ricord aboard.

When that had failed, Customs Agent Paul Boulad and Narcotics Agent Anthony Pohl had flown to Asunción to try again to bring about the "rapid, informal transfer" that seemed so necessary to the law enforcement men. But Ylitalo had declined to push for an immediate audience with President Stroessner for fear that it would give Stroessner an opening to request an increase in Paraguay's sugar import quota to the United States.

Ylitalo finally saw Stroessner on the morning of April 2 but was firmly told that Ricord would not be transferred to U.S. custody without extradition. The next day, he sent the Paraguayan government a note requesting Ricord's provisional arrest under a 1913 extradition treaty between the two countries. Frustrated and disappointed, Boulad and Pohl flew home.

It was not until April 29 that Judge Luis Alberto Bedoya of the

Court of First Instance issued the formal arrest order. Although Ricord remained in his Tacumbu cell during this maneuvering, the momentum of the initial quick arrest and the early attempts at a police-to-police transfer had been lost.

Late in May, two months after the incident at the Itá Enramada ferry, Ambassador Ylitalo finally sent President Stroessner a first-person note formally requesting Ricord's extradition. A week later, the long court proceedings began, and Auguste Ricord made his first appearance before a judge.

Justice, if that is what it was, was in no hurry. Not until late November did Solicitor General Rodney Elpidio Accvedo finish reading the case file and issue an opinion: Ricord should be sent to the United States.

On New Year's Eve of 1971, however, the pendulum again swung for Ricord. Judge Bedoya of the Court of First Instance rejected the Solicitor General's opinion and ruled against extradition.

In New York, Boulad was crestfallen. Nine months had passed, and each time it seemed that Ricord was almost in hand the situation reversed itself. "Ricord has got too many people dirty," Boulad told the authors in New York on January 5, 1972. "I feel he is effectively out of jail now. I don't think Auguste is coming back."

Some of his pessimism was warranted, but Ricord was not yet free. Five days later his bail was set at 40 million *guaranis*, or $317,000—the highest in Paraguayan judicial history. A month later, the Court of Appeals denied a Ricord motion to reduce the bail to $40,000. Ricord made no attempt to raise the $317,000; it seemed much safer to stay right where he was.

Official Washington, like Agent Boulad, was growing anxious. White House staff officials assigned to oversee the heroin battle even considered calling Ambassador Ylitalo home in January to discuss his failure to convince the Paraguayans that Ricord must be handed over.

Congress had passed a law in 1970 permitting extradition and prosecution for conspiracy for drug defendants, even if they had committed the crime against the United States from outside its shores. It had also provided, in the Foreign Assistance Act of 1971, that the President could deny aid to foreign countries that refused to cooperate in the drug war. Pressure was now mounting on Capitol Hill to make such aid cutoffs mandatory.

And Congress could not be ignored. In President Nixon's three and a half years in office, the legislators at his request had increased the Bureau of Narcotics budget from $14 million to $74 million and expanded its agent force from 600 to 1,600. The Bureau of Customs had been allowed to grow from 9,000 employees to 15,000. Progress was at last being made in drug law enforcement—but the tiny Paraguayan Government was thwarting a major test of whether the American giant might ever win the heroin war.

As the Ricord case dragged back and forth in Asunción, Washington officials prodded Ylitalo weekly to bring about a favorable solution, as if they thought he ran Paraguay himself. The $11 million that the United States provided to Paraguay annually in financial and military aid had not yet been halted. But requests for surplus uniforms and small arms were now being ignored or delayed. To the Paraguayans, it was beginning to seem tantamout to a cessation of American help.

About this time the Cabinet Committee on International Narcotics Control held a meeting to discuss the Ricord case, the continuing difficulties with Panama, and similar problems in Thailand and Burma. Drug diplomacy was indeed far-flung.

And on the Fourth of July, for the first time in 111 years, the American Embassy in Asunción did not hold an Independence Day party for Paraguayan officials. The message was plain: We want Ricord.

"As for the traditional party," an embassy aide told a *New York Times* reporter in Asunción, "you can say that it will be the first time since Charles A. Washburn, a Californian named by Lincoln, became the first permanent United States Ambassador resident here in 1861, that there will be no party. We believe that toasts to United States–Paraguayan friendship and all that are not in order at this time."

It was an unprecedented diplomatic slap in the face, but it did not produce the desired results. The court case dragged on, and a

State Department Paraguayan expert said, "They seem to be making up the rules as they go along."

By now the Ricord story had been reported extensively in the United States, Latin America, and particularly France. And columnist Jack Anderson continued to harpoon Paraguayan officials in print so forcefully that Paraguay formally asked the State Department to back up his charges with detailed information or find a way to shut Anderson up.

In the midst of one minicrisis precipitated by an Anderson column, the U.S. chiefs of mission for Latin American countries had been meeting in Bogotá, Colombia, to report to White House aides their progress on the drug front. Egil (Bud) Krogh, the President's "quarterback" in the drug war, bluntly warned them that "heads will roll" unless even more progress was made. For Ambassador Ylitalo, who was there, it was a fateful prediction.

In Asunción, some of Ylitalo's subordinates had suggested to the State Department that a special emissary be sent from Washington to soothe the Paraguayans' feelings over the Anderson charges and at the same time argue for the transfer of Ricord. Instead, officials in State's Latin American division had pulled Ylitalo out of the Bogotá meeting, told him to delay his home leave, and sent him back to Asunción with orders to see President Stroessner.

The maneuver was a failure. Krogh had not been consulted, and Krogh was angry. Furthermore, President Stroessner had refused Ylitalo an audience.

"That made it fairly crystal clear to the White House that Ray didn't have any clout," a State Department official said. Ylitalo's home leave was now granted. In Washington, he was reminded that he had missed one "deliver Ricord" deadline after another in June and July. His home leave was extended. Finally, he was sent back to Asunción.

"He did more in a few weeks than he had done in two years," the official said. "He did get to a couple of people who were key, and who did get to Stroessner." It still was not enough.

Late in July, President Nixon read an extensive memorandum on the Ricord case. It was attached to a draft of a proposed letter from Nixon to President Alfredo Stroessner. A plan was outlined: If Nixon approved, Nelson Gross, senior adviser to the Secretary of State and coordinator for international narcotics matters, would fly to Asunción with the letter. He held the equivalent rank of Assistant Secretary of State. Armed with the letter, he would be a special Presidential emissary, and he would seek an audience with Stroessner.

President Nixon signed off on the plan. Somewhere along the line, the permanent recall of Ambassador Ylitalo was also agreed upon. It was a Presidential election year and a delicate time for removing an ambassador from his post. But Senator Mundt, Ylitalo's patron, had been seriously ill and away from Washington for a long time. And all the polls indicated that Democratic Presidential candidate George McGovern (another South Dakotan) would not be much of a threat, even though he was accusing Nixon of inaction on drug addiction.

At the end of July the Paraguayan Government was notified that Ylitalo would be replaced by George W. Landau, who had served in Spain, Portugal, and Uruguay, was fluent in German and Spanish, and had helped handle the difficult negotiations with Spain over military bases there and with Portugal over bases in the Azores. The Paraguayans were also told that Gross was on his way. Both messages were intended to display intense dissatisfaction over the Ricord case.

At 8:30 A.M. on the morning of Tuesday, August 8, 1972, Nelson Gross walked into the Palace of Government in Asunción on a highly unusual mission. He was the first Presidential emissary in American history sent to request the extradition of an accused criminal who had never set foot in the country where he was charged.

The President's office was neither large nor pretentious. To the left of the desk stood a globe, a cabinet cluttered with objects that included a model of what could have been a *contrabandista* airplane (Stroessner himself piloted a Beech Bonanza), and a Paraguayan flag in an ornate stand. The President's high-backed swivel chair, marked with the state seal just at the point where his head rested against it, was not ornate by Latin standards.

Gross, a tall, dark-haired former congressman from New Jersey, handed the mustachioed President the letter from Nixon. It recalled the friendship of the United States for Paraguay and recognized President Stroessner's often-stated conviction that trafficking in narcotics was deplorable. And it expressed Nixon's own conviction that President Stroessner therefore would do all in his power to help the United States in its fight against drugs.

The letter did not mention Auguste Ricord by name. It did not need to. The Paraguayan President set the letter down on his desk, and a frank and vigorous exchange began. Gross had with him President Nixon's Spanish interpreter, and Stroessner had an interpreter of his own. Voices were never raised, but the debate sometimes moved so fast that near-simultaneous translations were required.

"It was not as simple as 'We want Ricord,' and 'O.k., you can have him,' " Gross recalled later. "It didn't go that way."

The Paraguayan chief told Gross of his great pride in his excellent relationships with the United States, where he had visited and trained, and of his fervent desire to stop the smuggling of narcotics through his country.

In his turn, Gross also spoke of mutual cooperation. He said that it could best be demonstrated by the extradition of Auguste Ricord. President Stroessner interrupted to say that, after all, this case was in the hands of the judiciary.

But Gross continued to speak of the $11 million annually in American aid and the help that had been given by the Inter-American Development Bank and the International Bank for Reconstruction and Development. President Nixon had now been empowered not only to cease direct aid but to instruct U.S. representatives to multinational groups like the two banks to vote against loans to Paraguay, should that become necessary.

Two implications were unspoken but unmistakably clear, Gross felt: The neighbor to the north was prepared to cut off the money flow; and the neighbor did not believe Stroessner's protestations that he had no influence over judges he had appointed.

If this was heroin imperialism that Gross was practicing, the U.S. Government felt the pressure was justified. Vietnam was one war. Drugs were another.

President Stroessner repeatedly insisted that the Ricord matter was not in his hands. But he ended the ninety-minute meeting by sending Gross, accompanied by the Solicitor General, off to separate meetings with Foreign Minister Raúl Sapena Pastor and the Chief Justice of the Supreme Court.

The meeting with the Foreign Minister lasted almost an hour, and the meeting with the Chief Justice about forty minutes. Gross told the Chief Justice that he was about to advance an argument and that if the Justice felt the argument was improper, he should say so.

"I told him there *was* a question here of foreign relations with another country," Gross later recalled, "and that there was no question that these relations would be impaired to some degree, if not by the Administration then by Congress and the public— which were determined to see to it that narcotics-trafficking was stopped."

Gross had already told the President and the Foreign Minister that the extradition of Ricord would serve as a signal to "other countries and other conspiracies that there is not going to be an immunity." He had pointed out that Paraguay had a chance to set an example for the fifty-six other nations that the United States had sought as allies in the war on heroin. These arguments he repeated to the Chief Justice.

The Chief Justice was no stranger to the United States. He held degrees from the Wharton School of the University of Pennsylvania and Columbia University. He remained polite, completely attentive, and noncommittal.

By 4:30 P.M. Nelson Gross's meetings were over and he was on his way to Buenos Aires and home.

On the same day Customs Agent Frankie DeSantis walked along a Greenwich Village street almost sputtering in his frustration over Auguste Ricord. He had invested many hours of his young life in the Latin cases and, he said, "this son of a bitch was a Nazi collaborator and now he's one of the biggest men in junk. He's had his finger up the world for twenty years and he sits there untouched!"

Six days later the Paraguayan Court of Appeals unanimously

granted the extradition request of the United States for Auguste Joseph Ricord. But two days after that, Ricord's lawyer filed motions in the Supreme Court and the Court of First Instance to delay the transfer. It was not yet clear whether the Gross mission had been a success—or whether it would turn out to be a case of overkill.

On August 1, 1972, Paraguayan General Patricio Colman was admitted to the Wilmington Medical Center in Wilmington, Delaware, for treatment. ("I bitterly opposed letting that SOB into the country," a government official said. "We even made a special Customs arrangement to be sure that he was 'clean' when he came in.")

At 7:40 A.M. on Wednesday, August 16—the same day that Ricord's lawyer filed motions to block his extradition—General Colman died.

The hospital listed one attending physician; the State Department listed a different one. The State Department said Colman had come for treatment of a suspected brain tumor, possibly a result of shrapnel wounds from the Chaco War in the 1930's. Other sources said the cause of death was gangrene of the small and large bowels and peritonitis, an infection of the abdominal cavity. The latter version squared with a story that Colman had gone to the Paraguayan border many weeks before to intercept a Paraguayan Communist who was trying to enter the country; that when he opened the trunk of a car the Communist hidden there shot him in the stomach; and that Colman emptied his revolver into the Communist.

Sources in Wilmington said General Colman's body was to have been flown from Dulles International Airport outside of Washington direct to Asunción, but was then diverted to St. Matthew's Cathedral in Washington for a memorial service. The State Department said that there had been no change of plans, that the Paraguayan Embassy in Washington had scheduled the memorial service all along.

Either way, Enio Anibal Varela-Segovia's defender and protector was dead.

Late in August, 1972, the Paraguayan Supreme Court and the Court of First Instance denied the latest Ricord motions.

On the first day of September, Ambassador J. Raymond Ylitalo, still in Asunción, received a first-person note from the Paraguayan Government granting the extradition of Auguste Joseph Ricord.

# 9 Trial in the Market Place

## December, 1972

*It was cold in New York.* A sharp, gusty wind whipped the December rain through the cavernous streets of lower Manhattan, across the drab openness of Foley Square, and squandered it against the windows and concrete walls of the Federal Court House.

In Courtroom 905 halfway up the towering building, a trial was in session. Yet the only sound in the room was the banshee wail of the wind against the windows. To the right of the judge's bench, the court reporter, the judge, and lawyers for both sides hovered together trying to smooth out one of the pretrial wrinkles.

Auguste Joseph Ricord, his wiry figure hunched deep in an ill-fitting blue double-breasted suit, sat behind the defendant's table gazing vacantly out into the wintry rain. Away from the warmth of Latin America or the sun of his native Mediterranean, in this cold and alien place, the man who controlled the biggest single narcotics-smuggling network ever penetrated by American agents appeared small and vulnerable, a pathetic figure.

The difficulties had begun long before Nelson Gross strode confidently into the Presidential Palace in Asunción. It had been as Ricord had often thought—when the Americans turned their full power on narcotics smuggling, disaster for him would follow.


The technique the Customs and Narcotics Bureau agents had used had been tedious and painstaking, yet starkly simple and dependent finally on the technological superiority of the United States and its clout as the big neighbor to the north. The ultimate device of the smugglers had always been to use fake identity papers, moving from country to country to avoid arrest. When pressures in one Latin American country became too great the smuggler would simply move on to another, changing his identity as he went. The police in the new country had little if any direct communication with the law-enforcement agencies of its neighbors, and the channels that did exist were often used to warn of the movement of political dissidents, rather than criminals. Utilizing the might of its sophisticated computers and communications systems, the U.S. authorities had begun systematically tracing each key figure in the narcotics trade from country to country. Once they learned that a suspect was in a certain country, they advised the local police of the charge against him and then attempted extradition or deportation.

The second weapon of the U.S. agents resulted from the accident of political atmospheres in different countries. Though wiretapping and bugging were fragile and legally hazardous techniques in the United States, police in most Latin and European countries knew no such limits. Thus U.S. agents could benefit from valuable intelligence data gathered from taps placed by foreign governments without endangering the legality of an American prosecution. By the same token, the interrogation methods used by certain countries were far more grisly than those permitted in the United States. But U.S. agents readily used the valuable information extracted at these sessions.

The most valuable break of this kind came in March, 1972, a year after Ricord had been caught in Asunción. The police of La Paz, Bolivia, made a series of drug arrests growing out of an internal investigation. At one point they had in custody five main suspects. The U.S. agencies immediately requested photographs and fingerprints of the people under arrest.

"The names of the people who were arrested didn't mean a thing," one Customs agent recalled, "but the faces and fingerprints sure did. But by the time we received the information from the Bolivians, they had already released most of the suspects."

Belatedly, the agents realized that the Bolivians had held two of Ricord's most important lieutenants—the very men who might take over his organization if he were killed or imprisoned in a country where he could not operate from his jail cell.

The older of the two, Lucien Sarti, had apparently been in La Paz with either his wife or his mistress (or both) when he was arrested. He was released and had left the country only days before the American request to hold him for questioning reached the Bolivians. Also held briefly in La Paz was thirty-year-old Jean-Paul Angeletti, Sarti's sidekick and an indispensable Ricord assistant.

Shortly after the two disappeared from La Paz, the American agents set up a trace on them. Through use of unusually cooperative Latin police informants and thorough border checks, the U.S. agents traced the pair northward, through Peru and across South and Central America. Forty-five days later the American pursuers had hard information that the two men were in Mexico City. Quietly, the Americans notified their counterparts in the Policía Judicial Federal, the tough Mexican FBI.

About 8:40 P.M. on the muggy evening of April 27, 1972, a well-polished European car pulled silently to the curb in front of 107 Temistocles Street in an exclusive residential section of Mexico City. The car was driven by an attractive, thirtyish woman in sporty, well-tailored clothes. She was later identified as Liliane Rous Vaillet, the wife of Lucien Sarti. A few moments after the pretty woman parked the car, and as she sat waiting behind the wheel, Sarti walked briskly from the house and approached the car on the driver's side.

As he paused to open the car door, two Mexican agents stepped forward from the shadows. According to the Mexican authorities, Sarti did not even wait for a salutation. Drawing a .38-caliber Colt

Cobra, the forty-one-year-old Frenchman bolted. He died a few seconds later from a hail of bullets fired by Mexican agents hidden in ambush near the house.

The same evening another team of Mexican police officers raided the hideout of Angeletti and surprised him in the act of making love. His surprise and disarray probably saved his life. The policemen grabbed him before he could reach the gun on the table nearby to shoot it out with them.

The Mexican authorities confiscated fourteen false passports, quantities of jewels, firearms, cash, and "several notebooks . . . with notes on large and small narcotics distributors." The Federales learned that Sarti, Angeletti, and their wives had arrived in Mexico from Panama aboard the small plane of a *contrabandista.* Furthermore, the Mexican agents learned, the group had been preparing to receive and smuggle into the United States some 100 kilos of cocaine.

Sarti's bullet-riddled body was never claimed and was buried in Mexico. The women, Angeletti, and another drug smuggler arrested with him that night were ultimately extradited to France and Italy.

At almost the same time that Sarti's life was flowing out on the Mexican street, his former mistress was about to supply American agents with their next major weapon in the war on drugs. Her assistance to the Americans was indirect and decidedly involuntary. Hélène Ferreira was a tall, statuesque brunette whose bikini-clad body had adorned the pages of more than one Brazilian magazine. She had been known as the sponsor for Sarti and for many another in the jet-set level of the Brazilian underworld. More important, Miss Ferreira had been arrested and identified in La Paz with Sarti.

Shortly after the La Paz incident she was rearrested in Peru and questioned about her paramour and his Corsican companions. She was uncooperative. For reasons that are unclear from a legal standpoint, Miss Ferreira was turned over to the Brazilian federal police at the border. "I don't know what they did to her," one American agent told the authors, "but it wasn't long before she started to cooperate." Indeed, Miss Ferreira became so cooperative that the Brazilians had to ask the Americans for help because they were running out of questions. "They didn't have any idea what to ask her, so we sent down seventy-five questions," an agent said. "She was answering all of them."

Among the things that the young model and showgirl told her Brazilian captors was the specific location of a telephone of a key Brazilian gangster whose home was a clearinghouse for the comings and goings of what the Brazilian press called the "Mafia." Unencumbered by the need for a court order to wiretap, the Brazilian police soon had the telephone "strapped" and were busily collecting the names and whereabouts of a veritable army of Corsican, Italian, and Brazilian underworld figures—including those of two forty-two-year-old Frenchmen, Christian David and Michel Nicole.

David had been identified by American intelligence officers not only as Ricord's one-time bodyguard and head of one of his five operating groups but also as an international criminal of particular daring and power who had lived with violence since his childhood in occupied France. In fact, David had once trod that strange never-never land between the French underworld and the Republic's supersecret political police. Of medium height and wiry, swarthy of skin like many Corsicans, he walked with the balanced, confident step of a fighter, favored carefully tailored Continental-style clothes, and never went anywhere without weapons. When the Brazilian police arrested him, he was carrying a grenade and a pistol with a silencer.

Michel Nicole was a smaller and seemingly less lethal man. The debonair Nicole had also been identified as heading one of Ricord's five subgroups and was regarded as a key figure in the drug trade. Posing as Miguel dos Santos, Nicole had entered the United States in 1968 and was later arrested for drug-smuggling. After his bail was reduced to $50,000 he fled the country, and there was a U.S.–issued Interpol warrant for the tiny Frenchman. David was also wanted in the United States on charges of conspiracy to smuggle narcotics.

The tough Brazilian federal police made their first sweeping set of arrests in October. Using Miss Ferreira's information and the material from the telephone tap, they snared David and Nicole along with a large number of Brazilian underworld figures. Almost all of them were carrying false identity papers, and the Brazilians were anxious to separate one from another.

According to American agents, the Brazilian police shipped David, Nicole, and another Frenchman by air to Brasilia, the nation's inland capital. There, in the headquarters of the federal police, they proceeded to obtain information in a way that has made Brazil notorious around the world.

David was first. Stripped of his clothing and hung upside down in the interrogation cell, he was, he later claimed, tortured with electric shocks applied to his testicles and the head of his penis. American agents do not know how long this torture was used, or even whether it was applied as David has said. But they do know that whatever happened to the Corsican in that torture cell, he tried to take his own life rather than undergo more. Apparently he swallowed a light bulb and later cut his wrists with glass fragments in hopes of ending it all. One U.S. agent who saw David a few weeks later said, "He was still walking bowlegged he was in so much pain."

Nicole was second. He too was stripped, hung upside down, and tortured with ends of hot electrical wires. Nicole became so despondent that he attempted to smash his skull by running his head into the walls of his cell. American agents said that his head showed bruises and bumps when he was examined in the United States, and there was evidence of permanent nerve damage. Both men have claimed they did not talk. In any event, they were identified as fugitives important to the United States—not after the torture but through the simple, mechanical expedient of checking their photos and fingerprints.

The third man tortured was not as strong, according to U.S. sources. He was tied to a chair in the center of his cell. His interrogator approached him and in a kind, almost conciliatory voice told the prisoner he would like to "introduce" some of the men who "would be looking out for his welfare" in the coming weeks. Then, as the interrogator called their names, a string of powerful police officers entered the room in single file. The first officer identified himself and smashed the prisoner squarely in the face with his fist. The second grabbed the prisoners' ears and twisted them violently. The third kicked the helpless man in the testicles. The prisoner began to talk with frantic insistence.

It was in mid-November that the Brazilians agreed to turn

David and Nicole over to the American authorities. The two Frenchmen, half-walking, half-staggering, were carried off a Pan American Airways jetliner at Kennedy International Airport shortly after 6 P.M. on November 17. Despite their condition, David was still proud. Boasting of his ability with a pistol, he challenged his captors to a shooting match at the first opportunity. The challenge was declined.

Less than a month later, both David and Nicole pleaded guilty to conspiracy charges (David to escape the French guillotine) and Nicole was reindicted on his narcotics charges and for bail-jumping.

Ricord's organization now was breaking apart as rapidly as an ice floe that has hit the Gulf Stream. William Perrin was arrested in France. André Condemine, first known to U.S. agents as Mario Deniz, was indicted by a Brooklyn grand jury and is believed to have been killed by rival gang members in Belgium. Michel Russo and Francisco Chiappe were arrested by Argentine police in Buenos Aires as they attempted to transport more than 100 pounds of pure heroin. Even the silent Aron Muravnik was to face arrest in Argentina shortly.

In the gloom of the wood-paneled U.S. courtroom that December morning, Auguste Ricord could not help but contemplate the shambles of his life and "l'organization" that had for so long flouted the powers of a score of nations. It had been as he had privately feared and half-expected. The subterfuges, the faked identities, the bribes to governments of a half-dozen countries, the secret Swiss bank accounts had come to naught.

In a sense, some of the more cynical observers of the Ricord case had noted, the United States had finally outbribed the wily Corsican. If it was accepted that Ricord, like some former Nazis and other exiles, had paid dearly for his haven in Paraguay, then it was as clear that finally the United States had simply outbid him. It had seriously threatened the little country's sugar income, military aid, and foreign loan possibilities and created a situation in which President Stroessner could safely defy Ricord's silent partners in the dominant Colorado political party.

For Ricord, nothing remained so symbolic of the power that

had finally wrested him from Paraguay as his trip to the United States. The American Government had chartered an entire commercial Pan American jetliner, complete with two crews. The jet had been flown from New York to Paraguay with agents of both the Customs Service and the Bureau of Narcotics and Dangerous Drugs, a movie cameraman, a doctor from the Treasury Department, and other officials.

In the relative luxury of the first class section of the plane, with the official entourage and Pan American Airways champagne, the diminutive Ricord, his daughter, and his niece had flown to the United States. Bureau of Narcotics press agents had quietly leaked word of the arrival time, and as the Corsican was marched in from the plane at Kennedy International Airport in New York, he had been greeted with photographers' flashbulbs. But though the government had tipped off the cameramen, it would not allow interviews for fear of "prejudicing" Ricord's court case.

That had been more than two months before. Now Ricord sat behind a defendant's table in the somber and austere courtroom. He was charged with conspiring to violate U.S. narcotics laws— even though the government was fully willing to stipulate that the diminutive Frenchman had never set foot in the United States. For a man of his years, suffering from heart disease, high blood pressure, and diabetes, the imprisonment—first at the Federal House of Detention at West Street and later at the Nassau County Jail—had not been good. One bout of illness had resulted in Ricord's being sent to the prison ward at Bellevue Hospital.

Obvious illness, the ill-fitting suit, and a sort of permanently perplexed expression from the strain of trying to understand the rapid English around him made Ricord seem a deeply sympathetic figure that first morning. The U.S. Government lawyers and officers looked far more forbidding.

The chief prosecutor was Assistant U.S. Attorney Walter M. Phillips, Jr., head of the narcotics section of the U.S. Attorney's office in the Southern District of New York. Phillips, tall, balding, appearing older than his thirty-three years, bore the diffident, detached air of the Philadelphia Main Line, in whose affluent, conservative upper-middle class he had been brought up. Throughout much of the trial, Phillips's attractive blonde wife, an actress and model, sat in the audience watching her husband's direction of the case.

Assisting in the prosecution was Eugene Bannigan, a handsome sandy-haired Assistant U.S. Attorney with considerable more courtroom experience. It was Bannigan who would conduct some of the most telling cross-examination. As the case opened, the government also introduced Customs Special Agent Paul Boulad and asked the court's permission for the investigator to assist in the delivery of the case. The request was not unusual and the judge granted it immediately.

Ricord's defense team was not impressive. He had chosen as his attorney Herbert I. Handman, a slightly built, balding, and nervous-seeming young New York criminal lawyer. The choice had deeply perplexed many of the more knowledgeable narcotics agents. "We expected Ricord to come up with one of the drug regulars or with some real high-powered guy," one agent told the authors. "We simply couldn't figure out, why Handman?"

There were two kinds of speculation. Some New York lawyers suggested that since the case was earmarked as a top-priority prosecution by the Nixon Administration, the possibility of bargaining or maneuvering was severely limited. "The government was out to get Ricord. They [the government lawyers] weren't going to make any deals. They wanted to put this guy away. When you take a case like that you can't look good."

Others in the New York law-enforcement community argued that Ricord's wealth had been so depleted by his jail term in Paraguay that he couldn't put up the enormous fees demanded by the top drug lawyers. Privately, some of the agents familiar with Ricord's economic status doubted this. "He's got plenty of money. He may be afraid to try to get at it for fear we're going to pounce, or some other country's going to get him for taxes."

In any event, Ricord ended up with Handman, who had been suggested to him by another prisoner in the West Street facility. If there was any single criticism of Handman, it was that the young lawyer was playing for the first time in a new league. The case began with something like slap-stick comedy. When Handman first interviewed his client at West Street, he discovered that neither his faltering Spanish nor Ricord's limited English was sufficient for the two to communicate well. Looking about, Handman engaged a prisoner sitting nearby who spoke French to translate. Thus the first intimate and vital conversations between the lawyer and his client were passed through a man neither knew who was in jail on a fraud charge.

The helpful prisoner immediately realized that he had something of value. First he called the Bureau of Narcotics and Dangerous Drugs and offered to sell what he'd learned in the conversations in exchange for leniency on his own charges. Later he called a newspaper reporter and tried to parlay the information into money.

The narcotics agents were intrigued and began sending men around town checking on the tips of the "translator." The only problem was that the information was fragmentary or out of date, and in a few weeks the narcs had completely lost patience. "They were so mad at this guy," one newsman learned, "that they planned to leave him in West Street and then let it be known he was a stoolie."

Handman finally engaged a discreet and respectable professional interpreter. Despite the government's rumblings about Ricord's vast wealth, Handman was later to claim that he saw little of it. He would not disclose his fee but some sources suggested it was less than $10,000, plus his expenses on a trip to Paraguay and office costs. Though Handman was an experienced criminal lawyer and had defended cases up through murder in state courts, he appeared unfamiliar with the Constitutional questions of Ricord's arrest, extradition, and interrogation.

The government appeared vulnerable on two aspects: the pressures it had used to have Ricord arrested and later extradited and the questionable motives of its two key witnesses, Cesar Mendice Bianchi and Felix Rogelio Becker—both of whom had made deals with the prosecutor in exchange for leniency. Handman had sought to attack these points in a series of pretrial motions but had been overruled both by the trial judge and by the U.S. Court of Appeals. Later, his efforts to subpoena and question State Department official Nelson Gross, the Ambassador to Paraguay, and others also failed.

Some of Handman's courtroom difficulties may have stemmed from the bench. The Ricord case had drawn U.S. District Court Judge John Matthew Cannella, a sixty-four-year-old Democrat who had been appointed by John F. Kennedy. Cannella, the great bear of a man who had played for the New York Giants after his graduation from Fordham Law School in 1933, was an expert on narcotics cases. As an assistant U.S. attorney a quarter-century before, he had prosecuted narcotics violations as a specialty, and in almost ten years on the federal bench he had heard a score of narcotics conspiracy and smuggling cases. In fact Cannella had judged the cases of a number of the men who would appear as witnesses against Ricord.

Cannella's experience produced not so much a prejudice for or against Ricord as an impatience with Handman's sometimes indirect courtroom style. Indeed, Judge Cannella on a number of occasions admonished the lawyer in the presence of the jury about his poor tactics.

The government's courtroom strategy was simple and clear-cut. Since it was undisputed that large amounts of heroin had been smuggled into the United States, the government must concentrate its energies on proving that Ricord, as "M. André," had masterminded and directed the smuggling operation. "This was really an organization, a business organization," Phillips told the jury of seven men and five women in his opening statement, "whose purpose was to import substantial amounts of heroin at substantial profit." At the "top" of this organization, the government lawyer sternly charged, was Auguste Joseph Ricord.

In any jury trial, almost no matter how strong the evidence, a good deal of the case becomes theater—drama designed to sway the jury, to capture the emotions, raise the anger, milk the sympathies, or stir the disgust of the twelve people chosen to judge. Rightfully, the prosecution has a harder time of it than the defense. The prosecution must persuade all twelve of those people to agree, beyond any reasonable doubt. The defense has only to sway the opinion of one to gain at least a mistrial.

Phillips and the government prosecution team had several clear advantages. They had the testimony of admitted heroin-smugglers who would identify Ricord as the man who sent them on their mission. They had the enormous emotional advantage attached to heroin itself. No American jury, certainly not a jury living in the New York metropolitan area, was going to display much sympathy for anyone who it believed to be trafficking in heroin.

Lastly, the government had on its side all that enormous atmosphere of official correctness that cloaks its cases. The trotting in and out of businesslike government agents and the testimony about the airplanes and the vast apparatus used by the law enforcement agencies to apprehend the accused could lead any jury to the belief that the government would not extend all this effort unless something was wrong.

Despite his limitations in exposing the weak points or procedural flaws in the government's case, Herbert Handman had a good grasp of the art of courtroom drama—and indeed, his appearance of being bumbling and slightly confused may have enhanced his defense.

Handman chose to present his client as the innocent victim of unscrupulous men. Considering the alternatives, it was not an unimaginative defense. Ricord at sixty-one, his face framed by gray-white muttonchop whiskers and his head nearly bald, looked like nothing so much as a shopkeeper or family doctor. The Frenchman's small stature meant that the marshals who marched him in each day and guarded him towered over him. Wally Phillips, a strapping six-footer, also loomed over Ricord, who was dwarfed as well by Boulad and most of the other agents who were to testify. The effect was of a man caught by mistake in the grasp of a powerful government.

Furthermore, Handman had the occasional advantage that goes hand in hand with most conspiracy cases. The key witnesses are themselves tainted. They have, themselves, committed the same crime as the man accused—and are testifying to curry favor and gain leniency from the government. In this case, Handman also enjoyed a clear added advantage—a number of the key witnesses were obviously professional liars. They told so many versions of the "truth" it was hard to choose which one to believe.

"Mr. Ricord is innocent," Handman told the jury in his opening statement, "The defendant will testify . . . he has asked to be given an opportunity to explain why he was innocent . . . why he couldn't possibly be guilty."

Handman launched his attack on the key government witnesses early. "If there were three people not to be listened to by a jury in this country, you could not pick a better three . . . these people are outright liars . . . They have a very good reason to incriminate someone. They're getting their freedom quickly because they're incriminating Auguste Ricord."

The trial began slowly, with little color and few revelations. The courtroom was packed. The first two rows had been set aside for the press. Along with such American publications as the *New York Times*, *Newsweek*, the *New York Daily News*, and *Readers' Digest*, this included representatives of the Paris daily *Le Monde*, *François*, the French wire service Agence France Presse, and the correspondent for a Latin American news agency. Behind the first two rows sat an audience—half courtroom "regulars" (the hangers-on who go from trial to trial for entertainment) and half government agents and lawyers.

Security was airtight. A few days before the trial, Phillips had told the court that Christian David had threatened star witness Cesar Bianchi in the Nassau County Jail, and Judge Cannella had ordered close screening of the audience. Newsmen and spectators alike were carefully searched with electronic weapons detectors each day and not even so much as a penknife was allowed in the courtroom.

Young Renato Balestra testified first, calmly describing the various flights he had made with Bianchi and his suspicion about the fact that what he was doing was smuggling. Handman probed with his cross-examination to establish whether Balestra had any complicity in the smuggling, but the fresh-faced, intense Brazilian made a good witness. Finally, Judge Cannella asked the witness whether he had actually been suspicious that he was doing something wrong. With stark candor, Balestra answered, "I closed my eyes to all of this, I ignored it." The judge had brought out more from the witness than the defense attorney had.

Next came Cesar Mendice Bianchi. He had shaved off his

mustache since his arrest and looked like a burly, prosperous businessman with a vague resemblance to Desi Arnaz. Unlike Balestra, Bianchi testified entirely through an interpreter, a pretty Spanish woman who gave his answers careful translation and studied impact.

The courtroom had the flavor of a mini-United Nations. While Bianchi's answers were being translated from Spanish to English, an interpreter in a low, droning voice was translating the proceedings into French for Ricord. Having an interpreter for the witnesses was as much tactical as necessary. Bianchi, Felix Rogelio Becker, and Pierre Gahou all spoke some English, but the period while the question was being translated gave them a few extra moments to contemplate the answer. It also denied Handman any opportunity for asking fast follow-up questions or making the witnesses appear to be confused.

Bianchi stuck tightly to a narrow version of the story that had obviously been well coached by government agents over his two years in custody. He answered questions with that same cryptic, terse style affected by policemen to avoid allowing the defense lawyer a handle or an opening. Handman came a cropper early in his attempt to break down Bianchi's testimony.

Asking the husky pilot why he had chosen to cooperate with American agents, the lawyer got this unexpected reply: "When I was arrested if I did not deliver [testimony] I would be more or less in the position of Mr. Ricord." The judge winced. He would later chide Handman for becoming so easily entrapped by a "why" question.

It was in his cross-examination of Bianchi that Handman began subtly to develop what would be his pattern of defense. If Ricord was not the mastermind of the heroin-smuggling, then Bianchi would be lying about having gone to Le Paris-Niza Motel to pick up one shipment. In classic scene-of-the-crime cross-examination, Handman attempted to show that Bianchi had a faulty and inaccurate memory of the layout of Le Paris-Niza. He was partially successful, and the pilot stepped from the stand a shakier witness for it.

Following Bianchi's testimony, the government swiftly shifted gears and put on a series of federal agents to establish the actual smuggling and the seizure of the heroin. It was a sophisticated though traditional conspiracy-case ploy. If the government had grouped the three conspirator-witnesses together, their obvious flaws—complicity and lack of complete truthfulness—would have been glaring. Instead, the government followed Bianchi with a string of federal agents, including Hoppy, Steve Csukas, and Tony DeGaglia.

The agents gave their testimony in that crisp, totally deadpan style of the professional law-enforcement officer. As one observer commented during a brief recess, "they're like walking tape recorders." And, indeed, the agents were growing tired of the story. They had had to tell it at several dozen pretrial hearings and rehearsal sessions with the prosecutors.

Even the disciplined disinterest of the Feds broke down when the evidence was trotted out. The government, to comply with trial law, had to bring into court the evidence in its entirety and to make a showing that it had been scrupulously accounted for in the more than two years since Hoppy had discovered it behind the auxiliary gas tank of the now notorious Cessna. So, with great huffing and puffing, the entire ninety-four pound shipment of pure heroin was placed on tables before the jury and unpacked from the three suitcases that had contained it on the fateful flight from Asunción.

Unexpectedly, at this point, Handman asked the court to order the witnesses—agents Hoppy Hopkins and Steve Csukas—to re pack the ninety-four pounds into the three suitcases. Undoubtedly Handman was convinced that the agents could not fit the heroin into the bags. As they worked trying to repack the three suitcases one of the tiny bright-colored plastic bags split, spewing white powder across the defense table and coating books and chairs nearby. Handman leaped back as if burned.

"I hope this is flour," he said to no one in particular as he tried to dust it off his briefcase.

"It is not, Mr. Handman," said District Judge John M. Cannella. "It is heroin."

The idea had backfired. First, the agents were successful in repacking the bags. More important, the jury had been treated to the indelible memory of a veritable fortune in pure heroin spread out and some of it spilled in front of them.

The government followed up the "official" testimony by placing Felix Rogelio Becker on the stand. Becker was to come off as the least convincing of the key witnesses. He spoke in a soft, almost inaudible voice and wore a cynical half-smile most of the time. Becker testified that he had personally seen Ricord at five meetings in Asunción in the summer of 1970 where the smuggling of drugs or movement of money had been planned or exchanged.

Handman sharply attacked Becker's credibility. When he asked Becker why the smuggler had told a different story in earlier grand jury and interrogation statements, the red-haired Paraguayan answered: "I told the truth in a great part of the statements, but I was confused at this time. I did not have a lawyer to tell me the laws of this country."

Pierre Gahou fared far better. As he described his relationship with Ricord and spoke of his knowledge of the narcotics traffic his gaze seldom wavered from Ricord's face and he spoke in clear, crisp French that the defendant clearly understood before the interpreter translated it for the court. The jury was clearly impressed. Some members leaned forward and craned to hear details from the translation.

The government's case took more than a week to present. Throughout, the weather in New York remained cold, rainy, and windy. The pre-holiday air of the city already adorned with Christmas decorations did not extend into the courtroom. As the trial unfolded, Ricord's niece and daughter sat in wooden chairs in the cold, marble hallway as though posing for the sketch of a French Impressionist. Since Handman had suggested he might call the two as witnesses, they could not sit in the courtroom itself.

Hélène Bonsignour, Ricord's thirty-four-year-old niece, her hair pulled starkly back from her face, had a look of melancholy in her deep brown eyes. Young Josephine Brigitte, at fifteen a beauty with soft perfect features and luxuriant blonde hair, seemed unaware that her shapely figure, already that of a woman, was catching the eye of every federal agent, newsman, and male spectator who passed through the hall. Despite the stares and whispers, the two women sat with a dignity and mutual gentleness that was soon to impress many of the trial observers. The bond between the two was clear well before it was brought out in testimony that Miss Bonsignour had cared for the young girl after her mother had left her father some years before.

The government rested its case midway through the second week of the trial, and Handman began the defense almost immediately. He had designed a two-pronged strategy. One prong, possibly the more important, was to establish Ricord as a man too innocent and harmless to have been involved in a plot of this kind. The other was a traditional "alibi" defense: to establish that it was not possible for Ricord to have been at the meetings and rendezvous the government witnesses claimed he attended.

Up through the testimony of Ricord's daughter, Handman's first objective was in reach. Indeed, Josephine Briggite Ricord's testimony provided the most effective moments of her father's defense. Quietly crossing herself before entering the courtroom, the lovely-looking young girl described her life as a Catholic seminary student in a Latin American city. It seemed like something out of the nineteenth century. Her father, she said, could not have been at some of the summer meetings because, as is well known, this is winter in South America and she remembered the family took a winter vacation to Buenos Aires. Under Handman's questioning, she suggested that no transfer of heroin could have taken place on October 11 because that is "an Indian festival . . . the day of the discovery of the Americas" and she remembered she had to be at her father's side because he was ill.

It was persuasive. The young girl's gentleness and demeanor were clearly effective. The government lawyers quickly realized that badgering her would make them seem like ogres, and they declined to cross-examine.

Miss Bonsignour did not fare as well. Phillips, the government attorney, pressed her closely about Ricord's financial investments and secret Swiss bank accounts. Much of the rest of Handman's defense was smokescreen—a series of confusing affidavits taken from witnesses in Paraguay meant to make it appear that Ricord could not have been at the meetings and heroin transfers described.

At this juncture, government agents privately agreed, the case against Ricord did not appear to be a sure thing. But then Handman chose to put Ricord himself on the stand. The defense attorney was reasonably confident that previous court rulings would deter the government from delving too insistently into Ricord's background prior to the period of the federal charge of conspiracy. Furthermore, Ricord was constantly pressing for a chance to tell his side of the story.

The result was disaster. It was not what Ricord said under direct examination, nor what secrets were wrested from him by the government lawyers. It was his demeanor. Sitting at the defendant's table, silent or occasionally whispering to his lawyer, Auguste Joseph Ricord had appeared the possible shopkeeper, the possible doctor, the possible victim of a terrible wrong.

But on the witness stand, angrily spitting out answers in gravelly-voiced French even before his interpreter translated the questions, his hands moving in furious emphasis of a point, he was the "commandante," the French Gestapo agent, the smuggler, the criminal. Each word, each gesture was that of a man who had lived all his life by cunning and force in a world of violent men. So convinced were the government attorneys that Ricord had torpedoed himself they even let the cross-examination dwindle away rather than evoke sympathy for the witness by appearing to press him.

It took the jury only two hours and twenty minutes to find the Frenchman guilty.

On December 16, 1972, two years and fifty-eight days after Cesar Mendice Bianchi's Cessna 210 set down at Miami International Airport with ninety-four pounds of hidden heroin, Auguste Joseph Ricord was convicted of conspiring to smuggle narcotics into the United States.

A few seconds after the verdict was read Ricord turned in his chair and gave a slight smile and shrug of resignation toward his daughter and his niece, Hélène Bonsignour, who was weeping.

As he was led from the courtroom he shook the hand of Paul Boulad, the collector, Customs agent in charge of the case.

*Postscript:*

On January 29, 1973, U.S. District Court Judge John Cannella sentenced Auguste Joseph Ricord to twenty years in prison and fined him $25,000. The sentence was one of the harshest possible under the narcotics laws.

U.S. Attorney Walter Phillips told the court that Ricord's rings were responsible for bringing at least 2,000 pounds of pure heroin a year into the United States. "The destruction he has wreaked on our society is unbelievable," he said.

In passing sentence, Judge Cannella told the court: "This is . . . a very large quantity of heroin. The end product in suffering and mortality from this quantity of drugs would probably equal the recent casualty figures given for the war in Vietnam."

On March 14, 1973, President Nixon repeated the judge's words in the course of a ceremony at the White House honoring Albert Seeley and the other agents who brought down Auguste Ricord and the *contrabandistas*.